JOSEL OF ROSHEIM

COMMANDER OF JEWRY

JOSEL OF ROSHEIM

IN THE HOLY ROMAN EMPIRE

OF THE GERMAN NATION

BY SELMA STERN

Translated from the German by Gertrude Hirschler

The Jewish Publication Society of America
5726 — 1965

FIRST EDITION

LIBRARY OF CONGRESS
CATALOG CARD NO. 65-17044
MANUFACTURED IN THE
UNITED STATES OF AMERICA
DESIGNED BY RICHARD PALMER

TO THE MEMORY OF

LEO BAECK

THE NOBLEST DEFENDER OF THE JEWISH PEOPLE

PREFACE

JOSEL OF ROSHEIM stands out as the representative figure of German Jewry at the threshold of an epoch commonly known as the beginning of the Modern Era. This period has been described as one of the most "anguished" in the history of German Jewry, and by virtue of this adjective it has been linked directly with the present time, to which it doubtless bears a certain historical and spiritual resemblance. One could easily compare the fate of the sixteenth-century Jews, whose social and economic situation was so radically changed by their expulsion from most of the Imperial Cities and larger territories of the *Reich* with the great social and economic changes in our own lives. It is possible to draw a parallel between the host desecrations and ritual murder accusations, which so gravely imperiled the lives of the Jews of Germany in the beginning of the Modern Era, and the horrors of the gas chambers and concentration camps which we have witnessed in our own time. The inexplicable eruption of primitive and irrational forces in a century in which "the arts flourished and the sciences awakened" resembles in many ways the breakthrough of sinister underworld powers in our own age, which boasts of having mastered all the mysteries of nature and of having conquered the unconscious passions and impulses of man.

Like our own epoch, the period of the Renaissance and the Reformation, which has been called a turning point in history, was marked by a massive upheaval which basically altered and reshaped every phase of political, social, economic, religious and cultural life. Unity gave way to multiplicity; the universal was replaced by the particular, community consciousness by universalism, the absolute by the relative, and permanence by rapid change. The concept of the eternal was superseded by *renascentia,* rebirth and reformation. And again, as in our own day, so then, this change did not take the form of drawing sharp and clear dividing lines between two cultures, the medieval-ecclesiastical on the one hand, and the modern-secular on the other. Even as the new spiritual and religious movements had already made themselves felt for some time during the medieval period, so the Christian dualist philosophy of life survived unbroken into the era of the Reformation. In practical life, these two movements interpenetrated and commingled; but they were never quite at peace: they were either in conflict or they existed side by side, unreconciled and irreconcilable.

This conflict and ambiguity, then as now, had a confusing and disconcerting effect as well on the general attitude toward the Jew. In keeping with the law of natural reason and the dictates of humanity, efforts were made to conceive of the Jew as a natural and human being. At the same time, however, it was firmly believed that the Jew was being used by evil and supernatural powers as a most dangerous and sinister weapon.

However, greatly as these two eras may resemble each other in many respects, no attempt will be made here to draw parallels between them. Every period in history runs its course in the path of its own historical laws; it evolves, in keeping with its own political constellations and economic character, and derives strength from those spiritual and religious movements which belong to it alone and to no other period. We merely wish to imply here that, as a result of the history we have experienced in our own day, we are better able than previous generations were to understand the personality of Josel of Rosheim, and we feel a closer kinship to this man—who was bound to his people with a magic bond and who served it with self-sacrificing devotion at a fateful turn in its history—than to our more fortunate ancestors of later centuries.

This book, which I once promised to a friend, I can now dedicate only to his memory. He in many ways felt akin to Josel of Rosheim. Both these men were keepers of that great faith "in which the finite eventually learns to experience something of the power of infinity . . . the hope above all hopes, the one which includes and unites all human beings within it."[1]

CONTENTS

INTRODUCTION

THE ERA of the Renaissance and Reformation may be regarded not only as one of the most anguished, but also one of the most tragic in the history of German Jewry. For it was then that the initial scenes were played in the dramatic encounter between German and Jew and Jew and German—that tragedy of love and hatred, attraction and repulsion, integration and segregation, on the final act of which the curtain has but lately fallen.

In the Middle Ages, Christianity and Judaism faced one another as two religious powers aware of their close kinship as well as of the irreconcilable conflict between them. Like two planets, circling the same blazing sun, each felt secure in its own prescribed orbit and each was sure of the infinite destiny ordained for it. If they came to grips, they would do so in the esoteric sphere, in the struggle for Divine rather than terrestrial truth.

It was only in the period of transition from the Middle Ages to the Modern Era that the locale of the dispute between Church and Synagogue was shifted from heaven to earth. It was only that century of humanism and religious universal theism, of Hebrew philology and cabbalistic studies, which saw the first earnest attempts by both sides at a rapprochement and better mutual understanding. Each sought to find in the other the natural moral law inherent in every human being, and to reconcile the aspects of eternal truth that are contained in both religions. It was then that, for the first time, men of both faiths jointly expounded the veiled tradition, the "miraculous word," and that the Hebrew language, the original tongue of mankind, was passed on with the same sacred zeal by the masters to their disciples. In those days the Germans discovered the Bible, which contained the original and genuine sources of Judaism and Christianity alike, and acquired it as their inalienable possession, while the Jews found in it new meaning for their existence as well as new instruction and exhortation.

But through their very efforts to delve into the secret of their common origin, the two faiths came to draw sharper boundaries and to isolate themselves from one another, to put greater stress on the irreconcilable character of their differences, and to deplore with increasing emotion what they felt to be the irrepressible conflict that kept them apart.

The reason why this debate now took on such dramatic forms was that it was no longer confined merely to the religious sphere, as it had been in the Middle Ages. In an era when the old states disintegrated and new political configurations arose, the Jewish problem, too, was lumped with all the political, social and economic factors and subjected to re-evaluation by a generation that had been awakened and put on the alert by revolutionary struggles and social upheavals.

Even when the most crucial problems of the nation came to a head, when the Holy Roman Empire was attacked by the Turks from the East and by the French from the West, and when the peasants rose up in bloody rebellions, the Jewish problem was debated just as heatedly as Luther's fight against Rome or Melanchthon's *Confessio Augustana* (Augsburg Confession), the battle of Pavia or the reign of the Anabaptists in Münster, the polemical writings of Ulrich von Hutten or the victory of Charles V over the Schmalkaldic League.

On the Jewish problem, minds would part. It seemed as if that period, when men still thought in terms of symbols and allegories, when sadness was depicted as "Melancolia" and usury as the *Judenspiess* (the Jew's javelin), was in need of a tangible figure which would reflect the differences and reveal the conflicts with which the era itself was beset.

The reigning princes who rebelled against the Emperor and sought to wrest the *Judenregal* ("royal prerogative over the Jews") from him, looked upon that sovereign right as a symbol of victory or defeat in their fight against the head of the *Reich.* The Emperor, in turn, interpreted such limitation of one of his Imperial prerogatives as an infringement upon the sovereign dignity of the anointed and crowned secular representative of God on earth.

In the *"Territorial Staaten"* then in the process of formation, the question of the admission or expulsion of Jews became a dangerous bone of contention in the power politics between the reigning princes and the Territorial Estates, again a conspicuous symbol of triumph for one side or the other in the struggle for superiority.

The Catholics came to see the Jew as the instigator of Protestantism, the guilty party in the schism and the accomplice of the infidel Turks, while the Protestants looked upon him as the Papist, the sectarian, and the heretic in league with the Devil.

The patrician citizen, the man of tradition and discipline, blamed the Jew for the outbreak of the great social revolution and for the ruin of the sacred order in the *Reich*; the "common man" in the towns and the peasant in the countryside, who strove for the legal equality of all classes and for the breakup of the large estates, branded him as a fellow-traveler of the capitalists and monopolists who to them represented wealth and property.

It was the controversy raging about the burning of Jewish books, the *cause célèbre* of sixteenth-century Europe, that divided Scholasticism from Humanism, the obscurantists from the tolerants, religious fanaticism from enlightenment —and the Middle Ages from the Modern Era.

When, due to their expulsion from the Imperial cities of the *Reich,* the serfs of the Chamber of the Holy Roman Empire had sunk very low indeed politically, socially and economically; when the erstwhile proud bankers and merchant princes of the middle class had turned into the despised moneylenders and pawnbrokers of villages and hamlets; when, practically week after week, Shrovetide plays, dramas, and passion plays presented to vast audiences gathered in open squares or spacious cathedrals the image of the Jew as a usurer and traitor, the killer of Christ and the ravisher of the Virgin Mary; and when broadsides and woodcuts informed the populace of every detail of the ritual-murder and host-desecration trials—that was the time when the Jews of Germany found a leader and advocate, a helper and a comforter, in the person of Josel of Rosheim, in Alsace. As their freely chosen "commander" and "chief," his authority resting solely on the affection and confidence of his community, he traveled the length and the breadth of the *Reich.* For a period of almost four decades, he pleaded the cause of his people before emperors and kings, princes and bishops, margraves and town magistrates, to stop trials for trumped-up ritual-murder charges, to obtain freedom for those condemned to death, to bring about the recall of expulsion orders, and to secure privileges and relief from trading restrictions for his brethren.

Josel raised the Imperial Diet, the most manifest and distinguished forum of the *Reich* in this period, to the status of a public tribunal. Acting at once as judge and advocate, he most impressively refuted before all the world the accusations brought against the Jews and insisted upon adherence to agreements which, having been confirmed by solemn oath, were irrevocable and inviolate.

In apologetic writings and public debates, he unequivocally refuted the charges brought by Catholics and Protestants alike against the literature of Judaism, and drew on the sacred texts to prove their attacks unfounded.

Keenly aware of the conflict between the forces of universalism and particularism within the *Reich,* he wisely took advantage of it, unconditionally taking the side of the Imperial Patron. In return for this gesture, the Jews received active support in times of grave external and internal stress.

With that same pious purposefulness he helped them make the difficult transition from urban to rural life, to give up the cities which they had so lovingly and proudly extolled in the past as the "Crown of Israel" and the "Shield and Mighty Pillar of the Torah" and to evolve, in their stead, on the pattern of the well-organized urban Jewish community, a new type of communal religious life in the form of the body corporate of the *Landjudenschaft* (Territorial Jewry). For the first time, and, except for the days of the Reichsvertretung (representative body of German Jewry), the last time in the history of the Diaspora in Germany, he succeeded in uniting the communities of the South and the West which until then had kept rigidly apart from one another and had zealously guarded their autonomy. He united them in one Jewish Imperial Federation, a sort of Jewish *Reichsliga.* He imbued them with a new spirit of cooperation, so that they reached a point where they could take counsel together at regular conferences on the problems raised by political, economic, social and religious change, and so guard Jewry against the dangers that threatened it.

In order to shore up this external reconstruction from within, Josel labored in that age of *renascentia* and Reformation to bring about an inner transformation in the individual Jew and to give his life renewed meaning and dedication through a moral and religious regeneration.

Thus Josel became the first social critic and social reformer of the Jews of Germany. His well-planned *Judenordnung* (Jewish by-laws), which was accepted by all the communities, represented the first large-scale attempt to clarify, reform and recast their unsettled social and economic situation by measuring it against the absolute and eternal standards of their Judaism and comparing it with the changed social and economic conditions of the environment in which they lived.

Even as the humanists acquainted the German people with their early beginnings in order that they might acquire a better understanding of their own times, so Josel led his brethren back to the wellsprings of their history so that they might gain a new awareness of their origins and of the Covenant which God had made with His people; that they might perceive once again, as they had in ages past, the words which the prophets and the psalmists had uttered both to judge and to sustain them.

Like the adherents of the *devotio moderna,* the "New Piety," who followed in the footsteps of the great Christian mystics of the Middle Ages, Josel patterned his own conduct and life on the standards set by the medieval Hasidim, the "Pietists of Germany." Josel thus demonstrated to them, by his personal example, how they should live and accept suffering, and so was able to impart to the Jews of his time the strength to calm the storm within their souls by contemplating the eternity of God and, if the need arose, to sanctify His Name by making the supreme sacrifice of martyrdom.

More than any other German Jew either before or after him, Josel, in the course of his long life, kept in close touch with the leading political figures of his time, including the Emperors Maximilian I and Charles V, King Ferdinand and his advisors, the Electors of Brandenburg, Saxony and the Palatinate, the Dukes of Bavaria and Wuerttemberg, the Bishops of Strasbourg and Wuerzburg, the *Landvoegte* (governors) of Alsace, and many town magistrates. But unlike the "Court Jews" of a later day, Josel never managed a public exchequer, nor did he conduct financial transactions or assist in the economic development of any territory.

He was actively involved in the most important political and military events of his century, such as the Imperial Diets of Nuremberg, Augsburg, Worms, Speyer and Regensburg, the Peasants' War, the Schmalkaldic War and the uprising of the princes against Charles V in 1552. But he never performed a political mission as the agent of either side and never acted as a war commissary to provision an army.

He did not fight for the rights of man or the political rights of his people, or for their civil and social equality, as later generations were to do after him. But he believed that by insisting, in accordance with the teaching of his prophets, upon the restoration of that "Divine right" and that "Divine justice" which rank above all man-made justice and right, he was fighting not only for the survival of Judaism but also for the survival of the whole world.

Josel's memoirs on the events of his time shed no new light on those decades which were the most tempestuous and discordant in German history. But they were written by a man who, as he himself admits, belonged to a people living dispersed throughout the world with neither land nor armies of its own, so that it was not up to him to take a stand in the fight between the conflicting powers. For this reason, he has left us a more objective and rational evaluation of the events which he witnessed and a more even distribution of the bright and seamy aspects of history than many chroniclers of his day, who advocated the cause of the Catholics or the Protestants, of the Imperial party or that of the Estates of the Realm.

It has been said of Charles V, Josel's most illustrious fellow on the stage of history that "all those forces which brought his achievements to naught are present even now, albeit in radically altered form, and their bearers no longer know anything of the inner law which guided the actions of that Emperor, their great opponent of the past, nor of the essence of his being, nor of the cogent idea which he personified."[1]

Applying standards of an entirely different character, it may be said also of Josel's political life-work that it was destroyed by forces which are present today, even as they were in the past.

After the death of Charles V, the world-wide monarchy in whose vast expanse Josel had sought a place for his Jews fell to pieces and was inherited by those powers which had mutinied against the Emperor and persecuted Imperial Jewry.

But the "cogent idea which Josel personified," this personification of a representative and heroic life, of a splendid *exemplar vitae humanae* (example of human living), must never be permitted to depart from the consciousness of his people over the generations.

JOSEL OF ROSHEIM

CHAPTER ONE

THE BEGINNINGS

THROUGH a strange quirk of circumstance, we know neither the year nor the city in which Josel of Rosheim was born; nor do we know where and when he died and where he was buried. It is odd that these two most important dates in the life of the man who was the most famous Jew of sixteenth-century Germany, who set down his memoirs with the painstaking accuracy of a chronicler, whose petitions to emperors and kings, electors and dukes, bishops and governors fill whole archives, and whose name appears year after year and indeed often month after month in the records of the *Reich* and in the Senatorial protocols of the Imperial towns, should not have been noted. Not even the Memorial Books dating from his time, which make loving mention of the good he did, give us any idea as to where to look for his final resting place. And despite the fact that pride in ancestry is a typical feature of the Jew, and there can be no doubt that Josel was of distinguished descent, no mention is made anywhere of his parental stock. Yet Wolfgang Capito, the reformer of Strasbourg, characterized him as an outstanding personality among his own people who revered him as their protector, and the

Jews proudly referred to him as their Prince and Chief, their Leader and Commander.

Tradition has it that Josel's family had immigrated into Germany from a place called Louhans in France, and as a matter of fact, the appellation Loans is often found appended to his name. On one occasion, at an assembly of Jewish delegates in Worms in 1542, he himself signed his name in Hebrew characters as Joseph ben Gershon of the family of Louans. His grandson, Eliahu Baal-Shem, rabbi in Worms and author of a commentary on the *Zohar,* was also known as Elijah ben Moses Loanz.[1]

One is easily inclined, therefore, to regard Josel as a kinsman of Jacob Jehiel Loans, personal physician to the Emperor Frederick III, not only because of the identical surname but also because of the many common traits the two men shared and the privileged position which both enjoyed, far above their fellow-Jews.

Just as the Emperor Charles V granted Josel favor upon favor, so the Emperor's great-grandfather, Frederick III, conferred knighthood on Jacob Jehiel Loans and refused to part with him until the end. Frederick, the most enigmatic figure in the Habsburg dynasty, bore the worst upheavals in his reign and in his personal life with an imperturbable smile. This ruler, who spent his leisure time studying metals and precious stones, inquiring into the course of the stars and interpreting the character and the future of men from their facial features and the lines on their palms, had held not only his physician but also the Jews as a group in such great esteem that one chronicler disdainfully referred to him as a "King of the Jews," and another complained that he had granted more protection to the Jewish subjects of the *Reich* than to the Christians. It is a moot question whether it was through Jacob Jehiel's influence that the Emperor first developed an interest in Judaism, or whether it was the

Emperor's own study of the mysterious forces of nature that served to bring him closer also to the more hidden and profound realms of religious perception and experience.

Johann Reuchlin, the most erudite classical scholar of his time,[2] referred to the Emperor's personal physician in admiring terms as "*homo ex Judaeis non parum literatus,*" as the "*humanissimus praeceptor*" who initiated him into the rudiments of the Hebrew language during a long stay at the Imperial Court in Linz in 1492. Reuchlin extolled not only the "*doctrina purissima*" of the "*doctor excellens,*" but to the same extent the goodness and the gentleness of his teacher, his search for unvarnished truth, his quest for basic and literal essentials which led him to look upon all outer sham and pretense with disdain. Reuchlin immortalized Loans in his major work *De Arte Cabbalistica* in a splendid and dignified manner, perpetuating his personality in the character of Simon, the wise and distinguished Jew. In fact, Reuchlin himself was surprised that he could look with such joy upon the face of "a Jew, begotten, nurtured, raised and taught by Jews, by a people which all others consider barbaric, superstitious, base, depraved and far removed from the brilliance of the sciences" and listen so eagerly to his words.

The Jew Simon is a new type of Jew who was not encountered in Germany prior to this time. He is a man of broad education and gentlemanly bearing, a person of great dignity and self-restraint. He is a profoundly erudite teacher of wisdom, a high-minded expounder of the Cabbala, a man well-versed in mysterious revelation and in a miraculous word which first made him aware of the secret origin of things, and gave him the key to the understanding of nature and of Creation. He is a microcosm, as it were, who reflects the macrocosm on a smaller scale and who, by means of words and numbers, symbols and figures, seeks to join the earthly and the heavenly, the physical and the spiritual, the natural and the supernatural, and to unite the soul of man with the Universal Soul.

It was probably due to the influence of this teacher that Reuchlin came to regard Hebrew as the language in which God had spoken to men and men had conversed with angels face to face. He came to consider it as the richest and most creative of all languages, in which every word, syllable, number and letter and even every dot and hook is replete with meaning and sanctity.

The only men whom we can name with certainty as Josel's paternal ancestors in a broad sense are his three great-uncles: Elias (Helya), Eberlin and Mercklin. A sad fate kept their names from oblivion; they are recorded to this day on the yellowed paper of ancient court records.[3]

In addition, drama and song, legend and art have preserved the memory of Josel's kinsmen with grisly forcefulness to our own time.

These three brothers lived in the second half of the fifteenth century in the little town of Endingen, which was then part of the ancestral territory of the House of Habsburg, known as Anterior Austria, whose landed estates lay scattered through Brisgau, the Black Forest, Switzerland and the Alsace. At that time Jewish families had settled in these areas in large numbers, because the Habsburg government had issued a decree in 1446 declaring that anyone injuring or slaying a Jew was liable to prompt prosecution by the law.

It was in this peaceful, sleepy town at the foot of the vine-covered *Kaiserstuhl,* not far from Fribourg in the Brisgau and the banks of the Rhine, which separates the fertile Alemannic plain from the Alsace, that there dwelt also the boy named Gershon, who was to be the father of Josel. We do not know whether he was an orphan and lived with his relatives, or whether his uncle Elias, who was a rabbi, had been the one to instruct him in the teachings of the Fathers.

One evening in the autumn of 1462, a migrant beggar family—a man, his wife and two children—passed through this little town. They wandered wearily from place to place because no one wanted to give them shelter. Sarah, the wife of Rabbi Elias, took pity on them and gave them lodging in the barn of her house. It was the season of the Feast of Tabernacles, and Elias had invited his two brothers and several Jews from Pforzheim, who happened to be staying at Endingen at the time, to pass the night of Hoshanah Rabbah at his home in prayer and hymn-singing.

Eight years went by. That Feast of Tabernacles and the beggar family had long since been forgotten. Then, one day, in the cemetery of the town, in the *Gerner,* where the remains of the dead were kept, there were found parts of four human bodies—a man, a woman and two children. They had been brutally murdered with a plow-iron. Elias' neighbor, a butcher who owed the brothers a great deal of money, testified under oath that, during the night of Hoshanah Rabbah, 1462, he had heard loud noise and unearthly screams, like those of children who were being bled to death, coming from the house of Rabbi Elias.

Under agonizing torture, the brothers made the confession which the Court wanted; namely, that they had obtained blood from Christians for use as medicine for various ailments and as medication after circumcision.

The verdict was handed down on April 4, 1470. The accused were found guilty as charged. They were placed on dried cows' skins, tied to the tails of horses and dragged through the narrow streets of the town to the execution site, a hill known to this day as "Jews' Hill." The four Jews from Pforzheim who were suspected of complicity in the crime met the same fate. The rest of the Jews of Endingen were banished from the area "for all time." As for the bodies of the murdered beggar family, they were enshrined in St. Peter's Church and worshipped as miraculous relics by devout pilgrims. The crime of the brothers was recorded for posterity in inscriptions on a series of eight picture panels painted on the house of Elias, the "Jews' House," and the character of Rabbi Elias was revived again and again in the *Endinger Judenspiel.* This drama, which dates from the beginning of the seventeenth century, portrayed Elias as the "plucky" man who felt called upon to attack helpless people "without arms or defenses" in order to have his revenge on the Christians for the insults they had offered his people.

Gershon, Josel's father, escaped the arm of the law by the skin of his teeth. It may be that he was not yet residing at Endingen in 1462, for there is no mention of his name in the court records; or perhaps he was too young to observe that Hoshanah Rabbah night with his kinsmen. However, the tragic fate of his uncles cast a somber gloom over his life. When his son reached the age at which other Jewish children heard from their fathers the story of the Exodus from Egypt or of the bravery of the lad David, Gershon gave Josel a moving account of the experience he had gone through in his youth; how the oppressors of Endingen had come and cast their nets over his kinsmen, how all of them together had been taken, how their souls had been tortured until they had been forced to make a false confession, and how finally they had gone to their deaths in order to sanctify the Name of Almighty God.[4]

At that time, Gershon had fled across the Rhine to the Alsace. Fribourg, which was nearer to Endingen, had already expelled its Jews in 1424 and Basel had denied them residence rights as early as 1397. The Alsace, on the other hand, had had a large Jewish settlement for centuries. This, the most fragmented region of the Holy Roman Empire, in which the reigning princes of Habsburg, Wuerttemberg, Baden, the

Palatinate, Hanau and Lichtenberg had their small Landgraviates, bailiwicks, counties and domains, in which the knights of the Empire and the bishops dwelt side by side as friends—or as foes—and in which the ten Imperial towns of Muehlhausen, Colmar, Tuerckheim, Munster, Kaysersberg, Schlettstadt, Oberehnheim, Rosheim, Hagenau and Weissenburg had united to form a confederation, was an ideal place of refuge for the persecuted Jew. If he was expelled from a city directly subordinate to the *Reich* or from the territory of a reigning prince, he could be certain of getting a friendly welcome from one of the debt-encumbered knights or noblemen or from the impoverished magistrate of some Landgravian village.

Moreover, Gershon knew this region well. The countryside was the same on each bank of the Rhine: a wide and fertile expanse on which grain and corn, tobacco and hops flourished, and green hills rose upon which "Bacchus dwells and the fruit of the vine ripens."[5] On either side there was the same temperate sky, the same southern sun. The blue mountains on which the somber dark fir trees grew offered the same broad vista at the snow-covered Swiss Alps. And the same massive colonnaded castles rose on the steep, wooded hillsides, ramparts, moats, and turrets from which the mighty nobility of old had defended the plains of the Rhine against enemies from the south and the west.

Gershon settled in Oberehnheim in the Lower Alsace, one of those trim Imperial towns of the country in which the finely wrought cathedrals, with their sumptuous stone ornamentation, and the sloping houses, with their black roofs, brown gables and carved balconies, proudly proclaimed the self-sufficiency, the piety and the affluence of the burghers within. But it was neither the charm of the architecture, nor the famed well, that attracted Gershon to Oberehnheim. What drew him there was the circumstance that this town, in which Jews had been living since 1215, had renewed the Jews' privileges at the beginning of the fifteenth century and had admitted to citizenship additional families "in the name of the *Reich*,"[6] so that Gershon encountered no difficulties when he made application there in 1470 for a residence permit.

However, his stay in Oberehnheim was not of long duration. This time, he was uprooted not by the superstitious intolerance of religious fanatics, but as a result of political developments in the warlike century in which he lived.

In those days Charles, Duke of Burgundy, a vassal of France and of the *Reich,* who lived under the spell of romantic delusions of a dying feudal civilization, cherished pipe-dreams of re-establishing the Empire of Lothar the Carolingian midway between the East and the West. He envisioned a united kingdom, or perhaps even an empire, which would be ruled by the will of one man, and which would extend from the English Channel, the shores of the North Sea and the Somme Estuary, through the Lower and Upper Rhine regions, south to Savoy, to Switzerland and as far south as upper Italy. Indeed, Sigismund, the Habsburg ruler of the Tyrol and Master of Anterior Austria, hard-pressed by the Swiss, had already mortgaged to Charles the Landgraviate in the Upper Alsace, the Southern Black Forest Region and the Brisgau, and Charles had succeeded in conquering the Duchies of Geldern and Lorraine. But at that point, those to whom the ambitions of Charles represented a menace, the Swiss Confederates, the Bishops of Basel and Strasbourg, the cities of Strasbourg, Schlettstadt and Colmar, and the Duke of Lorraine, joined forces in a defensive alliance. Thus it came to pass that little Switzerland was able to overpower the man who, until that time, had been unconquerable. He was defeated in the battles of Granson and Murten, and in 1477 the headstrong prince, whom his contemporaries had regarded as the Antichrist himself, met an untimely death in the fighting outside Nancy.

During that war the Swiss mercenaries, who for centuries had stood under the arms of their own country and under those of other governments, roamed through the Upper and Lower Alsace. Much like the Armagnacs before them, a pugnacious and rapacious lot, they, too, attacked the Jews. In Colmar, Schlettstadt, Kaysersberg and elsewhere Jews would be attacked and robbed of their possessions. Many were killed or forced under torture to accept baptism.[7]

Gershon, who had married in those years, fled from Oberehnheim with his wife and the other Jews. They hid out in two fortresses, Hohbarr and Luetzelstein, where they spent a whole year in "hunger and thirst."

Gershon told his child of this episode in the Burgundian War, of his flight and the sufferings of persecution, but he also told him the wondrous tale of how this little band, apparently doomed to death, was saved by the deed of a brave and pious man.

"It was very cold then,[8] colder than it had been for a long time, so that the Jews (mainly those of Colmar) could not seek shelter in caves and hiding places and therefore sought lodging in the houses in and around Tuerckheim. It was then that the foes came to throw them to the hangmen. Now there were some eighty souls all told, men, women, youths and maidens, all prepared to die. They cast themselves upon the ground to beg for their lives. At that time God sent His help and His angel, who disposed the chief of the robbers to have mercy. He said: 'If you can bring me eight hundred florins by noon tomorrow, I shall accept it as your ransom, ten gold florins for each one of you.' However, there was no Jew left in the territory, save one pious man, Judah Pamseh of Muehlhausen. All the other Jews had been either destroyed or dispersed, slain or drowned and robbed of all their possessions. Now when this pious man heard the evil tidings, he rent his garments, sat down on the ground and put on sackcloth and ashes, and all the people of his household did likewise. He took everything that he possessed and dispatched his servant Mordecai with the ransom money of eight hundred florins. The servant was delayed, so that he did not arrive there before noon. Thus they were all led away bound to a rope, rabbis, elders, women, youths and maidens. First the robbers seized one whose name was Paneth, tearing the clothes from his body so that they might cut off his head. They dealt likewise with the worthy Rabbi Zaddok and all the others. The people fell upon their knees to confess their sins, and they bared their necks to the sword. The hangman drew his sword to cut off their heads, one after the other. At that moment the servant arrived and cried out: 'Leave all these Jews alone. I have brought the money for the prisoners. Here it is.' And so the ringleaders took the eight hundred florins and permitted the Jews to enter safely into the house of Judah."

This near tragedy that had happened to his parents and to those who had shared their misfortune left a deep impression on the soul of the sensitive boy. Even as an old man, although he would render account in restrained and almost jejune language the happenings of his own eventful life, he could not suppress his emotions when he passed on to his own descendants the moving story his father had told him. It was in those early days that his great compassion for the defenseless victims of torture by human hands and of humiliation by human speech had first been stirred. All the moral instruction his father had given him did not impress him as powerfully as the parable of the praiseworthy Pamseh of Muehlhausen, who was overwhelmed by grief on first hearing the evil tidings, but who immediately strained every nerve to bring succor to his imperiled fellow-Jews.

Gershon and his wife were not able to return to Oberehnheim. After the war, the cities of Colmar, Muehlhausen, Kaysersberg, Schlettstadt, Rosheim, Oberehnheim and others had met in conference and resolved to ban all Jews from their gates. In a report which they submitted to their *Oberlandvogt*, the Count Palatine Philip, they claimed that the Swiss had forced them to drive out the Jews; if they were to permit the Jews to return to their former homes now, they said, they would only be exposing them to new danger. Even after most of the cities, yielding to explicit orders from the Count Palatine, had allowed their Jews to return, Oberehnheim stubbornly persisted in its refusal to readmit them and could not be persuaded even by the stern admonitions from the *Unterlandvogt* "to preserve and to practice time-honored custom."[9]

One of the few cities which did not participate in the conference of the allied Imperial Cities was Hagenau, in the Lower Alsace. Ever since Frederick Barbarossa and his successors had conferred generous privileges upon this city, it had frequently served as a place of refuge for persecuted Jews.[10] The Jews who had been driven from France by Philip August had already found shelter there, and those who had been expelled from the city of Strasbourg were readily admitted to Hagenau and its surrounding areas. Having gained wealth through lending money to monasteries, knights and noblemen, the Jews acquired homes in the best streets of Hagenau and built a handsome synagogue there. When the Black Death struck (1348-49), and most of the cities in the Alsace drove out their Jews, the Jews of Hagenau were permitted to remain in their homes undisturbed. At that time they received a charter of protection which has been preserved to this day, and which guaranteed them the inviolability of their rights and liberties as "domiciled citizens."

It was in Hagenau, the home town of his wife, Reislin,

whose brothers still lived there, that Gershon settled, and it appears that Josel was born there in the year 1478. Apparently Gershon and his wife were childless at the time of the Burgundian War, for when, at the end of his account of the persecution in the Alsace, their son Josel gives thanks to God for having preserved his father and mother, his friends and his kinsmen, he makes no mention of brothers, of sisters, or of himself.[11] In his *Sefer Ha-Mikneh,* he records that he spent his youth in Hagenau. "And I saw him (i.e., one of his uncles) in the days of my youth in Hagenau," he writes. "When I was six years of age, I was with him and with my pious uncle Rabbi Elijah, who moved to the Holy City of Jerusalem and wanted to take me with him. Then my father died . . ."[12]

In this text he makes mention also of the distinguished family of his grandmother Gitlin of Hagenau, who traced her descent to the Gaon Shelomo Spira, the progenitor of a dynasty of famous scholars, which included Yohanan Luria, a rabbinical authority and Josel's contemporary.[13]

The Imperial city of Hagenau, which headed the Decapolis, the League of the Ten Cities, was distinguished from the other Imperial towns of the *Reich* by virtue of the fact that it had been the capital of the *Reichslandvogtei* (Imperial government) of Alsace for centuries. There, in the "Holy Forest," Frederick Barbarossa had set up his Imperial palace. It was there, too, that Henry VI had hunted in the spacious *Reich* forests, and that Frederick II, who paid visit after visit to the Alsace, which he considered "of all his German hereditary lands the most dear," was married at his sumptuous palace to Agnes, his third wife.

In this palace, in the year 1236, the Emperor had handed down a wise and just decision in the ritual murder trial of Fulda, in which the Jews had been accused of having murdered Christian boys in order to use their blood for the Passover feast.[14] The Emperor had summoned before his judgment seat both the Jewish defendants and their Christian accusers, who had brought the bodies of the children with them as court evidence. He instructed the accusers to bury the bodies, since he considered them no longer of use for anything else. In addition, he had the accusation publicly refuted by calling together converted scholars from all over the world to attest once and for all to the innocence of their former coreligionists. For "these people, who once had been Jews themselves and had been converted to the Christian way of worship, were now their adversaries and therefore certainly would not conceal anything derogatory that they might know about them or about the Books of Moses either through their new beliefs or with the help of the Books of the Old Testament."

A remnant of the glory of the Hohenstauffen period still clung to the town of Hagenau. Surrounded by countless manorial estates, the Imperial Territory represented the sole central point, the only remaining symbol of the unity of the Empire, which still survived in theory. Representing the Emperor, the *Reichslandvogtei* was the effective Supreme Imperial authority and custodian of all the prerogatives pertaining to the *Reich*. Ever since 1408, when the *Vogtei* had been mortgaged to the Palatinate, the office of Governor of the Imperial Territory (*Reichslandvogt*) had been held by members of the Palatinate branch of the Wittelsbach dynasty. The Governor was judge, commander-in-chief of the armed forces, and receiver of taxes—all in one. When he took office, the Imperial cities were obliged to take an oath of allegiance to him and to pay him tribute. In return, the Imperial Governor was duty-bound to extend his personal protection to all the inhabitants of the Alsace who were directly subject to the *Reich* and to guarantee them their time-honored privileges.

It was in this country, through which traders carried their wares from Switzerland and Italy to the Rhine and Schelde deltas, and then brought back other merchandise from Flanders, the Hennegau, Bruges, and Ghent to Strasbourg, Basel, Zurich and Milan, that the lad Josel grew up. This was ancient Roman soil where, long ago, the Celts and Teutons had met and mingled. From their Alemannic-Frankish ancestors, the people of the Alsace had inherited an inclination to brooding, pensiveness, fanciful fabrications, religious inwardness and mystical ecstasy, but also a natural bent for defiant isolation and resistance to coercion and oppression. Their Celtic forebears, on the other hand, had bequeathed to them the gift of critical observation and sharp satire, a sense for clarity of expression and beauty of form, and the logic of alert, dispassionate reasoning which frequently clashed head-on with the irrational and mystical element of their Teutonic heritage. It was only natural that people living in a border and transit area of this kind, whose boundaries lay exposed on all sides, should also be susceptible to influences and stimuli from without.

From Italy came the new philosophy of religious-universal theism as taught at the Academy of Florence and particularly as expounded in the neo-Platonic doctrines of Ficino and Pico della Mirandola.[15] The ideal preached there was no longer that of the saintly, self-denying and self-sacrificing ascetic, of poverty and obedience; it was that of a natural, real and genuine human being who could develop freely and independently as the creator and shaper of his own destiny, guided by the dictates of his own innate reason.

The Alsace, and Schlettstadt in particular, has been described as "the real home" of what was known as "earlier humanism," because it was there, at the Latin School founded by the Rector Ludwig Dringenberg, that most of the Alsatian humanists had received their training. Like its Italian counterpart, this Alsatian humanism had rediscovered the literary sources of the past, based its studies on the pattern of the great historians of antiquity and, like the latter, sought to interpret the political and historical situation of its own time in terms of the experiences of the past. On the soil which had been the battleground for the struggle between the great rival powers of France and Austria, there came into being, for the first time in Germany, a nationalist approach to history which responded to France's attacks on the Alsace with impassioned verbal thrusts. By providing the "Divinely willed institution" of the medieval *Reich* with historical and legal foundation, this approach also imparted a solid basis to the dream the people had cherished for centuries: the dream of the return of the Emperor, who was envisioned as the redeemer of the oppressed, the comforter of the downhearted, and the restorer of the right.

However, unlike the Italian and the younger school of later humanism, the humanists of the Alsace were not aware of the uniqueness and originality of the individual personality They were still very much under the spell of the Middle Ages; they were Christian, bourgeois, modest and devout. They were educators imbued with high ideals whose aim it was to teach man common sense, frugality and self-control, to train him for a great mission and teach him to understand himself.

Dringenberg had come to the Alsace from Deventer, Holland, bringing with him the doctrine of the *devotio moderna,* the "New Piety," as exemplified in practice at the time by the "Brethren of Common Life" and the Augustinian Canons.

These non-ecstatic mystics did not seek to serve the Deity with the ardent wooing of Tauler and Seuse, nor did they wish to perceive God through the philosophical theorizing of Master Eckhart and Nicholas of Cusa. Instead, it was their aim to partake of the inner experience of the Divine by self-sacrificing service to their fellow-men, and to rid themselves of vices and passions through constant self-examination.

They sought peace of soul and the ultimate fulfillment in perfect love for every creature of God, in humble emulation of Christ.

What, if anything, did Josel absorb from these ideals, and how did he come by them? He had not been allowed to attend the school of the humanists or that of the "New Piety," nor did he have a teacher who could have familiarized him with the culture of his day. However, he was able to write in the vernacular of his country—in a pithy, graphic and expressive German, from which he could coax a tone both warm and somber, or gentle and harsh, or conciliatory and threatening. It was that heavy, Upper German dialect which we find in the farcical tales of Johannes Pauli, in Thomas Murner's *Schelmenzunft* ("Company of Rogues"), and in the romances of Joerg Wickram. Not only was Josel familiar with the legal concepts and the intellectual trends of his century, but he understood Latin as well, a language which was essential to him for interpretation of the Imperial and Papal documents of earlier centuries and for his debates at the Imperial Diets. But he does not reveal where and when he managed to acquire this learning. He mentions only on one occasion that, during a heated debate at one of the Diets, God enabled him to speak in the language of the scholars.[16] Elsewhere, he admits to having attended in Strasbourg the lectures of the erudite Wolfgang Capito, the most brilliant and noble personality among the Reformers, and a friend of Erasmus, who had been close to the "New Piety."[17]

In those days it was not too difficult for a bright lad to satisfy his thirst for learning. There were any number of sources on which he could draw, even without the benefit of teachers and schools. Month after month, the relatively new art of printing, which had originated in nearby Strasbourg, poured onto the market histories of the world and adventure stories, chronicles and books of devotion, political pamphlets and religious tracts, books on travel and texts on geography. Dramas and Shrovetide plays brought to the public the life stories of the Emperor Constantine and the Sultan of Babylonia, and tales of journeys to the Holy Land and of the changing fortunes of the Duke of Burgundy. Chapbooks gave graphic descriptions of far-off lands and cities, and of strange rites and customs. Even the *Ship of Fools* by Sebastian Brant, the erudite town clerk of Strasbourg, which was the most widely read book at the end of the fifteenth century, was intended not merely to lash out against the follies of the various classes of society, but also to educate the reader in politics, economics, religion and jurisprudence.

Josel tells us no more about his background in rabbinic studies than he does about his secular education. He was amazingly conversant in biblical, talmudic, philosophical and cabbalist literature; he had a good knowledge of medieval Jewish history and literature, and perfect mastery of Hebrew. He was skilled in the detailed interpretation of customs, rituals and ceremonies, and well-versed even in the most complex regulations of Mosaic and talmudic law. He had a sharp legal mind, and he was a master in the art of debating. These were all skills which he could only have acquired in one of the *yeshivoth* in the *Reich,* where the students, under the guidance of a gifted instructor, received training and exercise in refuting or defending the legal decisions handed down by illustrious commentators. And if Josel's self-control did not desert him in difficult situations, in danger and distress, and if he never showed arrogance in times of triumph and victory, he was simply putting into practice the precepts of Divine Law taught him at the *yeshivoth,* that Law which commands the pious man "to be heedful of his conduct and not to allow himself to be carried away by emotion."[18]

At that time there had been academies of this type in Swabia and Franconia, and on the banks of the Rhine, the Main and the Danube. The most renowned of these was the Academy of Regensburg, the seat of the Pilpulist school of talmudic studies.

It is probable, however, that Josel, for personal reasons, chose one of the *yeshivoth* in the Rhineland, not only because it was close to his home town, but because his entire philosophy of life indicates that he received his training from scholars who taught at these academies, scholars who were "men of exact, objective and scholarly inquiry," free of "all sophistry and casuistry."

Nor would it be out of line to conjecture that he received instruction from his kinsman, the Gaon Yohanan Luria, who mentions in one of his writings, a commentary on the Pentateuch entitled *Meshibat Nefesh* ("Restoration of the Soul"), that he had "purchased with his funds the permission to establish a *yeshiva* in the government seat of the Alsace." This "government seat" could only have been either the city of Ensisheim, the residence of the Habsburg rulers in the Upper Alsace, or the city of Hagenau, the seat of the *Landvoegte* in the Lower Alsace. Since sources show that Yohanan was in the Lower Alsace in the year 1483, we can assume that his house of study had been in Hagenau for some time, and that it was from this noted scholar, who also labored to defend Judaism from attacks by its adversaries, that Josel received his education in rabbinic lore.

However, it was not this world of Talmud and Halakhah that molded Josel's character, shaped his outlook and imparted to him the values and standards by which he was to live. When he looked for a pattern on which to model his future life, he chose as his model not the ingenious expounders of the Law, the learned authors of the *Responsa,* but the Jewish mystics who were known as the *Hasidei Ashkenaz,* the "Pious of Germany."

These "Pious Men of Germany," especially Yehuda he-Hasid of the Kalonymus family, the author of the *Book of the Pious,* and his disciple Eleazar of Worms, the author of a classic work entitled *Sefer ha-Rokeach,* exerted a significant influence on all elements and social classes of German Jewry during the twelfth and thirteenth centuries. They were influential not merely because of their teachings, but because of their way of life, an influence which persisted well into the modern era. Their original, powerful religious conviction and force stirred up the soul of the Jew, and gave it new life and form. They made him capable of accepting the suffering of persecution and of proclaiming the greatness and almighty power of their God in song and exultation, even as they stood tied to the stake.[19] They themselves could bear insult and humiliation with equanimity because they believed no mere human word can violate the purity of the human heart. They paid no regard to outward glitter and material gain, for, in their view, it was only by frugality and resignation that base desires could be kept in check and the commandments of God fulfilled. They overcame cruelty with gentleness, and thirst for revenge with forbearance; they replaced falsehood with truth and hatred with goodness because they believed in the inexhaustible strength of the human heart and in the all-conquering power of human love. They searched for insight into the mystery of God through ecstatic prayer, profound rapture and silent contemplation. They voluntarily placed themselves under a stringent discipline of penitence so that, by their repentance and contrition, they might be able to conquer the evil that had come into the world by reason of Israel's sin, to bring about a reconciliation between the upper sphere and the lower, and to unite God and His glory forever.

In 1473, shortly before Josel was born, there appeared in Coblenz the *Little Book of the Pious* by Moses ha-Kohen ben

Eleazar, which once again revived the ideology of the German Hasidim. But even as the "New Piety" could no longer attain to the lofty thoughts and ecstatic transports of medieval mysticism, so, too, this *Little Book of the Pious* lacked the visionary fervor and force of Yehuda he-Hasid and of Eleazar of Worms. The sole aim of this new work was to warn Jewish youth against wantonness, sensuality and greed and, at a time of upheaval when all values seemed to be disintegrating, to train them to live a life dedicated to God and to good works. Such a life the author, like the "Brethren of Common Life," valued more than the perfunctory fulfillment of the letter of the law and the mechanical observance of religious precepts. For God demanded the service of the heart, and all things were known to Him.

The tendency toward a *vita contemplativa,* a life of quiet contemplation, mystical rapture and inner meditation, was part and parcel of Josel's character. Even his political writings are replete with solemn observations on the transient nature of earthly things, on the justice and righteousness of God, and on the sin and error of man. When he stayed at the Imperial Court in Brussels in 1531, he rejoiced in the solitude which enabled him to meditate undisturbed on the most profound mysteries of the Torah, and, by contemplation of the eternity of God, to quench the thirst of his soul after ultimate bliss and repose and to fill it with inner joy. His mother's brother moved to the Holy Land so that he might there turn his thoughts to God alone and lead a life of penance and abstinence. His grandson, the "Baal Shem," became one of those zealous miracle workers who, by their entreaties, sought to move God to have mercy on His creatures, and by their own good deeds, hoped to bring about the deliverance of the world below.

The Christian environment in which the boy grew up also served to stimulate and augment the tendency to religious ecstasy inherent in his personality. The men he saw around him were not merely smug, self-satisfied burghers who traded off-color yarns from their dray-carts, or who reveled in drink and gambled in the bath houses or sat in the taverns and debated the magistrate's management of public funds. These people were torn by anxieties and agonies, plagued by nightmares, and set a-tremble by their dread of the Last Judgment. They were obsessed with a fanatical brand of piety; it was as if, at a time when the Church and the old order were collapsing and the absolute truth of Christianity was challenged, they were straining to conjure up once more the spirit of the saints and the martyrs of the Middle Ages. They produced glowing, frenzied, color-intoxicated paintings through which they witnessed their Savior's work of deliverance and his martyrdom again and again. They made wood carvings of sorrowful figures to immortalize the age-old tragedy of mankind and its unexpiated guilt; they composed ardent hymns to Mary, singing longingly of the gentleness and sweetness of the Queen of Heaven. They wrote stirring Passion Plays and Corpus Christi dramas which enabled them to retrace the path to Golgotha. And they delivered themselves of rousing penitential and revivalist sermons, of eery visions and prophecies announcing to the sinful people the coming of the Antichrist and the imminence of the end of the world and the Last Judgment.

The "Reformation of the Emperor Sigismund," in which God Himself was called upon to sit in judgment over the depravity of mankind, declared that all men would become equal "in freedom and deliverance before God". . . . "Obedience is dead," it was asserted, "justice is in distress, and nothing is in its rightful place. For this reason God has withdrawn His grace from us, and rightly so."

In the Alsace and in the nearby Black Forest, the people dreamed of the return of a God-sent Emperor of Peace, a crowned Messiah who would come forth from the mountains "in a garment pure as snow, riding upon a white horse, with a bow and a sword in his hand" to establish a kingdom of political and social equality and to deliver man forever from sin and sorrow.

Under the influence of the religious fervor of his century, Josel's innate penchant for the *vita contemplativa* might have led him to embrace wild visionary and eschatological concerns, had it not been kept in check by his equally strong tendency to a *vita activa,* a life of forceful action and practical interests. The mysticism which he had inherited from the pious of the Rhineland (from where his mother had come) was counterbalanced by a clean and sober sense of reality which had been passed on to his father by his French ancestors. This gift of common sense enabled Josel to analyze people and things with keen judgment and to evaluate them critically without pathos or distortion; to be willing to bury a dream if the time was not yet ripe for its fulfillment; and, in disregard of preconceived notions and abstract principles, to dare to take political action when the times demanded it of him.

No other place could have offered a more favorable environment for the cultivation of such a potential as this "Alsatian Land," which has been described as the land that shaped the destinies of the Holy Roman Empire. For in no other place was there such heated discussion of current political events or such loud clamor for social reform. Current problems such as the idea of a new German Empire, the creation of a good and stable *Reich* administration, the formation of a modern, centralized independent state, the question of a "Gallic" Alsace, the struggle of nearby Switzerland for independence from the *Reich,* the introduction of Roman law and the retention of time-honored statutes, were all debated with the same unflagging zeal as were the older conflicts between the Estates and the Emperor, the reigning princes and the cities, the cities and the knights, the guilds and the patricians and the peasants and their landlords.

There was still another thing that an alert and sensitive youngster with open eyes could observe. The "Song of the Parents and the Innocent Children,"[20] which the maid-servant would sing as she worked, would acquaint him, too, with the story of the murder that had taken place at Endingen, the tale of Jokle the Butcher, and the Jew-man who killed those poor people as they lay on their pallets of straw, them and "their children, even their children."

From Hans Folz's master-singer's song, which the journeymen would hum in their workshops, he could also learn that Judas, having been led astray by the Devil, was doomed to everlasting hell-fire because he had betrayed Christ, his Lord, and sold him to the "perfidious Jewish race."

During the Easter Season he was able to see dramas such as the "Corpus Christi Play of Kuenzelsau" or the "Alsfeld Passion Play"[21] performed in the town's market place almost every day. He could watch the Church Triumphant, a crown on her head and a cross in her hand, heap insults and humiliation upon the vanquished Synagogue, which stood before her with eyes downcast and scepter broken. In the "Drama of the Duke of Burgundy," the heathens and the knights were called upon to sit in judgment over the Jews, and could think of no more appropriate sentence than to advise the Duke to tie stones around the necks of the accused, to hang them, drown them, or perhaps burn the whole lot alive.

Moreover, there were woodcuts, passed from hand to hand by people filled with righteous indignation, which depicted such "happenings" as the "gruesome story" of the Jews of Passau, who, with evil intent, had pierced a sacred host and had therefore been placed under arrest, tortured, and put to death.[22] There was the scurrilous pamphlet about the "wicked, blackguardly Jews" of Sternberg in Mecklenburg, who, seeking to defy the holy Christian faith and to insult Almighty God, had violated the Sacrament of the Lord on St. Severus and St. Severinus Day in 1492, "because they had wanted to test the authenticity of the Blessed Sacrament"; and who "went to their deaths on the Wednesday before St. Simon's and St. Jude's Day, twenty-five men and two women all told, all singing psalms."[23]

At that time the lad still did not understand why such things should befall the people to whom he belonged and whom he loved. But his heart was afire with compassion for his people, compassion which made him wise before his time.

CHAPTER TWO

LEADER OF THE LANDJUDENSCHAFT

In 1493, when Josel was fifteen years old, the Emperor Frederick III died, after a reign of over five decades. For the Jews, the death of a ruler was an event of crucial importance. In the Alsace, particularly, the region of Imperial residences and Imperial towns, where the figure of the Emperor was enveloped by an aura of vision and legend, the Jews awaited the accession of a new sovereign with mingled fear and hope.

Since the days when the rulers of the Salic and Hohenstaufen dynasties had placed them under the Imperial protectorate and under the jurisdiction of the Imperial Chamber, the Jews of Germany had been linked to the person of the sovereign by a unique and singular bond. The force—or lack of force—with which the sovereign wielded his authority, and the moral strength or weakness he displayed, constituted a blessing or a curse for the destinies of his Jewish subjects. The prospering era when the Hohenstaufen rulers reigned supreme in the world was a period of economic prosperity and social advancement for the Jews as well; conversely, the decline of the *Reich* brought on a turn for the worse in the Jewish situation as well.[1] The sovereign's right of ownership with regard to the "Serfs of the Imperial Chamber" was never challenged, and the sovereign's obligation to protect them, as officially proclaimed and set down in Imperial privileges over and over again, was never disputed. However, in the centuries immediately preceding the death of Frederick, the Emperor's *Judenregal* (royal prerogative over the Jews), like other Imperial prerogatives, had been sold, temporarily granted, or ceded to the lower Estates of the *Reich.* Moreover, Louis of Bavaria's statement that the Emperor could do what he liked with his Jews, and take whatever action he saw fit with respect to them because their lives and fortunes belonged to the *Reich,*[2] was an assumption still widely held.

However, Frederick III had been good to his Jews. This emperor, whom neither perils from the west nor threats from the east could perturb, had never permitted any harm, whatever the cause, to come to his Jewish subjects as long as he was on the throne. True, he could not prevent their expulsion from Erfurt, Heilbronn, Rufach, Tuebingen, Schaffhausen, from the Bishopric and City of Bamberg, from the Bishopric of Wuerzburg, from Magdeburg, Mayence, Esslingen and many other cities during his reign. In addition, he was compelled to demand financial assistance from them in the form of taxes for his wars with the Turks, the Hungarians, the Burgundians and the Swiss. But he had rejected, indignantly and with a sense of shame, the charges of host desecration and ritual murder that had been made against them, particularly in Endingen, Passau and Regensburg; and insofar as he held mortgages from the guilty cities, he made the arrest, torture or slaying of the victims punishable by severe penalties of the law. For, as he once put it, he had "always been a foe of great deceit in all dealings, those of Christians and Jews alike."[3] In the ritual murder trial of Regensburg (1476-80), he ardently espoused the cause of the arrested and tortured Jews. According to a report sent to

Regensburg at the time by the then Bavarian Ambassador in Vienna, Frederick had been so enraged over the conduct of the city that he had divested the Magistrate of the power over life and death, and threatened to put him under the ban of the *Reich* unless he released the Jews at once. At that time the members of the clergy bitterly criticized the un-Christian attitude of their Sovereign Lord from their pulpits, and the Magistrate of Regensburg accused him of giving more credence to the "perfidious Jews, the enemies of God and of the Virgin Mary" than to the "pious, honorable, excellent people of this praiseworthy and ancient city."[4]

Certainly, the Emperor's attitude to the serfs of his Imperial Chamber was motivated by his innate tolerance and sense of justice. But he was motivated to an equally strong degree by his concept of the inviolable honor and sacred character of the Emperorship, and would tolerate no infringement on the prerogatives of the Imperial Sovereign. Just as he would never permit any encroachment upon any of his Imperial privileges, so, too, he would never allow anyone to interfere with his *Judenregal* (royal prerogative over the Jews), for he regarded the latter as the inalienable property of the Crown, since it was "directly subject and appertaining to him and to no one else by virtue of the fact that he was the Emperor of the Holy Roman Empire."

When the city of Erfurt made ready to expel its Jews in 1456, he forbade the authorities there "grossly to abuse the serfs of his Imperial Chamber in violation of the tradition of the *Reich*," and to encroach upon the prerogatives of the Emperor. When the *Reichsstadt* of Ulm imposed trading restrictions on its Jewish citizens, he ordered its Magistrate to have these prohibitions repealed, asserting that he would not tolerate the breach of Imperial justice that would result from the ill-treatment of Jews.[5]

Shortly after his accession, Frederick had already requested formal permission from Pope Nicholas V to readmit a certain number of Jews to those of his provinces from which they had been expelled in 1420. Moreover, tradition has it that on his deathbed, he urged his son Maximilian to treat the Jews with benevolence, justice and forbearance and to give no credence to their adversaries.

But the brilliant, talented Maximilian I was the opposite of his circumspect and irresolute father in almost every respect. The people who admired him, the women who loved him, and the humanists who fawned upon him called him "The Last of the Knights," because many of his traits and actions were reminiscent of the spirit of romance of the Crusades, the adventurous heroes of epic poetry, and the inspiration of the romantic minnesong. At the same time, however, Maximilian was a humanist of the modern type. He loved music, painting, architecture and poetry, wrote two novels, and gathered around him a group of scholars and artists, like himself restless, unstable men in quest of an unattainable goal.

But Maximilian also resembled the princes of the Renaissance era in that he was a crafty politician, an unreliable ally, a greedy trader, a believer and yet a skeptic at the same time, a lover of life and yet a mystic who yearned to be Pope and Emperor in one.

His contemporaries were unable to agree either in their evaluation of his personality or in their judgment of his policies. Some have called him the restorer of the Empire, while others have branded him as its destroyer. Some accused him of having entangled the Empire in constant warfare in the west, in the east and in the south solely to aggrandize the power of his own dynasty, while others extolled him for having made a display of the Empire's greatness and might for all to see.

The fact is that Maximilian did both; he damaged and strengthened the Empire at the same time. In order to recover the Burgundian inheritance of his wife Maria, the only daughter of Charles the Bold, he stirred up a conflict between France and the Habsburgs that was to continue for centuries. In this struggle he lost Switzerland for the Empire, but he acquired the Low Countries and the Free County of Burgundy in its stead. With his sanguine political-matrimonial maneuvers, by which he extended his territory into southeastern Europe, he caused the age-old Turkish question to become Europe's most crucial problem, and laid his ancestral territory wide open to raids by Turks and Hungarians. On the other hand, he won Bohemia and Hungary for Austria, and Spain and its colonies for the House of Habsburg.

The end of the fifteenth and the beginning of the sixteenth century have been described as the onset of the Modern Era, because it was at that time that the supremacy of the Church was first challenged by the Reformation, the absolute truth of Christianity by humanism, scholasticism by personal religious experience, and the social doctrine of the Church Fathers by the early capitalist economic system. It was at this time, too, that the State, which until then had been subordinate to the "Eternal Law," broke away from the tutelage of the Church and began its evolution into a national structure, secular in character and motivated solely by power politics and rational and material considerations.

The Holy Roman Empire of the German Nation lagged behind in this development. While the sovereigns of the Empire had lost almost all of their political significance in the course of the two preceding centuries, the institution of the Emperorship as such was still enveloped by an aura of near sanctity. In the minds of the people, the sovereign head of the Empire was still the preserver of justice and peace, the anointed and crowned secular representative on earth of God Himself, Whose commandments he was duty-bound to enforce.

But side by side with him and undermining his powers, there arose the Estates of the *Reich,* the Electors and the reigning princes, the archbishops, bishops, margraves and landgraves, who began at that time to unite the scattered domains, demesnes, and bailiwicks of their territories, to expand them by means of war, pillage, barter and seizure and then, by skillful management, to weld them together into autonomous political entities. No longer content to be vassals to the Emperor, they demanded that his executive powers be curtailed and their own position strengthened. It was their wish for the future to be able to stand alongside of the sovereign as bearers of public authority; not in order to dissolve and destroy the Empire, but in order to preserve and unite it and "to bind the Emperor more closely to the common welfare." It was their plan that the universal and feudal Empire should be transformed into a confederation of reigning princes with autonomous powers under a Government (*Reichsregiment*) which would stand above the Sovereign and the Estates, and which would advise the Emperor and exercise control over his authority. After a hard struggle, they compelled the Emperor to call an annual Diet, and to institute a *Reichskammergericht,* an Imperial High Court of Justice, which was an independent, non-partisan authority and to which the prerogatives of Imperial power, the preservation of justice and peace were transferred.

The dualism prevailing in the *Reich* had a crucial bearing on the political destinies of the Jews. In the course of the struggle for supremacy between the two forces, the Jews of the *Reich* became a bone of contention between the Emperor and the Estates.

Thus, too, in the final analysis, the roots of Maximilian's vacillating policy vis-à-vis the Jews lay in this political situation rather than in any instability or unreliability in his character. As long as the political situation permitted it,

Maximilian, like his father before him, conscientiously fulfilled the protectoral obligation devolving on him as supreme Lord of the Imperial Chamber. But when he was not strong enough to offer resistance to some powerful Estate, or when he was short of funds and therefore in no position to arouse the ire of some wealthy *Reichsstadt* to which he owed money, he would give his approval to the persecution and expulsion of Jews.

Thus he acceded to the request of the Austrian Territorial Estates that the Jews be expelled from Styria, Carinthia and the Archduchy of Austria, but he tolerated their presence in Eisenstadt, Marchegg and other border towns "as his Crown property which he did not intend to drive away." Thus in 1497 he ordered the ten Imperial towns of Alsace in very strong terms to readmit the Jews they had expelled during the Burgundian War.[6] But two years later he gave permission to the city of Nuremberg to "drive them out because of their many evil deeds," for "the excellent and renowned city of Nuremberg was more important to the *Reich* than those Jews." In that same year, the town of Ulm received permission to rid itself of its Jews in return for the promise that it would turn over to the Emperor the synagogue, the houses and all the real estate of the Jewish community.[7]

Many years later, we find Josel discussing the expulsion of the Jews from the German Imperial towns in his *Sefer Ha-Mikneh,* and the emotional coloration of his account, as well as its religious and moral implications, show what a profound shock these events had been to the young man.

In those days Josel had gone into the money trade, and had settled at Mittelbergheim, a small town in the territory of the diocese of Strasbourg, which was guarded by the mighty Vosges fortresses of Andlau, Landsberg and Spesburg.

Josel does not explain why he did not enter the active rabbinate, for which he would have been eminently qualified by both training and talent. In all probability, it was a purely economic consideration—his concern for his mother, who had been widowed at an early age, and for his young sister—which propelled him into this unpopular occupation. Josel, like the other Jews of his time, lent money to the citizens of neighboring towns[8] and to the peasants of nearby villages against securities or notes of hand, and charged the legally permissible rate of interest. He frequently had to request the help of town magistrates and of the *Landvogt* in order that justice might be done and he might collect the amounts he had lent. At one time, in 1504, during the Landshut feud of succession, it happened that Josel lost all his promissory notes and managed to save only a little over one hundred florins "from the teeth of the despoilers,"[9] so that he had great difficulty in providing for the needs of his family.

"In 1503, 1504, and 1505, many peoples fought against the Duke of Heidelberg in the name of our Emperor Maximilian and they drove him out in disgrace from many posts and fortresses. At that time they looted all the houses and stole everything in them, including my household goods, more than four hundred florins," Josel laments in his memoirs,[10] "and only a few pieces remained in my possession."

However, Josel was shaken less by this material loss than by his realization of the contempt with which his occupation was viewed everywhere. Wherever he went, in the city or in the countryside, he sensed a hatred out of all proportion to the insignificant role of the Jewish moneylender. The Church reforms and the canon prohibition against lending money at interest which had literally conferred a banking monopoly on the Jews were no longer strongly enforced. These prohibitions had enabled the Jews to become the ruling financial power in the Empire. Now the memories of the days long gone by, when Jews had been able to travel freely and unmolested to far-off Russia, to the Orient, to Italy, and to Spain, and when their commercial operations had served to increase the honor and fame of any city "a thousandfold," seemed almost unreal.

The Jews had almost forgotten the days when reigning princes, bishops, knights, noblemen, monasteries and abbots applied to them for loans in order to conduct their wars and to put their finances in order.

Due to the debt cancellations issued by the Emperor Wenceslas, the enormous tax demands of the Emperor Sigismund, and the expulsion of the Jews from the larger cities, their financial strength had been depleted to such an extent that they frequently were unable to raise the funds they needed to pay their own taxes to the authorities.

Of course there still were barons, patricians, clergymen and noblemen who continued to come to the ghetto to secure loans, and there were enough Jews who still were in a position to satisfy the requirements of these gentlemen. But by and large, in the city it was now mainly the artisan who deposited "silver utensils, tin, linen, a cap and whatever other things he might have in his home"[11] as security with the Jew, and in the countryside it was chiefly the peasant who took a loan from the Jew on grain and wine, on his horse, or his cow, or even on his cart and carriage.

Josel did not understand the historical causes of this social upheaval, nor did he suspect, any more than his contemporaries did, that he was living in an era in which the old social and class ties were breaking up, and new orders were forming in their place. He only noted with alarm how greatly the economic and social situation of his people had deteriorated. To be sure, like everyone else in Germany, he knew of the new financial powers in the *Reich*—the Fuggers and the Welsers, the Imhofs and the Hochstetters. These great trading concerns and banking establishments in Augsburg and Nuremberg owned gigantic silver and copper mines in Hungary, in the Tyrol, in Carinthia and in Carniola, operated branch establishments in Antwerp and Novgorod, in Portugal, Italy and Switzerland, and controlled the money market in Germany and Poland, in Sweden and in Hungary. He knew, too, as did everyone else, that these concerns lent large amounts of money to the Emperor and to the Pope, to reigning princes and cardinals, and that no thought was given in those transactions to the canon ban on usury, or to fair prices. to the immoral character of self-seeking gain, or to the "doctrine of adequate sustenance."

Josel also knew of the smaller competitors who had begun to pit themselves against the Jews, the "Christian Jews" who, as his countryman Sebastian Brant put it, charged forward with the *Judenspiess* (Jew's javelin). He had heard the complaint of the humanist Wimpfeling, another Alsatian, that the Christians were even worse than the Jews when it came to usury, and that they were no more concerned than the Fuggers about whether or not they were thereby jeopardizing the salvation of their souls.

Yet, all these complaints about the ruinous monopolies of the wholesalers and the contemptible usury practiced by the Christians which had "spread so rapidly that the Jews no longer could earn their living among the Christians"[12] were entirely different from the accusations hurled at the Jewish moneylender. It was from this time on that the medieval legend of the Jew who asked a pound of the debtor's flesh for security took on reality in the minds of the people, and that the mythical figure of the perfidious apostle Judas was transformed into the greedy and grasping Jewish usurer of their own day. It was only then that the Jew began to embody for them a demoniacal, dark and pernicious power, the "poisonous root"[13] of all economic and social troubles, and, indeed, the Antichrist himself, the Prince of Corruption who was to herald the downfall of the world and the end of the Roman Empire.

The problem of the Jewish usurer was a source of profound distress to Josel throughout his life. Indeed, it became the focal point of all his social theories and political activities. During those years, his own business activities afforded him an opportunity to gain deeper insight into a trade which, unlike commerce, had not only economic but also moral and religious implications. He became familiar with the threats that the power of property and the hunger for gold pose to the human soul. Indeed, he himself frequently crossed the narrow boundary that separated permissible profit from forbidden gain. In all probability, Josel, like the Jews in the drama of "Theophilos," had to wrestle with the Devil many a time when the latter sought to tempt him.

Moreover, he came into close contact with his customers. He learned of the "hunger, the want and the great duress" from which the "poor artisan"[14] suffered, and of the heavy imposts which spendthrift or debt-ridden magistrates demanded year after year. He saw many a peasant despairingly put up as security his only horse, his last farming implement, or his most precious heirloom, when hail had destroyed his harvest or lightning had struck his home, and he could not obtain the funds to pay the rental, the heriot, the forfeits, the duties, the tithes and the *Leibzins* tax to his landlords.

Impelled by his sense of justice, Josel would balance the distress of the common man and that of the poor tiller of the soil against the misery of his own brethren; but the scales always remained in equilibrium. The scale bearing the burden of the one was no less heavy than that which bore the load of the other.

As the figure of the Jewish usurer grew darker and more sinister in the minds of the people, the image of the peasant became brighter and brighter. It was at this time that the peasant first was crowned with the halo of the noble martyr, and became synonymous with the true and suffering Christian who "tended the produce of the field into which God Himself is transformed by the hand of the priest." Aroused by the sermons of the mendicant friars, who pleaded for a return to apostolic-like simplicity, and by the fight for freedom in Switzerland, where a small peasant people had been successful in their struggle for independence, men contrasted the trade of war as plied by the knights with the toil of the peasants, the morality of the rich with the morality of the poor, and the privileges of the governing with the powerlessness of the governed. The final verdict favored the little man.

Dissatisfaction was further increased by the actions of the small nobility and the minuscule princelings. Following the pattern set by the larger political units, these small powers began to gather around themselves jurists trained in Roman law, to impose stronger controls on their subjects, to raise their taxes, and to deal with the litigation of the peasants at their own manorial or ecclesiastical courts. The decisions of these courts were no longer based on the traditional, familiar law of precedent, but on the new and foreign Roman law. Popular resentment of these innovations led to unrest, uprisings and violence throughout the *Reich.* In addition, secret peasant organizations were formed, particularly in the west and the southwest. The *Bundschuh* was considered the most dangerous of these new groups; it was named after the strap of the heavy peasants' clog, which symbolized their powerlessness.

A group of conspirators, led by a former Councillor of Schlettstadt, met on the Ungerberg in the Lower Alsace and resolved to offer resistance to the demands of the authorities; to insist on a thorough-going reform of the judiciary; to abolish the ecclesiastical courts and the Imperial Court at Rottweil; and lastly, to put an end to the usury of the Jews and to their lust for litigation, to plunder them or drive them out. These plans were never carried out, for the conspiracy was exposed in time, and Hans Ullmann, the ringleader, was beheaded. But suppression by force only fanned the flames of discontent and revolt, and the danger to the Jews continued unabated.

In those days Josel's concern for the fate of his brethren in the Alsace was further increased by the news which he received from the northern part of the *Reich.*

"In that same year (1510)," he writes in his memoirs,[15] "disaster struck the March (of Brandenburg) and thirty-eight God-fearing people were burned at the stake in Berlin."

In 1447 the Elector had admitted several Jews to the March, particularly to the Uckermark, the Mittelmark and the Priegnitz, where Jews had not been permitted to reside since the Black Death epidemic.[16]

By permitting Jews to settle in this area, the Elector had hoped to gain new taxpayers to fill his ever-empty exchequer, and to relieve the financial and credit needs of the impoverished country. His successors had also adhered to this policy, despite the fact that the very powerful Estates of the Electorate, the knights, and the cities complained bitterly at all their meetings about the ruinous usury and the growing wealth of the Jews, deplored their own increasing indebtedness and impoverishment, and demanded in menacing terms that "the vermin" be driven out. Attempts to place ceilings on usurious rates of interest and temporarily to prohibit money-lending were of no avail because, as the Elector pointed out, the knights who needed the loans would then have more trouble from the Christians than from the Jews.

Gradually, the dispute as to whether the Jews to whom valuable real estate had been mortgaged should be retained or whether they should be expelled, threatened to lead to a dangerous and violent showdown between the Estates and the Electors, particularly Joachim I, who, in 1509, had permitted Jews to settle again in several border towns.

It transpired in those days that one Paul Fromm, a coppersmith from Bernau, stole a gilt monstrance and two sacred hosts from the church of the town of Knobloch. He attempted to escape, but was apprehended and confessed to the theft. He said that he had eaten one of the hosts himself and sold the other, for money, to a Jew from Spandau named Solomon. When questioned under torture, Solomon named a Jew from Brandenburg and one from Stendal as accomplices in the crime. By torture, the questioners wrested from these two men additional names, and as a result, Jews from Osterburg and Brunswick were also charged with complicity. Other Jews were accused of ritual murder, despite the fact that neither bodies of murdered children nor witnesses to the crime could be located. During the first four days of July, 1510, the Jury Court of Berlin tried one hundred defendants with great dispatch. Thirty-eight of those tried were found guilty of host desecration and sentenced to be burned at the stake.

The sentence was carried out on July 19 in the New Market, in the presence of a huge crowd. One informant, who had witnessed the grim spectacle in the capital of the March, reported in amazement[17] that he would never have believed the victims' actions if he had not seen them with his own eyes. The stubborn Jews had heard their sentence with laughter in their mouths, had sung their hymn of praise, and had not only laughed and sung but even leaped into the air and exulted at the stake, thrown up their fettered hands and thus, despite the miraculous signs [of the testimony] had gone to their end with great steadfastness.

The rest of March Jewry was driven out of the state for all time, lest, as the Abbot Trithemius put it, "*aut similia tentarent in futurum, aut necem illorum aliquo modo iniuste vindicarent."*

In that same year in which the Jewry of the Empire was shaken by the host desecration trial in the March, Josel reports that[18] "there arose enemies from among our own people to destroy the Torah and to bring grief to all Israel."[19] "The adversary and foe who was called by the name of *Trefe Katzav* (butcher of unclean meats)" was one Johannes Pfefferkorn, a moneylender and butcher of bad repute and unknown origin. All that is known of his life is that he first appeared in Southern Germany in 1504, and was converted to Christianity there together with his entire family. Eventually he moved to Cologne, where the erudite Ortwin Gratius and the Dominicans who controlled the University took an interest in him and secured for him the position of hospital overseer and measurer of salt. On the advice of his patrons, he published a series of writings[20] in which he "defamed (Jews) singly and collectively,"[21] proposing that the children of the Jews should be compelled to do hard and degrading labor, and that their holy books should be confiscated.

In 1509, through the good offices of the nun Cunegund, a sister of the Emperor Maximilian, Pfefferkorn obtained official authorization from the Emperor to confiscate all Jewish books except the Bible. Josel reports[22] that the Jewish community of Frankfort, the first to be affected by the Imperial decree, "sacrificed their lives and fortunes" in order to save their holy texts. They appealed to the Archbishop of Mayence, to the Magistrate of the City of Frankfort and finally to the Emperor himself, arguing that "it is not seemly to force a person to abandon his faith against his will."

Maximilian could give orders one day to confiscate the books, and request that they be restored to their owners on the next. Finally, he asked the Archbishop of Mayence to have the outstanding scholars of the day, especially Jacob

Hochstraten, the inquisitor of the Dominicans of Cologne, and Johann Reuchlin, Germany's best-known Hebraist, study the books and decide whether or not they contained any material that might be considered dangerous to the Christian faith.

In the treatise which he submitted to the Emperor, dated October 5, 1510, on "whether all the books of the Jews should be confiscated, got rid of and burned," Reuchlin asserted that the writings of Judaism were neither abusive of Christianity nor detrimental to it. He pointed out that, as a matter of fact, some of them, such as the cabbalistic texts, promoted a true understanding of the Christian faith, and he quoted a statement made by Pico della Mirandola long before their time: "There is no art that can make the deity better known to us than the art of magic and the Cabbala." Reuchlin further stated that the commentaries and grammar texts were essential for the reading of the Bible in its original language, and for its correct interpretation. It was most difficult, he went on, to understand the Talmud. How could an ignorant convert, a Jew who spread slander about his own people, presume to be familiar with this "proud stag of many antlers?" Judaism as such, Reuchlin asserted, constituted no threat to Christianity. "That they do not recognize Christ as God is their own belief, and they do not mean to insult anyone thereby."

As regarded matters pertinent to their belief, they were responsible to no judge but to themselves alone, because they were not members of the Christian Church and therefore it was none of the Christians' business what they believed. On the other hand, they were citizens of the German Roman Empire, and had the same rights of burgessship (and the same right to shelter in the castle precincts) as all other citizens of the *Reich.* For this reason, they were entitled to protection among the Imperial prerogatives and were not to be baptized by force.

Reuchlin's dispute with the Dominican friars of Cologne became an event of symbolic significance for all of German Jewry. It was through this incident that the Jews of Germany first came to know the two powers which had struggled for their souls from time immemorial: the forces of enlightenment and the forces of darkness; the "good and wise men" on the one side, and the "evil brood" on the other.[23]

In those days of insult and humiliation, the very fact that "one of the wise men of the nations" should have endangered his position, his good name, his health and his personal safety in order "to restore the Teaching of Judaism to its former glory,"[24] and that he should consider their sacred tradition the foundation of all knowledge and truth, the guide to ultimate perfection and bliss, the key to the understanding of the Creation and of God, seemed to the Jews "a miracle within a miracle."[25]

At the same time, however, this dispute revealed to them with glaring and relentless clarity the precipice at whose edge they stood.

To the Jews, Pfefferkorn, the baptized Jew, seemed an insignificant figure. They were accustomed to trouble from converts. But behind Pfefferkorn there loomed, dark and threatening, the full power of the Dominicans, who used him as their willing tool. And so the Jews began to compare their own situation with that of their brethren who had been expelled from Spain twenty years before. There, too, the mendicant orders, the Dominicans and the Franciscans, had been the ones to set up the segregated Jewish quarters, to institute the tribunals of the Inquisition, to force mass conversions, arrange exhibition debates, and clamor for the burning of the Talmud. They had finally succeeded in having the Jews expelled.[26] Like those of Cologne, the Dominicans of Spain were familiar with the Hebrew language and Jewish lore, and well-trained in dialectics and apologetics. The skills and knowledge which they had acquired in the monastic schools or at the universities in France or Spain had enabled them to deduce the truths of Christianity directly from the Jewish writings, and to expound them to both Christians and Jews in sermons and public disputations.

One of these Dominicans, Petrus Nigri (Schwarz) of Bohemia, had studied at the University of Salamanca, where he had taken instruction in the Hebrew language from a Jewish teacher. He moved to Germany in the 1470's and became a professor of scholastic theology at the University of Ingolstadt. From there he traveled to Regensburg, Nuremberg, Bamberg, Frankfort and Worms, in order to preach in public places and at outdoor gatherings, in German, Hebrew and Latin before municipal magistrates, bishops, prelates and Jews, "in praise of the Holy Trinity and of the Most Blessed Virgin and against the perfidy of the Jews." In 1475, he published a *Tractatus Contra Judaeos* ("Tract Against the Jews"), which he republished two years later in German with a Hebrew glossary under the title of *Stella Meschia* or "The Star of the Messiah." In this tract he drew upon the Old Testament text itself in an attempt to prove the existence of the Holy Trinity, the incarnation of Christ, the Virgin Birth, and the sufferings and resurrection of Jesus, so that the Jews might be persuaded by rational argument rather than by force to accept the everlasting truth. Furthermore, he invited the most erudite among the rabbis of Germany to engage in public debate with him about their religion, and when none accepted his invitation, he declared "Godforsaken Jewry" to be defeated.[27]

In 1504, another Dominican, Ortwin Gratius of Cologne, who had been Pfefferkorn's patron and to whom the famed *Epistolae Virorum Obscurorum* ("Letters of the Obscurantists") had been addressed, published an anti-Jewish tract in Latin and German, entitled *De Vita et Moribus Judaeorum* ("Concerning the Life and Customs of the Jews"). That same circle of obscurantists also produced the popular *Opus Aureum* ("Golden Work"), written by Rabbi Victor of Carben, who had been baptized,[28] a book which heaped venomous criticism on the Jewish festivals, prayers, customs and ceremonies. In the form of a disputation between a Christian and a Jewish scholar, this work refuted the erroneous beliefs of the Jews from their own sacred texts.

The fact that even the ordinary people viewed this dispute between Christianity and Judaism as a matter of vital and personal concern to each one of them is shown by the Passion and Shrovetide plays of the time, in which the Church and Synagogue strove to defeat one another in endless, heated, and in many instances, erudite debates. Thus, in "The Old Law and the New," a Shrovetide play by Hans Folz, the Synagogue, depicted as an aged matron with queenly bearing, "full of years," confronts the Church as one who was greatly honored by God long before the rise of Christianity. She demands of the Church, portrayed by a much younger woman, how she could presume to drive the Synagogue from pillar to post, to denounce her, to burn her at the stake and to hang her, when she is the one who gave birth to the prophets, reared the patriarchs, and nurtured kings at her breast. In the final scene of the play, however, a rabbi, in debate with a Christian, must shamefacedly concede that the Jews curse the Pope, the Emperor, the King, the bishop and the abbot three times each day, and that they implore God in their prayers to wipe out "all the cunning Christians" the world over "speedily and in our days."

The stern demands of the preachers of penitential homilies, who sharply criticized men in all walks of life, also served to inhibit economic progress. At a time when the agrarian state began to turn more and more to commerce, and the natural economy was making the transition to a money economy, when the new capitalist scheme, with its rational, planned methods of accounting and calculation, its modern concepts of financial transactions, capital, and credit had long since rendered obsolete the medieval systems of prices and trade, the Franciscan Brothers called for a return to the Christian economic ideal of the Church Fathers. As the new European spirit of commercial enterprise became increasingly independent, egocentric, and ruthless, they grew ever more insistent in their preachings on the biblical and apostolical doctrine of the barrenness of money, the immorality of the quest for gain and the sinfulness of lending money at interest.

The ascetic inclinations of the mendicant friars, and the aroused religious feelings of the people would not in themselves have been sufficient to bring about the expulsion of the Jews from nearly all the Imperial towns. There were other causes, economic and social ones; however, these, too, were inextricably bound up with religious and emotional factors.

As a result of the great revolutionary struggles that had taken place in the fourteenth and fifteenth centuries between the patricians and the craftsmen, guilds of large membership and great economic importance succeeded in displacing the ruling patrician class in many cities, and in taking over their administration—either by themselves or jointly with several members of the local nobility.

In the earlier days, the patricians, the wholesale traders and merchant princes, men of practical vision and long political experience, had utilized the wealth and business acumen of the Jews in the service of the flourishing urban communes; they had also availed themselves of loans and financial transactions managed by Jews in order to extend their commercial operations to Italy, France and Holland,

and to send their ships to the North Sea and to the Baltic. They had taken personal charge of the Jews, conferring upon them the full rights of citizenship and endeavoring to give them protection in times of persecution.

Now, in those cities where the guilds had taken over, there was a complete turnabout. Now the craftsman was at the helm. He was concerned only with making a livelihood and maintaining a standard of living in keeping with his station. Fearful of distant places and alien peoples, bound closely to custom and tradition, he shunned every form of competition and was intolerant of all beliefs other than his own. The craftsman set his stamp upon the city. Concern for the welfare of the entire city was superseded by concern for the welfare of the guild members. The fight for the attainment of civic freedom was subordinated to the struggle for the preservation of guild privileges. The city was transformed into a politico-religious, guild and legal authority which kept constant and unrelenting watch over the economic activities, the production, customs, habits, religion and morals of each and every one of its inhabitants.

Due to their exclusion from the guilds, the Jews were no longer able to continue the trading activities which they had carried on quite extensively until the middle of the fourteenth century. The only commercial enterprise in which they were still generally permitted to engage was the sale of unredeemed pledges. However, they frequently did not just sell such pawned articles as clothing, girdles, bonnets and household goods but had new articles made from these items which had been deposited with them as security and not redeemed. They sold these new articles without adhering to the fixed price standards set by the guilds. The impoverished artisans of Regensburg, in particular, complained bitterly that while they themselves had to go to so much effort and expense to produce their goods, the Jews were able to attract both local and out-of-town purchasers by their low prices.

Moreover, there were some liberal-minded governments which disregarded the rigid guild regulations. The Archbishop Diether of Mayence, for example, gave permission to a Jew to deal freely in remedies, the Margrave Albrecht Achilles of Ansbach-Bayreuth permitted all the Jews under his jurisdiction to engage in trading, and the Magistrate of Frankfort had no desire to "keep them from buying and selling."

These encroachments upon the rigidly circumscribed guild rights and privileges were all the more bitterly resented by the people, because Germany at that time was experiencing not only a commercial revolution, but a social upheaval as well, such as she had never seen before and has not witnessed since. As a result of the rise of new forms of enterprise, the boost in the mining industry and the exploitation of gold and silver mines, an intensive accumulation of capital had set in. However, the beneficiaries of this development were not the citizens in general, but the few trading companies and wholesale merchants. The small artisan and day laborer of the city was bewildered by the decline in the value of money, the rise in prices, and the lowering of wages, and at a loss to understand these "swift-moving times." All he could see was the great gap that had opened between the rich and the poor. Stirred up by the revolutionary broadsides of his day, he participated in violent uprisings against the ruling magistrate and the wealthy wholesale trader. The great constitutional struggles which had been fought out on the political front between the patricians and the guilds during the fourteenth century now recurred in the form of social conflicts between the propertied and the unpropertied classes. And even as the struggle between the patrician class and the guilds had been a determining factor in the fate of the Jews at the time of the Black Death epidemic, so now the revolt of the common man also spelled disaster for them.

These diverse motivations, disguised as charges of usury, illegal trading activities, host desecration or ritual murder, underlay the expulsion of the Jews from the Imperial towns of the Alsace.

Finally, the town of Schlettstadt, which had obtained a *privilegium de non tolerandis Judaeis* as early as 1479,[29] restricted the number of Jewish families allowed within its borders to two. The Imperial town of Kaysersberg followed suit. Munster had its old *Judenfreiheit* (freedom to expel Jews or to refuse them admittance) renewed in 1507,[30] and Colmar, which headed the League of the Ten Cities, sent one delegation after the other to Maximilian to obtain a decree permitting the expulsion of its Jews.

Most hostile of all the cities was the *Reichsstadt* of Oberehnheim, from which Josel's parents had had to flee during the Burgundian War. At that time the Count Palatine, as Imperial Governor (*Reichsvogt*) of the Lower Alsace, had made a vain attempt to persuade the town to have mercy on the Jewish exiles. As late as 1494, Oberehnheim had refused to obey the order of *Unterlandvogt* Jacob von Fleckenstein to readmit just one Jewish family. According to von Fleckenstein, it had "constantly rebelled, while the other towns of the Province proved loyal and obedient subjects of the *Reich.*"[31] It even ignored two strongly worded decrees issued by Maximilian himself. Only after the Imperial Fiscal Agent-General had requested the authorities of Oberehnheim to conform to the sovereign's will, did they finally agree, in the year 1500, to permit two Jewish families from Bischofsheim to reside within its borders as "citizens of the *Landvogtei.*"

However, when these first two families were followed by others, serious unrest ensued. The townsmen charged that the Jews were lending money on stolen articles, while the Jews complained that they were being hounded, persecuted, and forced to wear the Jewish badge.

At that point a decree from the Emperor put an end to all debate.

During a lengthy stay in Strasbourg early in 1507, Maximilian received a visit from the Councillors of Oberehnheim, who bitterly complained to him that the burghers of their city were being ruined as a result of the usury and theft committed by the Jews.

The Emperor was heavily in debt and easily influenced. He who only a few years before had ordered the city in no uncertain terms to admit the Jews, now was quickly prevailed upon to issue an order for their expulsion.

In a decree dated March 21, 1507,[32] the Jews were requested to leave Oberehnheim with all their possessions and to stay away for all time.

"In 1506-1507," Josel reports,[33] "the burghers of Oberehnheim importuned the Emperor to expel the Jews from the city. As a result, they obtained a decree that no Jew who worshipped the living God would ever be permitted to set foot in their city and on their territory. . . . They were turned out of their homes and their dwellings without mercy, driven out into the open and into misery and so came to great grief."[34]

This "grief held in common," which Ulrich von Hutten once said pained his heart more deeply than it did the others, moved Josel to make his first appearance on the political scene. Until that time he had led a quiet and secluded life in the little town of Mittelbergheim, devoted to his occupation and to the family which he had started in the meantime.

We know nothing about the origins or the personality of his wife. However, it would seem that she was a wise and valiant companion, who was a partner in her husband's business activities, his confidante in his political missions, and the firm and loving educator of his children, for whom she cared practically alone after Josel became the "Commander" of German Jewry.

In that year of 1507, when the exiles from Oberehnheim begged him for help and counsel, he heeded their call at once. Together with them he appealed to the *Unterlandvogt* (Governor of the Lower Alsace), who had long been their protector.

Josel did not come to beg for protection or to ask for mercy and clemency. Rather, he assumed the role of an impassioned advocate, pleading the complicated case of a client before a jury. At the same time, he played the part of the prosecutor, calm and dispassionate, publicly indicting a guilty defendant—the *Reichsstadt* of Oberehnheim—which he charged with ruthless breach of contract.

When the Jews had been admitted to Oberehnheim, he pointed out, they had entered into a contract which had been confirmed by solemn oath. In this contract, they had committed themselves to pay to the city a special direct tax known as the *Bede*. In return, the Magistrate had promised them "special protection." The Jews, for their part, had adhered to the terms of the contract, but the city had violated the agreement without rhyme or reason.

Josel cautiously pointed out that as of old, one Emperor after another had promised to protect the Jews of the Empire in keeping with time-honored custom and precedent. In the case of the city of Oberehnheim, he added, the Emperor was under a two-fold obligation to extend this protection. For the Emperor was not only the Sovereign of the Empire but also the *Oberlandvogt* of the Alsace, and hence obligated to guarantee all the traditional rights of the citizens of that country. When the *Landvogtei* was ceded as a hereditary land to the House of Austria after the defeat of the Count Palatine in the Landshut War of Succession, Maximilian had vowed to preserve the Jews safely "in their time-honored customs and station," and this provision had been duly inscribed in the Record Book of the town of Hagenau. Of course, the Emperor himself, Josel hastened to add, could not be blamed for the expulsion of the Jews. The guilt lay with the Councillors of Oberehnheim, who had insidiously forced the Emperor's hand by the baseless charges they had brought before him against the Jews. For if the Jews had indeed behaved in an unseemly manner, as the accusation had stated, and therefore had been expelled "with just cause," why, then, had they not first been indicted and given a fair trial in accordance with the law? Since this had not been done, the exiles from Oberehnheim refused to abide by this unjust procedure, and requested a court hearing at which they would be given an opportunity to defend themselves.

Josel's bold speech did not fail to impress the *Landvogt* and Maximilian. The Emperor issued a letter of safe-conduct to a Jew, one Phal of Dambach, and ordered the Magistrate of Oberehnheim to admit him and his family to the town, and to allocate two houses to him as places of residence.

Josel's first venture into political action brought far-reaching changes into his life, for it was then that the grateful Jews of the Lower Alsace elected him their Leader and Chief, or, as he put it in Hebrew, their *parnas u-manhig*.

"In the year 4270 (1510)," he records in his memoirs,[35] "I was appointed jointly with Rabbi Zadok, the Prince, and other men, to keep watch over the community with particular care and to lead it." This community was not the community of his own city, but the larger community of Lower Alsatian Jewry,[36] as indicated in a communication which he addressed to the Count Palatine Frederick in 1553, recalling that he had been "appointed and elected leader of All the Jewry" of this *Landvogtei* of Hagenau and other places nearly fifty years before and had had to take a great and solemn oath of office. By "other places" he meant the Imperial towns and villages of the Alsace which were subject to the authority of the *Landvogt* and probably also the counties and knightly manors in the Lower Alsace, as well as the Diocese of Strasbourg, where a large number of Jewish families resided. These widely scattered communities had already united in a loosely knit confederation some time before. However, it was only as a result of the breakup of the large urban Jewish communities in which the Jews of the rural areas had been able to perform their religious duties and to bury their dead that the problem of an organization of Rural Jewry became acute.

Until that time the Jewish community had been urban and middle-class in character. Within this framework, the old Jewish communal organizations and religious traditions of the past had blended with the legal and social institutions of the Christian environment in a unique and harmonious manner, molding the Jewish community into a slowly evolving, dynamic organism. The Jewish community had understood how to preserve its religious, legal and cultural autonomy and to safeguard its way of life from interference by government authorities. In each community there had been scholars who had given it laws, and God-fearing and righteous men and women who had been martyred, imparting to their community an individuality, fame, and glory all its own. Communities had vied with one another in loving pride for the honor of being known as the "Crown of Israel," "Shield and Armor of All Communities" and "Leader and Princess of Jewry," and to prove worthy of the noble deeds of their ancestors, which they valued beyond pearls and gold.

We know little today about the beginnings of the corporate bodies of rural Jewry. The meager documentary material that has been preserved from those days merely shows that they still did not then have the fixed patterns and regular representative assemblies which we learn of from the minute books dating from the era of absolutism.[37] However, there is no doubt that they evolved after the manner of the Jewish communities of the urban areas. The Jewish communities of the cities had been headed by a "Bishop," a "Grand Master" or a "Master Builder" *(Baumeister)* assisted by a *Judenrat,* a Jews' Council, frequently consisting of twelve members, who would represent the community before the municipal or national authorities, and who would be responsible for the enforcement of the law, the assessment of taxes, and internal administration. In the same manner, the corporate bodies of rural Jewry (*Landjudenschaft*) would elect a "Leader," "Grand Master," or "Commander," usually a rabbi, who in many cases was assisted by *parnassim* or tax administrators. As a rule, the officials chosen by the rural Jewish community were confirmed in office by the reigning princes, but in some cases the government imposed a "Commander" of its own choosing on such a corporate body to assure more efficient tax collection.

In his methodical way, Josel has given us further particulars concerning the functions of his office:

Dannach . . . ich nun der gemeinen juden vorgenger gewesen, dorum nun, was sich zwitracht oder irrung wider die billigkeit zwischen juden und christen erhalten hat und mir daselbig fuerbracht worden, alwegen die juden dohin gehalten, das si sich haben nach der erbarkeit miessen halten und der unbillichkeit miessen vermiden. . . . Derglichen auch, was minen verwanten von der uweren etlichen der unverstendigen und gitzigen den minen mit unbilligkeit entgegen geschehen, und so ich dasselbige E. Gn. fuerbracht, oder geclagt hab, - alwegen . . . dasselbig . . . glich abgewent.[38]

(Ever since I became the Leader of the Jewish community, I insisted that the Jews conduct themselves respectfully, and

I avoided prejudice whenever a discussion or discord arose between Jews and Christians with respect to the law, and they submitted the case to me. . . . So, too, whenever some of the imprudent and avaricious among the Christians treated my brethren improperly, I brought it to the attention of Your Grace or complained about it, and thus was always able to serve as referee between them and avert injustice.)

In a letter to the Magistrate of Colmar in 1541, Josel explained that [39] as Leader he had labored with the help of Almighty God and of pious, honorable men to settle all disputes and differences arising between Jews and Christians and to restore peace between them.

In addition to acting as general mediator between the two faiths, he was empowered to arbitrate in litigation between Jewish parties, and to exercise penal control in the form of excommunication.

In one document he states[40] that he had acted as judge at Rosheim, together with two other rabbis and judges under Jewish law.

Elsewhere[41] Josel writes that excommunication was the only secular penalty known to the Jews. He points out that the moment the three judges excommunicated a defendant, all his possessions were forfeited to the Imperial Fiscal Agent. Any decree of excommunication issued by the Jewish judges was regarded as binding also on the secular authorities. They were not permitted to give protection to those excommunicated; rather, they were obligated to expel them from the country. It was not seemly, Josel informed the Magistrate of the city of Strasbourg,[42] to inflict punishment on all the Jews of the *Landvogtei* for the crime of one evildoer, particularly since the man had already been excommunicated by himself and his fellow-judges.

There would be meetings, although sporadic ones, of deputies from all the rural Jewish communities (*Landjudenschaft*) of the Lower Alsace for the purpose of levying taxes, consulting on religious matters, or taking action against economic oppression—"even as we had recently met, in keeping with time-honored custom and tradition, in said *Landvogtei* of Hagenau at Rosheim."[43]

Even as the Jewish communities of the cities had patterned their organization on that of the Christian communes, so, too, the constitution of the *Landjudenschaft* in the Lower Alsace was clearly modeled on that of the territorial Estates there.

Toward the end of the fifteenth century, the territorial confederations, which had been rather loosely organized until that time, began to band together into more tightly knit Territorial Estates: those of the Upper Alsace in the territory of the Landgraviate of Austria, and those of the Lower Alsace in the District of Hagenau. These organizations would convoke separate Diets, independent of one another, to deliberate on economic and financial matters. Similarly, the Jewish communities of the Upper and Lower Alsace held assemblies under the chairmanship of the incumbent elders of the corporate bodies. Just as the Territorial Estates of the Alsace would hold joint meetings in times of emergency, for the purpose of "saving" and "preserving" the country, there were times when the corporate bodies of Upper and Lower Alsatian Jewry would also assemble in combined session to draft joint resolutions to defend their rights or to ward off a threatened attack.

The new Leader of Lower Alsatian Jewry soon had occasion to exercise one of the many functions of his office: namely, to settle "disputes and differences" arising between Jews and Christians. At the very outset of his career, he was exposed to the dangers that he was to face in the months and years to come.

"In the year 1514 the (Jewish) inhabitants of Mittelbergheim, including myself, were taken into custody on false accusations," Josel reports in his memoirs.[44] "Eight persons in all were kept prisoners in two places in the town of Oberehnheim for seven weeks until the affair was cleared up, when the treasurer admitted that he had been in error and that we were innocent."

These rather vague statements have been variously taken to indicate that the accusation was one of host desecration. However, this does not seem to be the case. Firstly, historical records from that period do not make mention of a host desecration trial in the Alsace. Secondly, Josel himself states only that he was arrested; he does not speak of torture, to which he would surely have been subjected had the charge against him been of that nature.

Then, too, the treasurer's admission of error would seem to indicate that the charge was one of counterfeiting or of forging bills of exchange, charges which were brought against the Jews again and again due to the profusion of currencies then in circulation and the absence of currency regulations at the time.

The possibility of an act of revenge on the part of the town of Oberehnheim should also not be overlooked. For it was at that time that the burghers of the town were up in arms against Phal von Dambach, the Jew who had been forced on them by the Emperor. On one occasion, when Phal appeared at the town hall, he was attacked, robbed of the cash he had on his person, and "almost drowned in water" so that he barely escaped with his life.[45] In addition, the Magistrate forbade non-resident Jews to visit the town fairs, to pass through the town, or to use the highways to which all other people had free access. The sons of the burghers would beat Jews traveling past the city without fear of being punished by the Magistrate. One former citizen of Oberehnheim, "an honest man, a Levite by the name of Jacob ben Judah,"[46] was killed by a plowman while traveling on the Imperial highway on some business. The neighbors followed suit and were guilty of the same "inhuman, violent and vicious conduct,"[47] treating the Jews in a manner that was "contrary to all fairness and in violation of every conceivable liberty."

When the Emperor learned of "this great distress and oppression," he directed Wilhelm von Rappoltstein (*Unterlandvogt,* 1514), to prevent any infringement on the safe conduct and rights of residence of the Jews.[48] However, the city of Oberehnheim heeded neither this Imperial directive nor the summons of the *Landvogt* to appear before him on a specified date so that he might act as arbitrator between Oberehnheim and the Jewish community. When, at the same time, the Bishop of Strasbourg and the Lords of Andlau also made known their intention to expel the Jews from the Imperial villages of Blienschweiler, Mittelbergheim and Nothalten, of which they were joint administrators,[49] the corporate body of Lower Alsatian Jewry sent its Presiding Officer to Coblenz in 1515 to put its situation personally to Emperor Maximilian.[50]

This was the first time that Josel had dealings on behalf of his brethren with their Imperial Patron. In contrast to his accounts of subsequent conferences with Charles V, he made no comments about this meeting. He simply states briefly and in impersonal terms that he had presented his complaint against the town of Oberehnheim before all the peoples and princes assembled there, and that he had succeeded in effecting a settlement with the Bishop of Strasbourg and the Lords of Andlau.[51] He also reports that on that occasion the Emperor had ordered the Magistrate of Oberehnheim to appear before him on a specified date for a hearing, but that the Magistrate had not only disregarded these orders, but also had refused a request from the Jews to permit Maximilian to act as judge in the dispute. For this reason Josel was compelled to make the journey on horseback to the Imperial Court two more times.[52]

However, Josel does not mention that, only a short time after these happenings, the Emperor, influenced by his petitions, issued an open writ strictly forbidding the *Landvogten, Stadtholders,* and Councillors of the Upper and Lower Alsace to give a hearing to denunciations and to turn the Jews out of their homes.[53]

It seems that this time Maximilian was serious about fulfilling his obligation as Protector of the serfs of his Imperial Chamber. For he also forbade the Count of Wertheim and the Archbishop of Cologne to carry out their plans to expel their Jews,[54] and he made a promise to the Jews of Rothenburg, who had been the victims of riots, brawls and violence, that he would take drastic measures against their enemies and not tolerate any encroachment upon their liberties.[55]

It was only in the year 1519 when the Emperor died, that the city of Rothenburg became free to put into effect its long-laid plans for the expulsion of its Jews which the Emperor had thwarted over and over again; and it was only then, too, that the Imperial village of Dangolsheim, in which a revival of the *Bundschuh* movement was taking place, got its longed-for opportunity to get rid of its Jews.[56]

"In the year 1519 the Emperor died, may his memory be a blessing," Josel relates in his memoirs.[57] "At that time the townsmen of Dangolsheim decided to drive out all their Jews and they actually carried out their plan. When their neighbors learned of this, they wanted to do likewise. Then God caused the *Landvogt* of Hagenau and the Bishop of Strasbourg to have mercy on us, so that they gave me a hearing. I therefore went to Dangolsheim with the *Landvogt* and spoke to them, although with great trepidation, until they gave up their evil intention and also revoked what they had done—namely, their breach of the agreements and of the Territorial Peace" (*Landfrieden*).

Josel also attributes to the Emperor's death an event which came as a great shock to him and his co-religionists: the "infamous expulsion" of the Jews from the ancient and renowned community of Regensburg, within whose walls they proudly claimed to have resided even before the birth of Christ.[58]

The inextricable mingling of economic, social, religious and psychological factors in this situation is clearly seen in the events that followed the expulsion of the Jews from Regensburg. This expulsion had been carried out at the insistence of the guilds, which charged the Jews with intolerable business practices, and at the demand of the common man, who had accused the Jews of scandalous usury. On the very day that the Jews left the city, the people of Regensburg, in a senseless outburst of fury, destroyed the fine old synagogue and later erected upon its ruins the chapel of "Mary the Beautiful," which eventually became the most popular shrine for pilgrims in the country.

"Crowds of people from every district converged on the glorious virgin who performed many cures and good deeds for the pilgrims who came there at that time," the Abbot of the Cistercian monastery of Aldersbach reported.

"It is marvelous to relate; lads, youths, maidens, mothers and men all came as if they were possessed. Whosoever had in his hand a tool or utensil would bring it with him, but none carried a traveling bag. And they came in such haste that many of them arrived in a state of complete exhaustion, half-naked, bereft of speech or senses, after they had rushed through days and nights without food or drink.

"And when they arrived at the shrine, most of them would fall sobbing to the ground as if in ecstasy. And when, after quite some time, they would arise, they found themselves dependent on the mercies of the townsmen, who were at pains to revive them and to send them back to their homes."

CHAPTER THREE

THE "COMMANDER"

IT was only reluctantly, and with considerable hesitation, that the Electors of the *Reich* chose Charles V as successor to his grandfather Maximilian. After one of the most dramatic election campaigns in German history, the Electors, bribed with the millions of the House of Fugger, finally gave preference to this youthful prince over the opposing candidate, King Francis I of France. They made it a condition of his election, however, that he would consult the Estates of the *Reich* on all matters of domestic and foreign policy; that he would appoint only native-born Germans as officials of the Court and the Empire; that he would use only German and Latin in both speech and writing; and that he would turn over the government of the *Reich* to an Imperial Council of Regency in his absence.

The Electors deemed these conditions imperative because they were alarmed at the enormous power concentrated in the hands of the young scion of the House of Habsburg, power which threatened to weaken their own authority and to involve the *Reich* in martial entanglements with the East, the West and the South of Europe. For this grandson of Maximilian's was heir to Austria, Styria, Carinthia, Carniola, the ancestral lands of the Habsburgs in the Upper Rhine region and to the Burgundian territories of Charles the Bold. He was the son of Philip the Fair of Habsburg, who had died at an early age, and of Juana, daughter of Ferdinand the Catholic and Isabella of Castile, whose reign had been marked by the defeat of the Moors, the expulsion of the Jews from Spain, and the discovery of America. As sole heir of the possessions of his demented mother, Charles was the sovereign lord of Spain, Naples and Sicily, of possessions in Africa, and of the conquests made on the new continent across the ocean, which was popularly called New Spain.

Charles of Habsburg had been reared in Burgundy, in the sumptuous world of medieval tournaments and solemn rites of orders of knighthood, of brilliant ostentation and pompous court ceremonial, which was slowly going down in a blaze of autumnal glory. But he had been bred, too, in an atmosphere of mysticism and of quiet and introspective meditation that marked the New Piety of the Low Countries.

At an early age, the introverted, deeply religious youth was already imbued with a strong sense of responsibility concerning the magnitude of his future calling, with an awareness of his chosenness and of his great mission, and with the belief that the Emperorship was "the highest honor instituted by God on earth."

When he came to the throne of Spain at the age of only sixteen, he was not only trained to conduct himself with restraint, courtesy and reserve, but also deeply committed to follow the strict Catholic tradition of his ancestors. It was impressed upon him that he had been chosen by Divine Providence to lead the crusade against the infidels and heretics, against the Mohammedans, the heathens, the Moors and the Jews, and to restore the holy kingdom of God on earth in its unity as of old.

The German people jubilantly hailed the accession to the Emperorship of this youth of twenty as the beginning of the golden Messianic Age foretold by the Prophets, and anxiously awaited the advent of "the Imperial Eagle," who would "stride forth from the clefts of Germany to spread his wings over all the German lands." For them it was the coming of the conqueror of the world, "who would march to Jerusalem and there lay down his crown upon the Mount of Olives."

The Jews of Germany, on the other hand, viewed the new reign with great alarm. What could they expect from a ruler who considered himself the "secular arm" of the Church, and whose ancestral country not only refused to admit Jews but still maintained the Inquisitions which claimed new victims every day? Was this choice not a dreaded omen of the same disaster that had befallen their brethren in Spain?

On October 20, 1520, Charles came to Aix-la-Chapelle to accept the crown and the homage of the princes. The young man, silent and aloof, clothed in armor and brocade robes, was met at the gates of the city by the Electors. Then, surrounded by Spanish grandees, the great and the nobles of the *Reich,* knights, heralds, ambassadors and the Magistrate of Aix-la-Chapelle, he made his triumphant entry into the city.

Two days later, the coronation ceremony was conducted by the Archbishops of Cologne, Treves, and Mayence amidst hymns and prayers in the incense-filled, festively-lit Cathedral of Aix-la-Chapelle, which had already been the scene of the pageantry of the reigns of Charlemagne and Otto I. Before the crown was placed upon his head, Charles solemnly pledged to preserve and to promote the holy Catholic faith, to reign justly over the empire which God had given him, and to remain properly loyal and obedient to the Most Holy Father, the Pope of Rome, and to his Church.

Among the thousands of spectators who witnessed this sumptuous pageant of sacred medieval ritual was the Leader of Lower Alsatian Jewry, who now called himself Josel of Rosheim, after the small Imperial town of Rosheim to which he had moved from Mittelbergheim in 1514.

"In the year 1520 Charles was crowned King," Josel states in his report of the rites in Aix-la-Chapelle,[1] "and I petitioned him and his servants in behalf of our people. We, that is myself and the man who was with me, were given (favorable) royal privileges for all of Germany. The townsmen of Rosheim and of the city of Kaysersberg had planned to expel their Jews, but with the help of God I managed to persuade the King to revoke the resolution of Kaysersberg.

"However, the decision with regard to the expulsion of the Jews from Rosheim was not revoked; by dint of untold effort, we succeeded in obtaining postponement again and again, but to this very day there has been no definite decision in the matter."

Presumably, Josel and his companion had come to Aix-la-Chapelle in behalf of German Jewry in order to have its privileges reconfirmed in keeping with the time-honored custom, and, at the same time, to confer with the advisors of the Emperor on the amount of coronation tax to be paid by the Jews.

Ever since Ludwig the Bavarian had proclaimed the principle that the Jews and all their possessions were chattels of the King, it had become customary for the Jews to pay a coronation tax or "tribute" to each sovereign on his election. This tax was a kind of fictional ransom for their survival, and for the conferring of new privileges or the reconfirming of existing ones.

Similarly, Sigismund, who also had required a tax on the occasion of the coronation of the Emperor, had summoned Jewish deputies to Basel in order to discuss the new tax with them, and Albrecht, his successor, had called the representatives of the Jewish communities to Nuremberg for the same purpose, so that he could confer with them while the Imperial Diet was held there.

However, historical sources make no mention of a request by Charles for the payment of such a coronation tax by the Jews of the *Reich*. The Emperor merely indicates in a document of a later date that, after being crowned in Aix-la-Chapelle, he had reconfirmed the pre-existing privileges of the Jewish communities in the *Reich* and in the Habsburg family domains of Austria.[2]

In the course of his negotiations with the Royal advisors in Aix-la-Chapelle, Josel took the opportunity to plead the cause of his Alsatian Jewry. For after the death of Maximilian, the Jews of the Alsace had cause to fear that the new sovereign, who was not familiar with German law and custom, might revoke the security agreements for which they had fought so tenaciously and which had been threatened again and again, as in the case of the actions of the Imperial towns of Kaysersberg and Rosheim.

At that time, when these two towns were seeking to rid themselves of their Jews, the *Reichsstadt* of Oberehnheim was preparing to deal them a new blow.[3] Leonhard Schuster, the town's energetic Burgomaster, and Councillor Johann von Heiligenstein, were dispatched to Worms, where Charles had gone from Aix-la-Chapelle to hold his first Imperial Diet on German soil. They persuaded the King to reconfirm the privilege which Maximilian had conferred on the town in 1507.[4] In March 1521, Charles also acceded to the request of Bishop William of Strasbourg, of the Lords of Andlau, and of the town of Schwaebisch-Gmuend for the "freedom against the Jews," meaning the privilege to expel their Jews or to refuse them admittance. He granted that same privilege to Rosheim in April and to Donauwoerth in May of that same year.[5]

Meanwhile, the Jews of the Alsace moved to ward off the blow which the town of Oberehnheim had struck them. They, too, sent deputies to Worms at approximately the time when Luther, at the historic meeting there, refused to retract his new doctrine "because it is a burdensome, pernicious and dangerous thing to act contrary to the dictates of one's conscience."

Josel was not among this deputation. But he states in a report of a later date[6] that the Jews of the Alsace had brought their grievance before Charles and the Estates of the *Reich* at Worms, and demanded that justice be done. At that time they were given the promise that justice would be done if it were indeed true that a violation of their privileges had taken place.

However, Burgomaster Schuster had only begun to fight. He now united with the Magistrate of Rosheim, where most of the Jews expelled from Oberehnheim had fled, so that together, they might be able to push for the expulsion of the Jews from the entire Alsace.

On learning of these intrigues, the Jewish community of Rosheim addressed a communication to the Burgomaster and Councillors of Oberehnheim. In this letter, which had been drafted—but not signed—by Josel,[7] the Jews inquired whether it was only his "own arrogance and envy" that had driven Burgomaster Schuster to hound them even in localities outside his jurisdiction, or whether the other Councillors were also implicated in this violation of their privileges. They threatened to bring another complaint against the town to His Majesty's Government if these insults continued. "For we, too, are men created in the image of God with whom Popes, Emperors and Kings have dealt kindly so that harshness is uncalled for."

The fact that the Jews of Rosheim had no more complaints to register in the years immediately following this incident would indicate that the alliance between the two Imperial towns may have worn a little thin by that time.

The Imperial Diet of Worms, which was the scene of a heated debate on the balance of power between Charles and the Estates, also had some bearing on the fate of the Jews.

The fact that the *Judenfreiheit* (the privilege to expel Jews or to refuse them admittance) had been granted to various cities seemed to confirm the premonition of the Jews that the Spanish King would be inclined in the future to deal with the Jewish problem in the spirit of his grandparents, Ferdinand and Isabella. It was well known that Charles, in a letter he had written to the Pope at the time of the Reuchlin-Pfefferkorn controversy when he was only fifteen years old, had delivered himself of the opinion that anyone favoring the Jews would incur God's punishment.[8] In addition, the final resolution of the Imperial Diet contained an order to the effect that "Jews who commit usury or make loans on stolen goods shall be given neither abode nor shelter, and shall have neither peace nor safe-conduct within the *Reich.*"[9]

On the other hand, Charles continued a time-honored custom which had been followed by the Emperors who had reigned before him. In keeping with a tradition dating back to 1407, he appointed Rabbi Samuel of Worms *Reichsrabbiner* over all of German Jewry. This so-called "Rabbi-General" had the authority to arbitrate in cases of dissension and dispute, and was responsible for the collection of the "golden tribute penny," the general *Reichssteuer* which had to be paid to the Imperial Chamber by every Jew or Jewess past the age of thirteen.[10]

Shortly after the dissolution of the Imperial Diet of Worms, Charles left the *Reich* and stayed away for a period of nine years. He handed over the reins of government to his brother, the Archduke Ferdinand, and to a Council of Regency (*Reichsregiment*), a body which included the most influential princes of the realm, with a permanent seat in the city of Nuremberg. This Council of States represented a concession which had been wrested from the Emperor by the Estates.

At the first Imperial Diet convened by the new government in Nuremberg in 1522, a proposal was made to shift the burden of maintaining the Council of Regency onto the Jews, by levying a heavy special tax on them for this purpose. Samuel, the *Reichsrabbiner,* was therefore summoned to Nuremberg to discuss the plan. When he stated that he alone was not competent to make commitments involving so heavy a tax without the consent of all the Jewish communities in the *Reich,* he was given permission to call a conference of Jewish deputies to Nuremberg. The conference was held in Nuremberg in 1523, and Josel of Rosheim attended as the representative of Alsatian Jewry.[11]

We do not know the final decision with regard to the proposed levy. However, it is known that Josel took the opportunity to complain to the Council of Regency about the conduct of the town of Oberehnheim, and successfully pressed for the appointment of a Royal Commission which, under the chairmanship of the Abbot Ruediger of Weissenburg, was to make an impartial investigation of the dispute.

It was to this commission that Josel, in behalf of all the Jews in the *Landvogtei* of Hagenau, handed a detailed bill of complaint.[12] In this document it was recalled that the Jews had been favored for many years with special privileges from Emperors, Kings and princes to dwell among the Christians and to carry on trade and commerce in their midst. It then went on to relate the manner in which the Magistrate of Oberehnheim had violated those decrees which had provided for the shelter, protection and safe-conduct of the Jews, and finally enumerated their specific grievances so that the entire matter could be "discussed in fairness and justice."

The action taken by the town, it was stated, was contrary to every custom and freedom. For every Emperor, immediately after receiving the crown, had made a solemn promise not to encroach upon the privileges of and to give protection to the Jews, the "serfs of his Imperial Chamber who had been committed to the Roman Empire." Oberehnheim was part of that Roman Empire, and therefore, by expelling its Jews, had violated the law of the House of Austria and interfered with its sovereignty.

Finally, the town was charged with having broken the Territorial Peace of the Province and the right of safe-conduct by maltreating Phal von Dambach, a "protected Jew" (*Schutzjude*), who had been admitted to Oberehnheim by order of the Emperor. Such an act, the bill stated, was considered criminal and liable to prosecution with regard to life, possessions and property. "For what else is the meaning of freedom and safe-conduct in the Roman Empire, adopted by all the Estates of the Realm, but to obey implicitly the order of the Emperor's Majesty on pain of severe penalty, so that the world may endure and injustice may not be done to any man."

Named in the bill of complaint was still another evil, contrary to all human and divine law—the barring of the Imperial highways and market places to the Jews. For each of the sovereigns had made the highways and market places "free to all" because "God, Who created us all, gave them to men for their comfort and benefit."

Josel demanded that, if the complaints would be upheld as justified, the town of Oberehnheim should be required to make restitution to its Jews for the damages they suffered and to restore their homes to them.

In March 1524, the Abbot of Weissenburg[13] invited the

Magistrate and Burgomaster of Oberehnheim and the representatives of the Jews of the district of Hagenau to a conference at Steinfels in order to effect an amicable settlement of the dispute. The *Landvogt* Jacob Baron von Moersberg proved an able mediator; he succeeded in bringing about an agreement between the two parties. The Magistrate of Oberehnheim and Josel (the latter representing the corporate body of Lower Alsatian Jewry) drew up a sworn agreement which, while it did not gain for the Jews the hoped-for permission to return to the Imperial town, did provide considerable relief from trading restrictions.

This "bill of complaint" which was drawn up by Josel is the earliest extant detailed document from his hand. It is an exceptionally faithful reflection of his personality and way of thinking. It is written by a sober jurist, who enumerates his complaints and then petitions for redress, point by point, in logical order. At the same time there emanates from these lines the genuine pathos of the position of a people's tribune, who carries on the valiant fight for unconditional justice and right, and who supports his arguments with biblical parables as well as with stories from the revolutionary broadsides of his own day. It is the writing of a serious scholar who is well-versed in the history of his people and wields this knowledge as an expert weapon with which to defend his brethren. He knows the exact terms of the privileges[14] in which the Emperors had avowed it to be the duty of the sovereign and a command of justice and prudence to preserve for the Jews their property, and to ensure permanence for their rights, safety for their lives and freedom for their commerce as for all other subjects. He was familiar, too, with the provisions of the King's Peace which at one time had assured to the Jews under oath, the same special legal protection that had been extended to the clergy, to merchants and to women, and which made any breach of that peace punishable by death.

Furthermore, Josel was fully cognizant of the original meaning of the concept of *Kammerknechtschaft,* or "royal prerogative to protect the Jews." It was only in the course of the past two centuries that *Kammerknechtschaft* had acquired its degrading connotation, demeaning the Jew to the status of a chattel and object of barter. In all probability, Josel also knew the terms of that privilege of 1236 in which Frederick II of the House of Hohenstaufen had extended to all the Jews of the Empire, to the "serfs of his Imperial Chamber," a privilege which originally had been conferred by Henry IV only upon the Jewish community of Worms. This was the earliest Imperial document to make use of this expression. There had been no intention at that time to degrade the Jews to the status of serfdom. The term *Kammerknechtschaft* had been used simply to express in definite legal form the long-standing attachment of the Jews to the Royal "Chamber" or Treasury, a relationship which entailed obligation for both parties. By virtue of the privilege of 1236, the Jews of the *Reich* as a group (not merely individual communities or persons), were made directly subordinate to the sovereign, thus providing a new legal and juridical definition of their relationship to him.[15] As a united association, set apart from all other subjects, and as "legally recognized protected members of the *Reich,*"[16] they received the solemn pledge of Imperial protection. The Jews, in turn, were required to pay certain taxes to the Imperial Chamber as a token of appreciation for that protection.

The term *perpetua servitus,* however, which had long been in use in official Church documents, had crept into secular legal documents as early as the thirteenth century. In 1237, therefore, Frederick II, in a privilege he conferred upon the burghers of Vienna, already spoke of the eternal servitude which "had been imposed upon the Jews from of old by the plenitude of Imperial power as a punishment for their crimes."

When Josel put particular stress in his "bill of complaint" against the town of Oberehnheim on the point that the Jews had been "committed to the *Reich* as serfs of the Imperial Chamber," he had in mind the original and not the current interpretation of this institution. It was his intention not only to point out the duties of the Emperor as protector of the Jews, but also to show that when the city caused harm to come to an Imperial prerogative, it was thereby insulting the Emperor himself and infringing upon his authority. For it had been written in the *Arenga* of 1236 that "the master is honored through his servants. Hence he who harms the servants also harms the master."

However, it was not only the knowledge of this time-honored privilege that impelled Josel to appeal to the Emperor for aid against the effrontery of the local powers. Like the people in whose midst he lived, Josel, too, cherished dreams of an Imperial shepherd "who would forsake self-interest, pursue the common good, and conquer all the earth in order to establish peace upon it." He, too, wished for "only *one Reich* and *one* Emperor who would free them all," so that "everything would be embraced by the Emperor's peace."

Josel would never have dared to speak out so defiantly, an action shocking in a Jew and tantamount to mutiny against the local authorities, had he not been greatly under the influence of the revolutionary atmosphere of his time. His petition to the Royal Commission exudes the same spirit that pervaded the broadsides of that period, and the Articles of the rebellious peasants. The peasants also demanded freedom of the highways and proper administration of the market places, so that "the poor man might have his full Christian freedom and receive what is justly due him."

"The earth is free and was given to men by God, Who

created us all, for their comfort and benefit," Josel preached to the members of the Royal Commission.

"Although by right every man is born free, our masters seek to keep us as chattels as if we had been born slaves," the peasants of Stuehlingen grumbled in that same year of 1524.

"We, too, are human beings created in the image of God," Josel angrily admonished the Magistrate of Oberehnheim.

"God created the peasant in the image of Adam, free and with the same rights as the other Estates, and it is only because of the injustice of men that he must suffer oppression," was the slogan that passed from mouth to mouth during the Peasants' War.

When Josel made reference again and again to "Divine right" and "Divine justice," he had in mind the fulfillment of the word of God as he learned it in the Holy Scriptures, and particularly in the writings of the Prophets. But, like the Hussites and the peasants, he, too, understood this fulfillment to imply the replacement of historical law by ideal law, of secular order by the Divine order, and of the law of the State by the law of God.[17]

In his bill of complaint against the town of Oberehnheim, he stated that the Jews had been beaten, thrown into water, and robbed of their cash by servants and by sons of the town's burghers; and the Magistrate had allowed the evildoers to go unpunished.

The peasants of Allgaeu in the Abbey of Kempten testified at court that they had been "insulted, injured and terrorized by the Bishop of Kempten with regard to their persons and property by imprisonment, incarceration, blocking, chaining, and exorbitant fines."

It was probably this similarity in the situation of these two most oppressed classes in the *Reich* that led public opinion at the time, as well as later historians, to accuse the Jews of having made common cause, or at least of having sympathized, with the peasants.[18]

Actually, however, the differences dividing these two classes were greater than their similarities. The Peasants' Movement, which flared up in 1524 in the southern Black Forest and the Lake Constance area and swept like wildfire through Swabia, Franconia, Bavaria, the Danube, Rhine and Main territories, Saxony, Thuringia and the Alsace, had caught up so many different classes of the population in its path that the resulting upheaval was more of a social revolution than a Peasants' War. In addition to the rebel peasants, the motley mass consisted of the urban proletariat, the "common man," who had been restive for so long, impoverished knights and men of letters, Protestant preachers and other adherents of the new doctrine, whose participation in the movement was motivated by an infinite variety of political, social, economic or religious causes.

In the Black Forest and the Lake of Constance region, the unrest had been caused by local grievances of an agrarian nature. In Bavarian Swabia, the Allgaeu and the Danube region, the land of bishoprics and abbeys, the aim of the movement was to abolish the manorial domains and to restore the free Germanic native communities. In Franconia, where it was led by men of considerable political ability, the movement marched on the castles and estates of the landed nobility. At the same time, plans were laid for thoroughgoing reforms in the *Reich* and for a Peasants' Parliament, with the Emperor as the one sovereign lord.

All of these groups were in agreement, however, when it came to such issues as the authority of the Gospels, the freedom of the Christian individual as proclaimed by Luther, and the demand for the right to choose their vicars in free elections and to have their ecclesiastical affairs set in order by reformers such as Luther, Melanchthon, Zwingli and Osiander.

The Jews had no part in these innovations. The agrarian demands, the evangelical regulations, the secularization of Church goods, and the founding of a theocratic-communistic Kingdom of God such as Thomas Muenzer had just established in Thuringia were of no concern to them. Why should they have desired to have all the political, social, and religious affairs of the land managed in accordance with the Gospels? And in view of the fact that they were not permitted to own landed property, what advantages would have accrued to them from the establishment of free rural and market communities? Furthermore, why should they have wished to destroy the castles of the ecclesiastical and temporal lords, where they had found shelter and refuge in times of persecution?

Rather, they had ample cause to view with deep concern the swelling of a movement which, like the *Bundschuh* Uprising and the revolt of the common man, threatened to bring them new troubles.

Balthasar Hubmeier, the canon who had branded the Jews as "usurers" and "ravishers of the Virgin Mary" from the pulpit in Regensburg, and who had helped to bring about their expulsion, had turned into a zealous Anabaptist, and, as Master of the town of Waldshut, had incited the peasants of the Black Forest region to cease paying their tribute and to rise up against their manorial lords.

The learned Doctor Johann Teutschlein,[19] who had roused the populace of Rothenburg to such a frenzy with his sermons on social revolution and his condemnation of usury that the Jews of the city were "beaten in many quarters and in their homes," terrorized and finally expelled altogether, had become a fervent follower of Luther and goaded the common man to mutiny against the "honorable Magistrate" of the city.

The peasants of Franconia promised the Jews protection "for the time being," and only forbade them to carry away their possessions, and the peasant bands of Speyer vowed that all confiscated property would be returned to them. The Estates of the Rheingau, on the other hand, insisted that Jews should not be permitted to reside in the Rheingau, and that no judge should give them a hearing in the courts.

In the Alsace, the land of minuscule manors, where the ground for revolt had been prepared by the conspiracies of the last centuries, and where the hostility to the clergy took on more vehement forms, the uprising swept "from village to village, like a forest fire." The burghers, too, became infected with the agitation of the peasants, and in many areas they either joined the insurgents or opened the gates of the towns to them.

Even the Articles of Confederation adopted by the peasants of the Alsace were couched in more radical terms than those of the bands of Franconia and Swabia. It was their aim, the peasants stated, to be independent of all non-resident jurisdiction, especially that of the ecclesiastical courts and the Imperial High Court of Justice (*Reichskammergericht*). They further proposed to cease paying tithes, rents, tributes, *Umgeld,* hunt taxes and imposts to their lords, and to give tribute monies to the Emperor alone, whom they acknowledged to be their sole sovereign lord.

And even as they robbed the churches of gold and silver, of altar ornaments and chalices, and burned the priceless manuscripts and books of the abbeys and monasteries, so they also ransacked the dwellings of the Jews, assuring the frightened townspeople that they had come only "to punish the priests, the monks, the nuns and the Jews."

The peasants of the Sundgau demanded that the knights of their region have all the Jews expelled from the Alsace and that the authorities cease protecting them. The knights, while firmly rejecting the liberal demands of the peasants, stated that, "for their part," they would be "in favor of" the articles pertaining to the Jews.

"The monsters committed many outrages against the Jews,"[20] Josel relates with regard to his own experiences in 1525. "It was their intention to swallow us up alive, and they had already made a good start in this direction."

In the Lower Alsace, the hotbed of rebellion was the region on the Odilienberg, at the foot of which was located the Imperial town of Rosheim. There one Erasmus Gerber of Molsheim, an impetuous man of no mean abilities, had become leader of the band of peasants which Josel estimated to be fifteen thousand strong. Gerber had appointed one Diebold von Dalheim as his deputy, and Peter von Nordheim as captain over the peasants living in the Imperial villages. He had gathered around himself a committee of twenty-five peasants and burghers.

As a self-styled "Christian regent," seeking to "support the Divine right, the sacred Gospels and justice," Gerber was the only peasant leader in the *Reich* able to unite the splintered and unregimented masses of the Upper and Lower Alsace, and to weld them together into a compact and menacing force.

It was from Altorf Monastery, only half a mile away from Rosheim, that he directed his schemes, aiming primarily to bring the larger cities, especially Strasbourg, Hagenau and Rosheim, into the movement.

The attempt of *Landvogt* Hans Jakob von Moersberg to open negotiations with the peasant leaders, so as to gain time until he would receive military assistance, ended in failure. Gerber did not even grant him an audience. The deputies from the city of Strasbourg, among them the Councillor Martin Herlin, with whom Josel frequently had occasion to confer, also received no answer from Gerber to their repeated requests for a meeting. Likewise, Martin Butzer, Wolfgang Capito and Zell, the three reformers from Strasbourg who had called at the camp of Altorf to convince the peasants, who adhered to the word of the Gospels, that their insurrection was not justifiable in accordance with the Holy Scriptures, had to leave without achieving anything.

Such was the situation when, late one evening in the spring of 1525, Josel received the news[21] that the peasant armies were planning to attack the town of Rosheim the next day. His brief report, which was corroborated years later by the Magistrate of Rosheim, does not indicate the reason why Erasmus Gerber should have chosen to send so important a message to Josel. Did he think perhaps that Josel, the most influential Jew in the Alsace, whose dispute with the town magistrates of Oberehnheim and Rosheim had become widely known, would betray the city (whose Mayor, Ittel, had joined the insurgents) and that he would become his ally?

Josel, ordinarily calm and collected in the hour of crucial decision, rushed to the homes of the two burgomasters Hans Mangen and Jacob Wagner in the middle of the night to warn them of the danger that threatened their people. Thereupon the Magistrate had the gates of the town locked, temporarily staving off the raid planned by the peasants. But soon thereafter new mobs of insurgents joined the band of Altorf, strengthening the numbers of the peasant army to such a degree that the city had reason to fear a new raid, against which it would not have been able to hold out.

Josel then decided "with the help of God"[22] to go to Altdorf to talk with the leaders of the insurrection. We can only surmise what he discussed with Erasmus Gerber and his two comrades. During those hours in the old abbey (whose patron saint was St. Odilie), he somehow managed to put the "ringleaders of the conspiracy" in a favorable mood. We have no picture of him which would reveal how majestic his forehead was, how commanding his look, or how firm and steady his hands. However, according to reports from many historical sources, he had the gift of inspiring oratory which few opponents could withstand, and he had the ability to attract people from a great many walks of life and win their respect and devotion. At any rate, he succeeded where both the *Unterlandvogt,* who was skilled in the art of political intrigue, and the Burgomaster, Martin Herlin, who had a sound, practical approach, had failed. In return for a gift of eighty florins, the leaders of the insurrection promised Josel in a written document that they would not attack the city of Rosheim unless all the Imperial towns made common cause with the peasants. "And they kept this promise for me,"[23] Josel wrote. Overjoyed at his success, Jakob Wagner, the Burgomaster of Rosheim, promised Josel that his deed would never be forgotten while he or his children were alive.[24]

Josel also tells in his memoirs that he was able to persuade Erasmus Gerber in Altorf to have mercy on the Jews and to spare them in the future.[25] "And even though they subsequently failed to keep their promise, this statement of theirs came as a great relief to us at this time."

Shortly after these events, the peasants of the Alsace were defeated near Lupstein and Saverne by the mercenaries of Duke Anton of Lorraine from Spain and from the Low Countries. They fell victim to the same cruel revenge that had been executed upon the peasant armies of Swabia, Franconia, Thuringia, the Rhineland and elsewhere, who had been suppressed without mercy by the Swabian League and the reigning princes.

"Here in the Alsace the Duke of Lorraine attacked them and destroyed them; in the other provinces, too, they were slain and drowned by the thousands and tens of thousands." In these words, Josel describes the sad ending of what was the most tragic revolution in German history.[26] He was happy that the Jews had not been harmed by the "evil plans" of the peasants. He failed to realize, however, that the suppression of this Estate, which had fought for its time-honored rights and for equality with the other Estates, also meant the end of the dream of a free and united *Reich,* headed by one Emperor of Peace as sole sovereign of the people. For the defeat of the peasants meant victory for the modern, secular, authoritarian and autonomous State which, in league with the Lutheran Reformation, had overrun not only the "murderous and predatory mob of peasants," but also the only viable democratic movement in Germany.

In this struggle, the peasants fought primarily for relief from their social burdens and for their rightful share of the political rights in the *Reich.* But beyond this, they considered themselves the representatives of the natural and agrarian economy of the Middle Ages, which had been imperiled by the rise of the monetary system of capitalism. By revolting against these new powers, they rose up also against the Jews, who for so many centuries had been the privileged bankers of both Church and State.

In those tumultuous times, for reasons similar to those which motivated the peasants, the impoverished and debt-ridden landed nobility of the Alsace also turned against their Jewish subjects.

These small landowners and knights formerly had almost always protected the Jews. One might almost say that they had welcomed with open arms the Jews who had been expelled from the Imperial towns. This was not only because they were gaining new taxpayers and good salesmen for their farm products, but also because with their new subjects they were able to harass the neighboring cities, which by their *Meilenrecht* (freedom of towns extending one mile round) and economic privileges barred the rural population round about from engaging in trade and the crafts.

Like the peasants, these landlords were imperiled by the new type of State, which sought to abrogate the basic rights of feudalism, to abolish the jurisdiction of the nobility, and to force the independent nobles of the *Reich* into the tightly knit framework of its new order. Similarly, the new credit system, which began to "supplant the economic system based on feudal land ownership," posed a menace to them as well.

Moreover, like the peasants, the landowners regarded the Jews, their principal creditors, as the most obvious representatives of the capitalist system, and therefore held them responsible for the changes in their living conditions, for their impoverishment, and for their loss of independence.

Thus, in 1528, the landed nobility and the knights of the *Unterlandvogtei* of Hagenau turned directly to King Ferdinand with their grievances, and obtained from him an edict ordering the expulsion of the Jews.[27]

As in 1515, the corporate body of Lower Alsatian Jewry again requested its leader to plead its cause with the sovereign and to intercede in its behalf. As Lord of Anterior Austria, Ferdinand was thoroughly familiar with economic and social conditions in the Alsace. He listened to Josel's representations at his castle in Prague with sympathy and understanding. He agreed to recall the decree which he had issued to the knights, and assuring Josel of his good will, he reconfirmed the privileges that had been issued to the Jews of the Alsace. "The adversaries again planned to stir up enmity and to undo what had been achieved. But God sent angels of destruction so that three of the plotters fell victim to a sudden illness, and the fourth fell into the hands of his own enemies at his residence, Hochfelden, and was put to death."[28]

It was Josel's firm belief that this miraculous rescue of his brethren had been brought about by the stringent regimen of sacrifice and restraint which he had imposed upon himself.

When an accident had befallen his horse during the journey to Prague, he had resolved to travel on foot the rest of the way and not to mount his horse again until he arrived at the court of the King. "My real reason [for this] was my hope that by much toil, prayer and supplication, it might be possible to bring about a change for the better in the situation."

The fact that he undertook this long and arduous journey from the west to the east of the *Reich* on foot, as would a penitent pilgrim, threatened by drunken mercenaries and brawling students, and never certain if he would find shelter for the night in the cities through which he passed, shows the great importance Josel attached to this change in the attitude of the knights.

The personal relationship which Josel established with King Ferdinand at that time stood him in good stead in the following year, when he was faced with an even more difficult task.

In 1529, in the small Hungarian townlet of Poesing, not far from Pressburg, a wealthy Jew by the name of Esslein Ausch was accused of having "cruelly tortured, beaten, stabbed, cut and murdered" a nine-year-old boy. After terrible tortures, the unhappy victim confessed that he and his co-religionists had sucked the blood from the child with the help of goosequills and reeds, and had rejoicingly taken it to the synagogue for use at wedding feasts. The accused, around thirty in number, named several other Jews from Marchegg, Lower Austria, as accomplices, and were sentenced to be burned at the stake.[29] But before the Jews arrested at Marchegg could be tried, the child whom Esslein Ausch had allegedly murdered was found by some Jews from Vienna, safe and sound, with an old, nearly imbecile woman. It turned out that a certain Count Wolf von Poesing, who owed a large amount of money to Esslein Ausch and his business associates, had removed the boy from Poesing and proceeded to instigate the ritual murder charge. Upon this discovery, the Jews from Marchegg were released, but it appears that the true facts of the case were not then divulged to the public; for the news of the Poesing murder, that "horrible affair," as it is described in a broadsheet of the times, caused a great stir far and wide. In nearby Moravia, which had been stirred up to a fever pitch by the wars with the Hussites and the Turks, and by the change in its ruling dynasty, the ritual murder of Poesing was exploited as a pretext for throwing a number of Jews into prison.

The only information we have of these events in Moravia is in the memoirs of Josel of Rosheim.[30]

"In the year 1529, the saintly martyrs of Poesing, thirty-six souls,[31] God-fearing men and women, youths and maidens, were arrested on mendacious charges and burned at the stake on the thirteenth day of Sivan. On this occasion, the Jews of Moravia were put into prison." He also relates that, at the request of the rabbis and scholars of the *Reich,* he had brought all the existing papal bulls and Imperial privileges to Guenzburg on the Danube, and had drafted a paper of justification, which he sent, together with the other documents, to King Ferdinand, who had been sovereign lord of Bohemia and Moravia since 1526. As a result, "our innocence became known to them and they said to the captives. 'Go forth, free.' "

It may be assumed that, at that time, deputies from the Jewish communities called a conference at Guenzburg on the Danube in order to take common action for the release of their brethren in Moravia, and that they requested Josel, who had successfully negotiated with King Ferdinand only the year before, to draft a memorial for them.

Like so many of Josel's other writings, this memorial was lost. But we can surmise the character of the petition, and which papal and Imperial documents he would have selected to convince Ferdinand, who was so deeply devoted to the Church, of the absurdity of the blood libel.[32]

There was, for instance, a bull sent by Pope Innocent IV in 1247 to the bishops and archbishops of Germany, in which the Pope harshly condemned all false accusations made without confession or conviction. Next, the bull of 1272 by Gregory X, in which the Christians were charged with hiding their children and then accusing the Jews of robbery and murder. Finally, there were more recent bulls, issued by Martin V and Nicholas V, and Imperial privileges conferred by Frederick II, Rudolph of Habsburg, and Frederick III, all vigorously condemning accusations of ritual murder.

It was not merely concern for their brethren in Moravia that motivated the Jews of the *Reich* to send their deputies to Guenzburg. They had a vague suspicion that the increasing incidence of host desecration and ritual murder charges was caused by motivations much more complex than the envy of their business rivals or the machinations of ambitious priests, who sought to gain new saints, new miracles, new martyrs, and thus added power for the Church. The accusations originated in the depths of the souls of severely shaken men, men who delved into the realm of the sinister and the supernatural to find the reason for the mysterious events that were happening to them: the disintegration of the old order to which they had been accustomed from time immemorial. They really believed that magical powers were at work in their destinies, and that the stars determined the course of their lives for better or for worse. They beheld with their own eyes the Horsemen of the Apocalypse sweeping through the land, bringing famine, war and pestilence in their wake. At night they saw blazing meteors streak through the sky, and knew this meant that ruin and disaster were about to strike. During the day, crosses rained down upon their clothes, portents of a new Flood or perhaps even of the End of the World.

Water sprites and demons begat offspring with their wives and daughters, and the witches that danced atop the Blocksberg put a hex on the cattle in the stables and brought want and illness to their homes. And the Devil, with whom the witches had intercourse, made a pact with man so that he might learn about the "elements" and strip God of His mysteries.

Why, then, should they not also have believed that the Jews would make use of the blood of Christian children to bring healing to their bodies and salvation to their souls, to help them defeat nature and to crucify the hated Christians, even as they once had crucified the Savior Himself?[33]

It was probably at this memorable conference at Guenzburg, at which he made his first plea in defense of Jews living outside the Alsace, that Josel was elected "Leader" and "Commander" by the deputies from the Jewish communities of Germany.

To this day, no explanation has been found for this unique event in the history of German Jewry. At no other time, either before or after, had the Jews of the *Reich* ever voluntarily given up their zealously guarded autonomy in communal organizations and corporate bodies of Rural Jewry to unite into one community, no matter how loosely knit.

There had been other synods and conferences of rabbis and *parnassim* throughout the Middle Ages,[34] necessitated by persecution such as occurred during the Crusades or in the Rindfleisch Insurrection, and by intolerable taxation or cancellation of debts. Those conferences represented attempts to deliberate jointly on concerted action to avert the threatening peril and to give moral and legal guidance to the communities. As recently as 1510, shortly after the Jews of the March had been burned at the stake and the survivors expelled and threatened by Pfefferkorn's attacks, the officers of the Jewish community of Frankfort had asked the Emperor

Maximilian for permission to call a conference of deputies from the *Reich* to discuss the many encroachments that had been made on their time-honored civil liberties.[35]

Thus the conference at Guenzburg does not in itself represent an innovation. But what distinguished it from all previous conferences was that in this instance the Jews of the *Reich* put themselves under the authority of a leader, without having been compelled to do so by the Emperor or some other official.

A similar attempt to unite the Jews of the *Reich* under the leadership of a Chief Rabbi, or *Hochmeister,* had already been made over a century before, an attempt which was probably patterned on an analogous development in France at that time.

In 1407, Ruprecht of the Palatinate had appointed Rabbi Israel of Rothenburg *Reichsrabbiner* (Imperial Rabbi), and had put all the other rabbis and *Hochmeister,* as well as all the Jews and Jewesses of the *Reich,* under his authority.[36] This official was empowered to ensure the prompt and proper payment of the various fines which the Jews had to remit to the King as penalties for delinquencies, denunciations and deliberate procrastination in court proceedings. He was further authorized to summon Jews before his tribunal at his own discretion, and to sentence to penalties or to excommunication anyone who proved delinquent in the payment of the tribute penny or other taxes.

The *Reichsrabbiner* was bound by oath to perform the duties of his office in an unimpeachable manner, and to safeguard the privileges of the Jews to the best of his knowledge and conscience. The Jews, in turn, particularly the rabbis and the *parnassim,* were admonished to comply with the directives of the *Reichsrabbiner* and to obey his orders implicitly.[37]

The fiscal stipulation in the *Reichsrabbiner's* certificate of appointment—his duty to ensure the prompt payment of all fines to the Royal Treasury so that "the rights of the *Reich* pertaining to the Jews be not impaired"—had a prominent place also in the certificates of appointment issued to the three *Reichsrabbinern*, Nathan of Eger, Jacob ha-Levi (MaHaRIL) of Mayence, and Yohanan Treves, who were appointed in 1426, and to Anselm of Cologne, a rabbi in Worms, who was named "Supreme Master and Rabbi" in 1435.

We have no information on the functions of "Levi Jud, of Nuremberg, the Supreme *Hochmeister* of Jewry in the Holy Empire,"[38] but they were probably similar to those of his predecessors and of his successor, Samuel of Worms.

Josel's prerogatives exceeded those of the *Reichsrabbiner* by far, and, unlike the latter, he had a political role of considerable significance. It is clear, too, from the numerous official documents of that time, that he acted as the plenipotentiary of German Jewry as a whole and that he was recognized as such by the highest authorities in the land. Yet, in contrast to the certificates of appointment issued to the *Reichsrabbiner*, there is no document to show who had appointed Josel to this important office.

Beginning with the year 1530, or shortly after the Guenzburg conference, we find Josel adding to his signature such titles as "Regent of All Jewry in Germany," "Commander of All Jewry of the German Nation," "Governor of All Jewry," "Provost of All Jewry," and "Advocate of All Jewry."

The *Landvogt* of the Upper Alsace addressed him in a letter as "Chief of All Jewry of the German Nation."[39] The Hereditary Marshal Joerg Wolf von Pappenheim called him "Chief in the German *Reich*."[40] The Burgrave of Rotenburg applied a request to Josel, addressing him as "Governor of All Jewry"; the records of the *Reichshofrat* referred to him as "Commander of All Jewry,"[41] and the Emperor, in a written mandate to the *Unterlandvogt* of Hagenau, made mention of Josel as the "Commander of All Jewry."[42]

In 1551, Duke Christopher of Wuerttemberg signed an important treaty with Josel as the "Advocate and Commander of All Jewry," "by virtue of the power and authority vested in him."

Like these titles, the definition of Josel's functions as set forth by the authorities indicate that his position in the Jewish community was officially recognized.

Mathias Held, the Imperial Vice-Chancellor, stated[43] that the Emperor Charles had been induced by Josel's "frequent and assiduous importunings and solicitations" to preserve the liberties of the Jews, and Dr. Christoff Hoss, Josel's lawyer, stressed that Josel "had been appointed by all Jewry to defend their liberties and *confirmationes* at every Imperial Diet."[44]

Yet, despite all these indications that Josel was the legally recognized leader of German Jewry for many decades, we have no certificate of appointment to give us more detailed information concerning the manner in which he was chosen for this office. It is difficult to believe that a document of this character, if it ever existed, should have been lost. Numerous copies of nearly all the Imperial privileges granted to the Jews during that period are still preserved in many of the archives in Southern Germany. And if Josel himself had been in possession of so important a document, he certainly would have mentioned it, in keeping with his methodical manner of recording important events, even as he set down the facts of his appointment as *manhig* and *parnas* of Lower Alsatian Jewry. Josel liked to cite official documents for added emphasis upon the legitimacy of his demands; hence, he surely would have cited this document as well whenever the Jews were faced with a crisis. Even in 1534, when he had to engage in costly litigation with the Supreme Court of Justice, and an important Imperial privilege of this sort would have placed him at a considerable advantage, we find no mention anywhere of such a document.[45] Furthermore, Charles V, in his reconfirmation of Josel's safe-conduct in 1548, does not indicate that he had been appointed Commander of German Jewry by Maximilian, as some historians have presumed.

It must therefore be assumed that, unlike the *Reichsrabbiner,* Josel had been appointed to his office not by the Emperor but by the Jewish community.[46] The fact that he did not have to assume any fiscal responsibilities vis-à-vis the Imperial Treasury, and that he was neither compelled to collect taxes nor authorized to excommunicate, punish or pass sentence on any Jews other than those of the Alsace, would support this assumption. He never carried out a single mission without first receiving a request from the deputies of the communities.[47] In 1551, when he had to conduct involved negotiations with Bavaria and Wuerttemberg, the rabbis and *parnassim* assembled in Frankfort gave their "veteran Leader and Commander" appropriate powers plenipotentiary and approved the arrangements he had made previously.[48]

Internal factors, too, would indicate that Josel probably owed his office to voluntary election by his own people. Israel, the *Reichsrabbiner* whom Ruprecht had foisted on the Jews, was furiously persecuted and even excommunicated by the other *Hochmeister* because his appointment by the Emperor and his power to excommunicate was not in keeping with their traditional laws and customs. Josel, on the other hand, never lost the magic link that bound him to his brethren, even though his authority was founded solely on the confidence of those who had chosen him, and on the affection of the people whom he led.

As in the days of the Judges, the office held by Josel was an outgrowth of the demands of the century in which he lived. A Jewish population, deeply humiliated, in danger of losing its very foundations of survival, beset by fanaticism and superstition and grown unsure of itself, set about to elect a leader, even as the peasants, the knights, the Protestants and the Anabaptists, and all others seeking a new kind of faith and way of life, had named men of their own choosing to lead them.

How it came about that the reigning princes, the *Landvoegte,* the magistrates of the cities, the royal and ducal officials and even the Emperor, accorded official recognition to this "Commander" appointed by the Jewish community, and safeguarded his position and strengthened his authority, will be discussed in the chapters that follow.

CHAPTER FOUR

CRITIC AND REFORMER

IN 1530, Charles V returned to the *Reich* after an absence of nine years as the victor triumphant, the lord of the greater part of the universe. He had just been crowned Emperor by the Pope in Bologna. His *conquistadores* had conquered Peru and Mexico for him. He himself had quelled the revolt of the *comuneros* in Spain; he had defeated his most implacable foe, Francis I of France, in the Battle of Pavia. He had then marched on Rome, humbled the Pope, who had been the King's ally, and compelled both Pope and King to sign a peace treaty at Cambrai.

The shy, reserved youth, whom Josel had last met at Aix-la-Chapelle in 1520, had become a mature man, fully aware of the responsibilities of his high station. As the secular Vicar of God on earth, duly anointed and crowned, Charles was driven by a consuming ambition to restore to the Holy Roman Empire its former supreme position and religious unity, to suppress the mutiny of the Protestants, and to rout the Turks, who had swept over the Danube region and were actually laying siege to Vienna.

These two major projects, the showdown with the Lutheran movement and the preparation of a crusade against the Turks, were on the agenda of a great Imperial Diet that was to be held in Augsburg in June 1530.

Charles had come to Innsbruck from Bologna to discuss with his brother Ferdinand, his chancellor, and his ministers how best to break the power of the Estates without losing their aid in the campaign against the Turks or jeopardizing the unity of the Empire.

During the latter part of May, while Charles was thus occupied with affairs of State, he received word that one "Josel of Rosheim," a Jew from the Alsace, had arrived at Innsbruck and was urgently seeking an audience with him.[1]

This time the reason for Josel's journey on horseback clear across the *Reich* to Tyrol to appeal to the Emperor for help was more pressing than just another charge of ritual murder.

"In the year 1530," he wrote, "a rumor spread and persisted among the nations that 'the Jews were reporting calumnies about us to the Turks.' These defamations came to the attention also of our sovereign lord, the King and Emperor. As a result, we were outlawed and denied admission to many lands."[2] Josel goes on to relate that he had drawn up a paper of justification "with the consent of the communities," and had presented it to the two sovereigns then meeting at Innsbruck.

Like all his other apologetic writings, this document, too, was lost, and unlike the papal bulls and Imperial privileges, it cannot be reconstructed from other sources. However, we may safely assume that this new accusation, which was tantamount to one of high treason, must have posed a threat to the safety of German Jewry much greater than any trumped-up charge of ritual murder or host desecration. For the Turks were the most dreaded scourge to afflict the Empire since the days of the Mongol raids.

Seen in the light of the eschatological mood prevailing at the time, the Jews and the Turks appeared to the people to be none other than Gog and Magog. It was widely believed that the fire and death, famine and pestilence which these sinister tribes from the far-off East carried in their wake heralded the coming of the Antichrist. For prophecy had it that before the advent of the Messiah, Gog and Magog, the peoples of the end of the world, would break through the walls that Alexander the Great had built to confine them and would sweep on toward Jerusalem to conquer the Holy City. There they would be met and routed by the Antichrist, the Roman Empire would crumble, and an era of evil and disaster would begin.

It was further related that the Antichrist, the Prince of Iniquity, would be the son of a Jewish whore descended from the tribe of Dan. Even the Tiburtine Sibylla had already announced that *in illo tempore surget princeps iniquitatis de tribu Dan qui vocabitur Antichristus* ("In those days there will arise a Prince of Iniquity from the tribe of Dan, who will be called the Antichrist").

In Johannes Lichtenberger's famous prediction from the second half of the fifteenth century, the date of the coming of the Antichrist was set for 1488. In that year, it was asserted, the Antichrist would unleash a wave of terror to last for a period of five years, and he would bring great trouble upon the world by causing the tainted and pernicious Jews to be appointed to high positions in many lands. They would occupy strategic places at the courts of princes as governors, physicians, artists and counselors, and great and famous people would love them "due to the elevated position of Saturn in this astronomical constellation."

Such were the supernatural and mysterious associations by which Christianity's most implacable foes, the Jews and the Turks, were linked together. Both were held to be implicated in the impending era of doom, and both were regarded as the causes of the End of the World, the deeper meaning of which no one could comprehend logically or interpret with any degree of reason.

Even so enlightened a humanist and so accomplished a statesman as Konrad Peutinger, the Town Clerk of Augsburg, was not immune to the climate of superstition in which he lived.[3] He actually declared it to be common knowledge that the Jews had been guilty of vile treason during the last Turkish War. He asserted that they had acted as spies for the Turks and had probably given them financial support as well.

This general atmosphere of mistrust was not improved by the great expectations which the then rife Apocalyptic fantasies associated with a Turkish victory. The Anabaptists, Luther's vehement antagonists and the victims of cruel persecution, who sought to put the Evangelic ideal into practice in everyday life, hoped that the Turks would "reform corrupted Christianity and chastise all the Godless, particularly the ruling powers."[4]

Augustin Baader, a furrier by trade and a zealot by conviction, proclaimed that the Turks would "set up a new empire composed of Christians, Jews, heathens and Turks" in which he would reign supreme, patterning his rule on that of the kings of the Bible. The Anabaptists, whose faith was based on the "inner testimony" of the individual, derived this doctrine of "inner testimony" from the authority of the Bible itself. Hence it was the Bible, and the Old Testament in particular, that served them as a guide for their personal conduct and for their Utopian State, which would be subject to no human authority, religious or secular, but solely to God. Thomas Muenzer, the spiritual leader of the movement, who was executed during the Peasants' War, consistently identified himself with the prophets and heroes of the Old Testament. Thus he would imagine himself to be Gideon, wielding the sacred sword entrusted to his care. At other times he was Jeremiah, waging the good fight against mighty and godless tyranny. Then, like Daniel, he would prophesy that the End of the World was at hand and the Kingdom of God was about to begin.

It was said that Augustin Baader had associated with Jews in Worms who had initiated him into the mysteries of the Hebrew language, and that he in turn had revealed to the Jews of Leipzig and Guenzburg the hopes and expectations he cherished in connection with the coming of the Turks. Oswald Lewer, another Anabaptist who predicted that the new Kingdom would be established in 1530, had also taken instruction in Hebrew from Jews, and in turn had attempted to win them over to his new doctrine.

It cannot be denied that in those years of distress and persecution, the Messianic yearnings of the Jews received fresh nourishment from the Apocalyptic visions of the Anabaptists, and that there were many among them who hoped that a Turkish victory would bring about a change for the better in their fortunes.

Had not the Sultan given a warm and cordial welcome to the Sephardi emigrés, and had he not honored and exalted them so that they had become advisors to the sovereigns and ministers of finance almost as they had been in Spain?[5] And had they not received letters from them to the effect that it was better to live among Mohammedans than among Christians? They wrote of a land where people were not burned at the stake, where monks and priests did not run rampant, and where everyone was dressed in sumptuous robes and could dwell in peace beneath his own fig tree.

All arguments against the Jews notwithstanding, Josel succeeded in convincing Charles and Ferdinand at Innsbruck of the baselessness of the accusations that the Jews were serving the Turks as spies. "Joseph found favor in their eyes, and they reconfirmed all our privileges as of old."[6]

On May 18, 1530, the Emperor issued an edict at Innsbruck

in which he reconfirmed, as Roman Emperor, all the rights and freedoms which he had granted the Jews at the time of his coronation at Aix-la-Chapelle.[7]

On June 15, Charles, accompanied by a great retinue, entered Augsburg, that festive and cheerful southern city whose broad and stately avenues were lined with the picturesque homes of the Fuggers, the Welsers, the Hochstetters and the Eggenbergers. These dwellings were filled with works of art from all over the world, and surrounded by magnificent gardens.

A stranger, gazing in amazement at the painted Tuscan pillars and the Venetian arcades of these palatial mansions, must have thought himself transported to Renaissance Italy. The Italian spirit permeated this worldly wise Imperial city.

However, the Electors and reigning princes, the deputies from the various cities, and the theologians, Protestant and Catholic, who had come to Augsburg in large numbers to hold the most important and decisive Imperial Diet of the century, were more concerned with the heavy responsibilities of their task than with the atmosphere of pagan-like opulence which surrounded them.[8]

To Charles, the political, religious, and psychological aspects of the work before him were altogether different from the task he had faced in Worms in 1521. To excommunicate and ostracize an obstinate apostate monk was one thing; to deal with reigning princes who had acquired self-confidence and political importance was quite another. These were men who had introduced the "new doctrine" into their realms, had abolished the Holy Mass, done away with the monasteries, and confiscated the Church properties.

The Emperor had wanted to give priority in the agenda to what he considered the most pressing problem; namely, the financial and military aid to be rendered by the Estates in the campaign against the Turks. The Evangelicals, however, declared that they would support Charles in his war only after the religious problems were settled in a manner compatible with their consciences.

The danger facing the lands of the Habsburg dynasty made it imperative that Charles make compromises and concessions. Thus, only a few days after the opening of the Diet, he gave a hearing to the *Confessio Augustana,* composed by Melanchthon, a basic tenet of the Protestant Church to this day. It was refuted by Catholic theologians in a written rebuttal entitled *Confutatio.*

While these heated debates kept emotions in suspense, the Catholics made the charge that the Jews were to blame for the outbreak of the Reformation, "because they had taught their faith to the Lutherans."[9]

The notion that the Protestant movement had been brought about by the Jews was just as absurd as the claim that they used the blood of Christian children for medicinal purposes. But the superficial or hostile outsider, who did not grasp the deeper implications of the new doctrine, was very likely to assume that there was indeed some close connection between Judaism and the Lutheran movement.

It was the first time that a movement of world-wide importance had made an impassioned effort to come closer to Judaism and to understand it, to discover in its doctrines the mystery of their common origin, and, guided by them, to interpret the hidden meaning of the revealed word. As the Reformers discovered anew for themselves the Bible, the original and pure wellspring of their religion, and found it contained all the knowledge and wisdom in the world, they came to regard the Jews as the descendants of patriarchs, prophets and kings, and the Jewish people as the nation chosen and distinguished among all others, since it was to the Jews alone that God had entrusted the Holy Scriptures.[10]

The pronounced biblicism of the Reformers, which led

them to seek out learned Jews and to consult the writings of the ancient Jewish commentators, their fight against the hierarchy and the "graven images" of the Church, and their political-secular theories modeled on those of the Old Testament, had long earned them the charge of "Judaization" from the Catholics. Luther was suspected of being a "patron of the Jews" and a "half-Jew"; Zwingli was accused of having obtained his knowledge of the Bible from a Jew from Winterthur, and it was said that Butzer was of Jewish descent.

The Reformation had also caused a great stir among the Jews. The fact that the new religion was based on the text of their Holy Scriptures, that canon law had been abrogated and the absolute rule of the Church badly shaken, seemed to them the promised sign that the Messiah would indeed come and that Israel would rise again in all its ancient glory.

It was as the representative of *Reich* Jewry that Josel came to Augsburg, and it was there that he refuted the accusations of the Catholics before the greatest forum in the world and in the presence of the Emperor and the Bishop of Strasbourg. "For it was never heard that we presumed to decide for others," he said. "We abide by our ancient Law."[11]

This terse remark reflects very little of the manner in which Josel pleaded the cause of his people. It is not likely that he foresaw at that time the great fight against the Jews upon which Luther was to embark a decade later. But it is likely that Josel, as the friend of the Magistrate of Strasbourg, the spokesman city of the Reformation, was sufficiently familiar with the basic features of the Protestant faith to be able to explain to the Catholic Estates the fundamental differences between Protestantism and the Jewish religion. For how could Luther's doctrine of justification through faith be related to the ceremonial law of the Old Testament, the Evangelical doctrine of predestination to the Jewish concept of free will, or Luther's interpretation of Divine grace to the Jewish teaching of individual moral responsibility? For what relationship could there be between the ideas of the one religion and those of the other? It would seem impossible even to find a resemblance between them, let alone make one dependent on the other. And could the *res publica Christiana,* that "Christian State" organized by Martin Butzer, that God-willed and God-ordained commonwealth imbued with the spirit of the true Gospels, be expected to tolerate within its borders a community that differed from it with regard to both nationality and religion, a community which, as Josel stressed, was determined to "abide by its ancient Law?"

It appears that these discussions consisted only of private conversations between Josel and several Catholic leaders, to whom he explained the differences which set Judaism and Lutheranism apart from one another.

The situation was altered when Josel was requested by the Emperor himself to refute, in a public disputation, some serious accusations which had been made against the Jews.

In March 1530, three months prior to the opening of the Imperial Diet, there had appeared in the city of Augsburg an anti-Jewish tract written by a lecturer in the Hebrew language. The work created such a stir that a second edition was printed only a month later. The book, entitled *The Whole Jewish Faith,*[12] was full of glaring errors and inaccuracies of grammar and style as well as deliberate distortions of fact. Moreover, it contained a good deal of material borrowed from Victor von Carben's *Opus Aureum.* Nevertheless, this book, which represented the first attempt to explain to non-Jews all the prayers of the Jews and interpret all their customs and ceremonies, furnished the Christian scholars and theologians with the ammunition they needed in their fight against Judaism and the Jewish religion until well into the modern era.

The popular appeal of the book was due primarily to the fact that the author, Antonius Margaritha, was descended from an old, well-known Jewish family. He was a grandson of the distinguished talmudical scholar, Jacob Margolis of Nuremberg, the son of Rabbi Samuel of Regensburg, and related by blood and marriage to several renowned Jews in Prague. It was not surprising that, at a time when minds were so receptive to Jewish literature, his knowledge of Jewish customs and ceremonies, the ingenious manner in which he set down recollections from his childhood in the home of his pious parents and recalled events that had taken place in the Jewish community of Regensburg, his historical and cultural comparisons, and his descriptions of the Messianic expectations and cabbalistic visions of his former co-religionists, all should have aroused great interest.

It was only to be expected that his "great zeal for the Christian religion," which had led him to abandon his blind, stubborn and obdurate people in order to worship the true Messiah, should create the impression that this man had indeed undergone a "true rebirth." This is what he called his baptism, which had taken place at Wasserburg, Bavaria, in 1522.

The Jews, however, considered this lecturer in the Hebrew language a much more dangerous adversary than the ignorant butcher Pfefferkorn. Margaritha was thus right in his prediction that the Jews would call a conference in Worms immediately after the publication of his book, to discuss with their *Reichsrabbiner* Samuel how best to suppress this piece of literature, or to disparage it in the eyes of the Christians.

Margaritha had taken great pains to translate all the Jewish prayers into German, in order to prove that the Jews prayed to God every day of the year, morning, afternoon and evening, and particularly on the Day of Atonement, that He might tear out the Roman Empire by its roots, destroy all the Christian authorities and all the Kingdoms, and "spatter the blood of the Christians upon the walls."

"Remember, O Christian reader," he writes, "that when the Jews pray for vengeance and curse the Edomites, Esau or Seir, they always mean all the authorities, together with the subjects of the Roman Empire. . . . In fact, they have prayers, particularly the *Alenu,* in which they dare to curse even Christ. When they say in their prayer that 'they (the Christians) kneel and bow down to folly and vanity and pray to a god who cannot give help,' they are clearly uttering prayers against Christ and the Christians. For by 'folly' and 'vanity' they mean Jesus; the numerical value of the letters in these words [in Hebrew] corresponds to that of the letters in His name."

At the end of his treatise, Margaritha accuses the Jews of theft, usury, counterfeiting and other vices, and requests that the government prohibit them from lending money, and give them neither protection nor assistance in safeguarding their rights.

The contents of this tract were made known to the Emperor soon after his arrival in Augsburg. He had just given a hearing at Innsbruck to Josel's defense of his people. Now a scholarly apostate had brought evidence to show that the Jews were cursing Christ and even the Emperor himself in their synagogues, and that they were attempting to win the Christians over to Judaism.

In his book, Margaritha had expressed the wish that he might be permitted to discuss his charges with the most erudite among the Jews. "I know," he wrote, "that the Jews will attempt to distort many of these facts, but while I am there, and with the help of God, none of these subterfuges, no matter how cunning, will avail them."

Perhaps it was this challenge that prompted the Emperor, "full of wrath,"[13] to demand that Josel refute Margaritha's charges before a learned commission.

It was a difficult situation for Josel. Public religious disputations were almost unknown in Germany. True, discussions between Jews and Christians, or between rabbis and clergymen, took place quite often, as can be seen from the Passion and Shrovetide plays of the period. As early as the beginning of the fifteenth century, Lipmann Muehlhausen had explained in his work, *Sefer ha-Nitzachon* ("Book of Victory"), how texts from the Old Testament could be employed to defeat a Christian opponent in debate. At the end of the century, Victor von Carben had engaged in a heated dispute on religious problems with learned rabbis from the Rhineland in the presence of the Archbishop of Cologne. But these had been spontaneous discussions with no political implications or repercussions.

In Spain, however, debates of this type were common and evolved into public exhibitions and arguments, which continued for weeks and frequently even over a period of months, in which the King and his ministers, nobles, clergymen, Jews and Christians eagerly participated, much as they did in knightly jousts or tournaments. The most learned Jews of the land would be forced to engage in debate with Christian opponents of equal erudition, mostly converts, and many of these disputations carried in their wake severe penalties, acts of violence, the suppression of certain prayers, the expulsion of Jewish philosophers from the country, and mass conversions.

Therefore Charles V thrust an enormous burden of responsibility upon Josel by introducing this Spanish practice into Germany. In his arguments, Josel would be forced to suppress his feelings of hatred for apostates and traitors to his faith, lest one heated word from him should endanger all of

Jewry. In addition, he would be required to cite verbatim texts from the Holy Scripture without laying himself open to suspicion of casuistry, equivocation or distortion of fact.

The disputation took place on June 25 before a learned commission, with the Emperor, several princes and representatives of other Estates of the realm in attendance. Josel was challenged to "defend himself with regard to three counts":[14] namely, that the Jews were slandering Christ and Christianity, that they sought to make proselytes, and that they were out to destroy the authorities to whom they were subordinate.

In his metaphorical, cumbersome and frequently awkward language, which made it appear as if he were wresting each and every word with great effort from his very heart, Josel proceeded to take up the defense of his people. In all likelihood, he did not base his arguments solely on his knowledge of the Holy Scriptures, but also consulted those apologetic texts with which the Jews had fended off similar attacks for centuries.

Countering Margaritha's arguments that the Jews had been defaming Christ and Christianity, Josel was able to explain to the members of the commission that the Law of Moses had unequivocally forbidden them to curse the gods, and that this prohibition was applicable in the case of every non-Jewish religion. In addition, it was taught in the Talmud[15] that all pious men who served the Lord on earth would be considered equal to the Priests and would have a portion in the world to come. "The heathens do not say to us: 'May the blessing of the Eternal be upon you'; but as for us, we still call out to them: 'We bless you in the name of the Eternal.' "[16]

In answer to Margaritha's assertion that the Jews considered the Christians their enemies, Josel could prove directly from the biblical text that the Jews were commanded to love the stranger as themselves,[17] since they themselves had once been strangers in the land of Egypt.[18] Besides, he could quote Mar Samuel's statement that Jews and Christians were equal before the throne of the Creator, since there were noble and virtuous men also among the followers of the Christian faith.

Furthermore, as their great teacher Rashi had said so eloquently: "No matter what the Egyptians have done to you—they have enslaved you and cast your sons into the river—the fact remains that at one time they took you in."[19]

To counter Margaritha's charge that the Jews were mutinying against the governments of the countries in which they resided, and were betraying them to their enemies, Josel could cite the historic fact that the Jews had always given loyal obedience to the Emperors of Rome and of the Roman Empire. For they had been commanded by none other than the Prophet Jeremiah to "seek the peace of the city whither I have caused you to be carried away, and pray to the Eternal for it, for in the peace thereof shall you have peace."

Josel did not have the broad philosophical education and scholarship of Moses ben Nachman of Gerona who, in 1263, had been forced to engage in disputation on the divinity and the Messianic nature of Christ, and on the ceremonial laws of the Old Testament, at the palace of the King of Aragon with Paulus Christiani, a baptized Jew.

Yet, compassion for his brethren endowed this simple, God-inspired man, who argued more from his heart than with logic, with such persuasive power that in the end the Imperial Commission had Margaritha arrested as a dangerous troublemaker and finally expelled him from Augsburg. Josel recorded exultantly[20] that Margaritha had to promise on oath never to set foot in the city of Augsburg again. Josel names as witnesses to this total victory Mathias Held, the Imperial Vice-Chancellor, Dr. Brandt, and the Magistrate of Augsburg, who "had to advertise said disputation."[21] The accuracy of Josel's statement is verified by the fact that from that time on, Margaritha was not heard from again in southern Germany. He moved to Meissen, but settled in Leipzig as early as 1531, where he took a position as lecturer in the Hebrew language. It was at that time that the third edition of *The Whole Jewish Faith,* which was to exert a powerful influence on Luther, appeared.

"Thereafter Margaritha allied himself with Luther and they became as thorns in our side."[22]

"But that which has befallen me thus far on account of this little book shall not long remain untold," Margaritha himself laments in the closing passages of the third edition of his work. "However, I pray to God, my Creator, and to Jesus Christ, my Redeemer, that He may save me and preserve me from the stubborn, crafty Jews and their designs."[23]

Charles V knew of Josel since the days of his coronation as King at Aix-la-Chapelle. But he had been impressed no more by the simple Jew from the Alsace at that time than he was later, at Innsbruck, when he reconfirmed for him the privileges of *Reich* Jewry.

It was only in Augsburg that Charles first came to observe Josel more closely. To be sure, Josel's exposition on the nature of the Jewish religion would certainly not have been sufficient to persuade the Emperor, "who could think only within terms of Catholicism and theocracy," to view Judaism as something other than heresy, which he tolerated only with reluctance in a land where he so longed to bring about religious unity. As late as 1522, he had declared to the Imperial Council of Regency that he would offer no resistance if the Council should decide to drive the Jews out of the *Reich* altogether "for the glory of God and the Christian faith." At the time of his accession in Spain, he refused the ardent pleas of the Marranos for relief from the horrors of the Inquisition, and for a ban on the secret denunciations which brought hundreds of "New Christians" to the stake each day.

Yet Charles, who had been reared in the religious ideals of the "New Piety" that prevailed in the Low Countries, and whose greatest wish was that the Catholic faith should experience a "rebirth from within," was neither fanatical nor cruel. At the Imperial Diet, Melanchthon, the reformer, admired the Emperor's "great moderation," asserting "there was no word or action on his part that could be described as unseemly in any fashion."

The motives that impelled the Emperor, who was ruler over all the world, to be drawn to Josel, the member of a degraded and despised people who, in this crucial hour, had spoken out in defense of his brethren, had their origin in those strata of human consciousness which cannot be fathomed by the rational methods of logic. Despite all the differences in station, philosophy of life, religion, and educational background which set these two men apart, the Emperor still was bound to recognize or sense their shared qualities: the same self-effacing readiness to wage the good fight, even at the risk of danger and death; the same devotion to a self-chosen task, which transcended all personal considerations; and the same mystical bond with the heavenly and the divine which irradiated, warmed, and hallowed their lives of toil and sacrifice.

Nevertheless, it would be incorrect to assume that it was this personal sympathy alone that led Charles subsequently to grant privilege after privilege to Josel for the Jews of Germany.

"In 1530, the princes of the people, the officials and noble ladies without number held a conference in order to adopt resolutions and ordinances," Josel writes in his terse account of what took place at the Imperial Diet of Augsburg.[24]

"However, I was on the alert, and I succeeded in having the ancient rights from the days of the Emperor Sigismund reconfirmed, in silencing our accusers, and in restoring peace to the land."

By this he meant that he had succeeded in obtaining from Charles the renewal and confirmation of an important and liberal privilege which Emperor Sigismund had granted to the Jews of the Alsace in 1433.[25]

By virtue of this privilege, the Christians were required to honor all debts that they had contracted with Jews by verbal or written agreement, and the Jews were given permission to sell or pawn any pledges still unredeemed at the end of one year. The Emperor had thus undertaken to protect the lives and property of the Jews, not to burden them with taxes other than the conventional duties, to permit them free movement from one city to another, and to safeguard their freedom and security in both war and peace, even as he would do with his Christian subjects. Forced baptism of men, women or children was strictly prohibited, and the Jews were given the right to request trial by the secular court of the city in which they resided, and to accept as witnesses only Christians or Jews of unimpeachable character.

In reconfirming this privilege on August 12, and broadening it to include all the Jews of the *Reich,* Charles admonished the princes and the magistrates of cities and towns to comply with the stipulations of the document on pain of severe prosecution and disfavor, so that the Jews "may dwell and remain at peace in the future in the Holy Empire."

Sigismund had issued this and similar patents of freedom to the Jews by way of compensation for the enormous regular and extraordinary taxes which he had imposed upon them in order to finance the wars with the Hussites and the settlement of the Church schism. In addition, he had obligated them to cede to the Royal Treasury ten per cent of the value of their movable property in return for the privileges issued to them.

Unlike Sigismund, Charles did not demand payment for confirming these privileges of August 1530. Beyond the golden tribute penny which every Jewish man and woman had to pay, he imposed no additional financial burdens on them.

Josel's success in obtaining important concessions at this critical period was due to the "time-honored tradition of the *Reich,*" of which Charles speaks over and over again. Like Frederick III and Maximilian I, Charles, too, maintained that the *Judenregal* (the Emperor's prerogative over the Jews) was an inalienable right of the Crown which could not be contested by any power in the world. When, in the 'twenties of the century, the Imperial Council of Regency made plans to impose a capitation fee on the Jews and to forbid them to engage in the money trade, Charles advised the Council in very sharp terms "that all the Jews in the *Reich* belonged to the Imperial Chamber and could be taxed only for the profit of the Sovereign." At another time, in a controversy with the Supreme Court of Justice, he asserted that he considered the Jew Tax his own money to use as he saw fit.[26] He ordered the Imperial town of Esslingen to permit a Jew named Baruch to reside within its walls, since "according to time-honored tradition, the Emperor may send Jews to any city he chooses, whom that city must then admit."

Charles' policy vis-à-vis the Jews, like that of his predecessors, shows that he felt a greater sense of duty toward "time-honored tradition" than toward his own deeply rooted conviction of the necessity for religious unity within the confederation of states over which he reigned. Seeking as he did to revive the concept of one *Reich* from the medieval Empire, he felt it his duty also to readopt and to maintain the policy which his ancestors had followed with regard to the Jews in their day.

Contrary to popular conception, the Imperial Diet at Augsburg did not confine itself to a discussion of political and religious problems. The same vehemence which characterized the struggle of the Protestants and the Catholics for the new doctrine versus the old was manifest also in the dispute between the representatives of the fixed, corporate and closed urban economy on the one hand, and the adherents of modern free and capitalist enterprise on the other. Both sides drew their arguments from the voluminous pamphlet literature of their day, in which the rigid views of the Church Fathers and canon law were either defended, or carried *ad absurdum* by way of theories which practice had long since rendered obsolete. In the main, there were two problems for which solutions were earnestly sought: monopolies and money-lending.

By dint of their immense drive for expansion and their ruthless exploitation of every opportunity which offered itself, the great trading houses and banking concerns had obtained from the Emperors and the reigning princes, in return for huge loans granted them, the right to exploit the rich silver and copper deposits of the Tyrol, and the Spanish quicksilver and silver mines, as well as exclusive trading rights for certain categories of goods, particularly overseas products. It was this monopoly that aroused the wrath of the moralist writers and the common man, who blamed this *Fuerkauf,* or barter, as they called it, for the rise in prices, currency depreciation, increased food costs, and thus for the troubles of the retailer. At Territorial and Imperial Diets, demands were heard again and again that the governments take action against the "forgeries and frauds," inflict severe penalties on the monopolists, and confiscate part of their assets.

At the Imperial Diet of Augsburg, the Town Clerk Peutinger, in a treatise which was to become famous, spoke out in opposition to public opinion and in behalf of freedom of trade for the individual, who should be responsible only to himself, provided that he observed the *honestas* and the laws, and refrained from "fraud, forgery, deceit and falsehood." Like Professor Eck of Ingolstadt, he demanded that the conventional five per cent allowance for capital invested in large enterprises be accepted as legitimate, and as a capital investment that it was in no way contrary to either business ethics or common law.

However, the Imperial Diet's Commission on Monopolies, persuaded by prevailing public opinion and by the stern demands of the social and economic moralists, unanimously turned down Peutinger's recommendation.

It is not surprising, therefore, that in the debate on moneylending which ensued, and in which the problem of Jews in the money trade was discussed in detail, the Jews should not have fared well.

In actual practice, the canonic ban on usury was widely disregarded. Like the trading concerns, the monasteries and even the clergy accepted deposits and paid interest on them. Christian merchants everywhere, in the mountains, in the valleys, in the market place and in the street, as a pamphlet then in circulation stated, were demanding interest rates much higher than those charged by the Jews. The triumphant Roman law had stressed the necessity for the profitable utilization of capital, and advocated the payment of standard rates of interest to be established by appropriate legislation.

Nevertheless, as late as the end of the fifteenth century and the beginning of the sixteenth, many territorial and municipal codes of law still carried in their revisions the ban on usury that had been pronounced by the Church Fathers and by canon law.[27]

Further, despite all the religious differences that divided them, Catholic and Protestant writers were united in their heated fight against merchants and moneylending. Erasmus considered the merchants the most sordid class, plying its trade in what he felt to be a most vile and contemptible fashion. Wimpfeling decried the rampant greed which led to secularization and to the widespread contempt of God. Hutten declared that the merchants were robbing the public. Luther, in his books on usury, branded moneylending as the greatest evil ever to have befallen the German nation. He demanded that usurers should be denied absolution and sacraments, and that they should not be given burial in Christian cemeteries.[28]

All this must be taken into account if we are to understand the import of the memorandum which was submitted to the Imperial Diet of Augsburg at this time by nineteen "honorable free Imperial cities,"[29] decrying the great havoc which "shameless and abominable Jewry" was causing in the High and Low German states. Their main grievances were as follows: first, the Jews evaded the local courts in matters of litigation and compelled their unfortunate debtors to seek justice from the Imperial and other non-resident courts, to the detriment of the other party and to the advantage of the creditor. Next, it was claimed that, in order to avoid charges of unfair usury, the Jews added the "heavy interest rates" to the total amount lent and recorded that amount in their agreements and debentures. Or, they would give indirect loans in the form of credit, for which they would also charge compound interest. It was further asserted that, while the Jews had been expelled from the cities and towns, the manorial masters of neighboring rural areas still tolerated them, with the result that their subjects were being ruined, and the municipal authorities were receiving less revenue. But the greatest damage of all, they claimed, was done by the so-called *juedische Hehlerrecht* (Jewish law respecting concealment of stolen goods), the right of the Jews to deal in stolen goods, by which they were allowed to accept stolen goods as pledges.

The cities petitioned the Emperor "to take action against such evil goings-on, and either to drive the obnoxious Jews from the High German lands, or at least to forbid them to engage in usury which was prohibited by the Holy Scriptures, and to make them earn their living by the work of their hands." Should this not be feasible, the Emperor should forbid them, on pain of severe penalty, to cite Christians before non-resident courts. Furthermore, the cities asked the Emperor to establish an "appropriate" rate of interest (1/8 farthing on the gold florin), to prohibit compound interest, to have bonds issued to the Jews sealed by the authorities of the debtor's place of residence, and to force the Jews to restore stolen goods to their rightful owners.

Wuerttemberg had already expelled its Jews in 1498.[30] Nevertheless, the Councillors, who ruled the state in behalf of the exiled Duke Ulrich, felt called upon to submit a special bill of complaint to the Imperial Diet. They claimed that the Jews in the Imperial towns, manors and territorial domains surrounding the duchy would ruin the unfortunate subjects of Wuerttemberg and drive them out of their homes by their unfair moneylending practices, forged bonds, and fraudulent debentures. In response to these plaintive cries for help, Charles confirmed and broadened a privilege which had already been issued to the Councillors of Wuerttemberg in Brussels in 1521. [31] According to this privilege, the Jews were forbidden to reside in the state, to engage in commerce or give loans on immovable property there, and to cite residents before non-resident courts of justice. The judges were directed not to honor their bonds and debentures unless valid proof was submitted that no compound interest had been charged.[32]

Josel followed these debates at the Imperial Diet with a good deal of anxiety. What was more, his conversations with deputies yielded complaints that his co-religionists were conducting themselves in an unseemly manner and were ruining the Christian citizens by their unfair business practices. Vice Chancellor Mathias Held's primary complaint was that the Jews gave preference to the Imperial Court of Rottweil (*Hofgericht*) in the settlement of their lawsuits, with the result that the "poor common man" was so sorely oppressed that the Emperor felt compelled to take action to put a stop to this practice.[33]

For many years, no problem had troubled Josel so deeply as that of whether a Jew had the ethical right to lend out money at interest. It was not only the disrepute attaching to this trade, and the contempt in which the world held the Jewish moneylender that preoccupied Josel with this compelling question. Like other deeply pious Jews, Josel brooded over whether the practice of moneylending at interest was compatible with the text of the Holy Scriptures and the precepts of the Talmud.[34] True, the Jews were strangers in Germany, and the Law of Moses permitted them to charge interest on loans made to strangers. But had not the Talmud, which was more stringent than the Bible, adhered more closely to the spirit of the Scriptures when it declared that the fortune of him who lends out money at interest was bound to be lost, even if the debtors were non-Jews? Besides, was it not written that "he who lends out money at interest will not rise from the dead?" And did not Judah ben Samuel explicitly state in his *Book of the Pious* that a Jew was not permitted to accept interest, even if he were to use it for purposes of charity?

On the other hand, had not the scholars of more recent

times, taking into account the changing economic conditions, made allowances for reasonable rates of interest, seeing that Jews were no longer permitted to own fields and vineyards,[35] and had to raise huge amounts of money to pay the many taxes demanded by the King?[36]

Deep in his heart, Josel agreed with the opinion of Judah ben Samuel. Yet, in actual practice, he felt that it was necessary to accept the views of the later scholars, for he, too, was becoming more and more convinced by the harsh realities of life that the Jews were forced to charge interest on loans made to Christians if only to make ends meet.

There was one other accusation that was made again and again in all the complaints against the Jews; namely, that they were abusing the *juedische Hehlerrecht,* the rights which the Jews claimed in connection with the disposition of stolen goods.[37]

This right was based on a privilege which Henry IV had conferred on the Jews of Speyer in 1090, in order to safeguard their commerce. According to the privilege, they were required to restore stolen goods which they had acquired in good faith, only if the owner paid them the price at which they had purchased the article. The Jews were required to submit a sworn statement of the amount originally paid. It was true that this privilege, which subsequently was conferred also upon the Lombards to safeguard their commerce, represented a special boon; for Roman law, which sought to protect the interests of the victims of theft, had always insisted that stolen property be returned to its rightful owner without any compensation.

All the privileges enacted subsequently, as well as the territorial and municipal edicts and the letters of safe-conduct issued to communities or individuals, incorporated this commercial right in their articles. Of course, due to opposition from the clergy and from trade and business circles, the privilege underwent considerable modification in the course of time. In some territories, the Jews were forbidden to lend money on ceremonial and other objects concerning which suspicion could arise that they had been acquired by the seller in an unlawful manner.

As the years passed, the privilege became subject to increasingly strict interpretation. The Jews were forced to purchase or give loans on suspect goods only in public places, they could not transact such business in secret or at night, or deal with nonresident individuals not personally known to them, unless such persons were accompanied by honest witnesses, and confirmed by a complicated sworn statement their own good faith and the amount paid for the article in question. In some municipal decrees, Jews were forbidden to accept pledges from farm laborers, maids, journeymen or minors, i.e., from any persons considered irresponsible or liable to commit theft. Nevertheless, the "law respecting concealment of stolen goods," if accepted in good faith, survived as a commercial privilege until Josel's time. It was still incorporated in the letters of safe-conduct issued to Jews by the town of Oberehnheim in 1437, and by the city of Colmar in 1468.

Like the exemptions from the canon ban on interest, this special privilege also gave rise to bitter resentment. The Jews were not openly accused of having knowingly acquired stolen goods, however, for it was well known how seriously they regarded the stipulated oath, which entailed the most odd and cumbersome formalities, and the most humiliating requirements.

What aroused the ire of the Christian population, and particularly of the poor artisans, was the fact that this special privilege made it possible for Jews to gain possession of costly merchandise in a simple and entirely legitimate manner, and then to sell this merchandise at prices far below its original value, to the insufferable detriment of the "common man."[38]

Unlike the practice of moneylending at interest, the right to have traffic in stolen goods did not run altogether counter to any one commandment in the Holy Scriptures. Contrary to what was popularly thought, however, it also had not been derived from Jewish law. Jewish laws actually unequivocally prohibited the acquisition, in any manner, of stolen goods or of robbers' loot. For example, Jewish law prohibited the purchase of fruit from suspect individuals, such as overseers of orchards, because it might be assumed that fruit sold by such persons could have been stolen.[39] In addition, it is explicitly stated that if the purchaser becomes aware that the merchandise he has bought was not the seller's lawful property, he must restore the article to its rightful owner without demanding or accepting payment of any kind. "However," the Talmud stipulates,[40] "if a man finds his own clothes or books in the hands of another and it is known that the items had been stolen (and sold to said person by the thief), the purchaser shall make a sworn statement of the amount he paid for them, and he shall be reimbursed for the sum he spent."

As far as the religious aspects of the problem were concerned, Josel could set his conscience at ease. But he had cause to fear that, due to the many complaints about the abuse of the "law respecting concealment of stolen goods," some of which were justified, the Jews would eventually be forced out not only from banking, but also from retail trade, and thus deprived of their only remaining means of making a living.

Josel was not a *homo capitalisticus.* He could not understand the viewpoint or the restless drive of those venturesome modern enterprising merchants, who ignored the order established by God Himself, in order to satisfy their own creative impulse, to gain wealth and power, authority and status in their attempts to bend kings and emperors, princes and cardinals, popes and patricians to their will. It seemed to him a matter of course that one allowed one's fellow-citizen the same sphere of existence required for one's own living, did not deliberately force up the price of merchandise or pocket excessive profits, and guarded the property of one's neighbor as zealously as one's own.

On the other hand, Josel was not a dreamy theorist, a man secluded from the world. Unlike Luther, Wimpfeling, Erasmus and Franck, he was not a rigid social philosopher, pondering and passing judgment on economic life from a remote ivory tower. He was possessed of common sense and an alert and accurate gift of observation. He made his home in the Alsace, that geographical link connecting the north and the south, the east and the west. He had now been living for months in Augsburg, which was then Germany's center of international commerce and banking. Here in this city were the counting houses, where operations were methodical and well-organized, speculation was calculated, and plans were made on a long-range basis. It was from Augsburg that loans and bills of exchange were sent to Lisbon, Antwerp, Constantinople, and Naples, and that funds were raised for the fitting of ships that sailed for the East Indies and the new West Indies. It was in Augsburg, too, that the agents were paid who gathered political information in Spain and England, in Brabant and in Italy, for the greater glory of the House of Fugger.[41]

Josel was well aware that these new enterprises could no longer be judged from the standpoint of the agrarian economy of the biblical era, or, for that matter, of the natural economy of the Middle Ages. He knew that international commerce had to be conducted according to laws other than those governing the trade of a small, self-sufficient Imperial town, or some other self-contained territory.

Yet, he wondered, was there not some way in which to reconcile the new economic system with the precepts of the holy Torah? Was there no way in which Jews could continue to engage in commerce and money trading without detriment to their souls? Could not some way be found to extricate them from their disoriented state, to place their existence on a firmer foundation, and to turn them again to the purpose for which God had originally created them—a people observing the way of the Eternal "to do righteousness and justice?"

Josel's deliberations led him to a bold decision. He wrote to all the Jewish communities and corporate rural Jewries of the *Reich,* requesting them to send their deputies to Augsburg so that, together with him, they might draw up an "honorable regulation and statute" for the Jews of the cities, villages and market places.

The Jews "obeyed" and sent their authorized representatives "from many places" to the city where the Imperial Diet was being held. After exceedingly tedious and detailed deliberations, which ended only a short time before the Imperial Diet was recessed, the following articles and regulations were drawn up to be submitted to all the Estates of the *Reich* for their approval:[42]

1. If a Jew sells merchandise to a Christian on credit, he shall not practice indirect usury by charging higher prices, not even if he must wait for a considerable amount of time for his money, lest the purchaser suffer damage thereby. If he does not observe this regulation, the *Parnas* of his community shall ask him to pay a fine of three gold florins; of these, two florins shall go to the authorities of the place in which the offender resides, and one to the leader of the Jewish community there. Moreover, a Jew engaging in such fraudulent practices shall be compelled to refund to the purchaser that

amount of money paid in excess of the actual price of the merchandise.

2. If a Jew lends out money in smaller or larger amounts, he may charge a moderate rate of interest in accordance with permission granted him to do so by Imperial and other privileges. However, he must refrain, on pain of severe penalty, from adding the interest every quarter or half year to the principal, lest the poor man be overcharged and handicapped in providing for his sustenance.

3. Should the debtor be unable to return the borrowed amount at the time specified, the creditor shall not immediately institute legal proceedings against him in a non-resident court of justice. Instead, he shall attempt to arrive at an amicable settlement with him before the local bailiff or mayor. Should the creditor be unable to arrive at such settlement and therefore be compelled to appeal to a non-resident court of justice, he still shall not inflict any undue expense on the debtor, but shall ask of him only that which may be required "out of necessity and in all fairness."

4. If a Jewish man or woman lend money against security, they shall not accept pledges of suspicious character or purchase merchandise which may have been stolen. If such a thing should "befall them by accident," they shall not ever again make purchases from such "thievish and pilfering" individuals, and they shall neither lend them money nor do business with them again. If they violate this statute and gain possession of stolen merchandise, they shall return all of it to its rightful owner without payment of any kind. If a Jew has purchased horses, cows or sheep and it is proven, even after many a long day, that these had been stolen, he shall return said livestock to the victim of the theft without compensation of any kind. If he has already sold said livestock, he shall turn over to the rightful owner the proceeds from the sale. If he refuses to do so, he shall pay a fine of six gold florins.

5. No Jew shall accept goods as pledges from minor sons or daughters, man-servants or maid-servants of a Christian burgher, purchase any object from such persons, or lend them money, unless the parents or the master, as the case may be, are informed of the transaction. If a Jew transgresses this law, the money shall not be refunded to him and he shall be liable to severe punishment.

6. In the event that a debtor dies and his heirs refuse to acknowledge his debt or have no knowledge of it, the creditor shall not institute proceedings against them immediately before a secular or ecclesiastical court. Instead, he shall calmly discuss the matter with his *parnas,* heed the latter's counsel, and in some cases even waive his legal claim altogether.

7. If a Jew should accept merchandise or pledges from a Christian and then go abroad in bad faith and sell these goods, the *parnas* of the place where this occurred shall excommunicate the swindler and divest him of all his Imperial freedoms. No one shall be permitted to marry him, to eat or drink with him, or to give him shelter. He who, in violation of all the foregoing, will still have dealings with such a swindler, shall be obligated to make restitution to the victim of the fraud "with all the property and assets in his possession."

8. If a Christian should have a legal complaint to make against a Jew, the *parnas* or the chief judge of the Jews shall help the plaintiff obtain his just due and let the Law of God prevail "as is just and righteous also in keeping with natural law, without regard to differences between men on earth."

9. Any Jew who learns that a fraud or other unlawful act has been committed (by a member of his community) is duty-bound to report such act to the *parnas* of his community.

10. The *parnassim* of the Jewish communities shall take great care to see that the statutes of these Jewish Regulations are strictly observed by every individual. They shall exercise stringent supervision over the conduct of all the members of

their communities and severely discipline all violators of these ordinances. For "our Jewish custom and canons, laws and statutes from times immemorial and our Holy Scriptures require justice and honesty and have no use for fraudulent schemes."

In the closing passages of the regulations, Josel requested all the Estates of the *Reich* to follow the lead of the Emperor, who had reconfirmed all the privileges of the Jews. He asked them to protect the Jews, out of justice and mercy, from oppression in the future, not to expel them from the places in which they reside, and to permit them to live and work among the Christians as of old. "For we, too, are men, created by Almighty God to dwell on earth, and to live and work together with you and in your midst."

Josel's "Articles and Regulations" represent the first large-scale attempt within their own group to purge the life of the Jews, to improve their deteriorating social and economic position, and to help them adjust to the changing social and economic conditions under which they lived. Josel was in a position to set up such a practical and "positive program of reforms" because he himself was involved in practical life and aware of the economic conditions, the social relationships and also the spiritual foundations of both the Jewish and the Christian worlds.

Unlike the generations that were to follow him, Josel did not dream of seeking to effect a synthesis between these two worlds. Deriving his knowledge from the original and uncorrupted sources of Judaism, he insisted rather on the unconditional fulfillment of the precepts and commandments set down in the Holy Scriptures and on their practical application in everyday life. Yet, from the environment in which the Almighty had placed him in order that he might dwell, live and work there, he derived and came to understand certain ideas and concepts that had been alien to the Jew of an earlier day. This pious man, who modeled his personal way of life on that of the mystics of the Middle Ages, could not, like them, humbly accept the insults dealt to his people. Addressing an audience gathered from all over Europe, he demanded openly and with pride that the human dignity of the Jew, too, be acknowledged, since there was no difference between men on earth, and since Jew and Christian alike had been created in the image of God. On November 19, Josel put his seal on these "Articles and Regulations." Two days later, the Imperial Diet ended on a "note of shrill discord." There had been no reconciliation between the Catholics and the Protestants, chiefly due to the Emperor's insistence on the restoration of the confiscated Church properties to the Catholic clergy. For this reason, Josel was unable to present his "Articles" to the Estates and thus to avert the incorporation into the final resolution of the Diet of those harsh decrees by which the governments were forbidden to extend protection, safe-conduct and legal assistance to Jews who practiced usury. This referred, of course, to any Jews who made a living from moneylending, who gave loans on high debentures, and lent money on stolen goods.

However, Josel refused to accept defeat. Immediately after the close of the Diet, he submitted the Articles "in person" to Christoph von Stadion, the Bishop of Strasbourg,[43] and sent copies of the document to the Public Clerk of the Margraviate of Burgau, to the Senate of the town of Ulm, to the Secretary of the *Landvogt* of the Lower Alsace, to the magistrates of the towns of Rosheim and Oberehnheim and to the Estates gathered in convention at Hagenau, so that they might all desist from enforcing the ordinances of the Final Decree of the Imperial Diet in the areas within their jurisdiction.

His request for permission to submit the "Articles" in person also to the Councillors of Wuerttemberg and to travel through the state in order to follow the Imperial entourage foundered because of the strict prohibition of the government against the issuance of a letter of safe-conduct to him.[44] Thus he was not able to catch up to the Emperor, who had proceeded from Augsburg to Cologne in order to crown his brother Ferdinand as King there.

CHAPTER FIVE

MEDIATOR AND LIBERATOR

EARLY in 1531, the Emperor Charles left Cologne for the Low Countries, where he planned to hold court until the spring. At that time Burgundy was "the center of learning, the metropolis of the painter's art and the spiritual home of the Reformed faith," and the city of Antwerp was the world's most important center of international commerce and finance. It was there that the spices of the Far East and the treasures of the new West were bought and sold, that the merchant princes of England, Germany, Italy and Spain had their counting-houses, and that Charles obtained the funds needed to finance his campaigns and to maintain the Imperial household. There, too, as in Spain, the Protestants and the Anabaptists were ruthlessly persecuted, and the Jews were refused admission on pain of death.

In the first half of the sixteenth century, Marranos from Portugal began to settle in the Low Countries, and particularly in Antwerp, not only because they were drawn to that great center of international commerce, but also because King John III, following the lead of Spain, was planning to set up tribunals of inquisition in Portugal. These wealthy merchants, who knew the ways of the world and of commerce, were received favorably by the magistrates of the cities in which they settled, but they were eyed with considerable suspicion by both the Imperial authorities and the Catholic clergy. Only those who had wholeheartedly embraced Christianity quite some time before were tolerated, since there was no reason to fear that they might move on to Italy or Turkey and there openly profess Judaism again.

In the beginning, Charles, in the interest of commerce, had endeavored to protect the "New Christians," who continually complained about the annoying difficulties that were being placed in their path. However, in the early 1530's, several "Judaist heretics" were already accused of observing the precepts of the old doctrine and of coming to Burgundy under false pretenses, using the state merely as a stop-off on their journey to the Orient.

"In 1531," Josel reports,[1] "the slanderers accosted the Emperor in Brabant and Flanders, where there are no Jews. But, I, unlike others, set out to travel to those countries in order to plead our cause with the help of God. From the beginning of Adar until the beginning of Sivan (February 18 to May 17), 1531, I remained at the Emperor's court to work for the common good. A knight named Ruthard (or Rotraut) made an attempt on my life, but God in His great mercy saved me from all those who sought to slay me. In fact, I was granted an audience with the Emperor and received favorable replies [to my requests]."

This report from Josel, which cannot be supplemented by data from other sources,[2] is basically different from both all his earlier and his subsequent statements. He does not describe the nature of the slanderous reports that had been made, and he also omits his usual declaration that he had carried out his mission in agreement with the officials and scholars of the Jewish communities. Does the statement that he traveled to Brabant and Flanders "unlike others" indicate that he had been advised against attempting to make this perilous journey? Or are we to surmise that he made his plans without taking counsel with the rest of Jewry?

Since the matter for which he placed his life in danger had to do with "the common good," as he termed it, it would be logical to assume that he made the journey to intercede with the Emperor so as to prevent the enforcement of the provisions set down in the Final Decree of the Augsburg Diet. Since Josel had been unable to catch up with Charles in Germany, he had had to follow him to the Low Countries in order to acquaint him with his "Articles," which, he believed, would render the Imperial Police Regulations of 1530 superfluous.

Albrecht Dürer, who visited the Low Countries several years before Josel, left a thrilled and excited description of the city of Brussels in his diary. He wrote of "an exquisite city hall, large, hewn of handsome tracery with a splended pellucid tower . . . ," and he believed "that he had never seen anything in his life before that so gladdened his heart" as did the wondrous treasures, brought over from the New Spain across the ocean, which he was able to view there in those days.[3]

Josel's description of his stay in the Low Countries is somewhat different.[4] "During those three months when I was free of all business concerns and was permitted to remain alone in my chamber, I wrote a little work to which I gave the title *The Holy Path (Derech ha-Kodesh),"* he relates in his memoirs. "Great was my delight in those days of solitude, and I said in my heart: 'Happy were those great men of the past who bent their minds and their thoughts to removing themselves from the vanities of the world and to occupying themselves with things Divine.' "

It is likely that the solitude which so gladdened Josel's heart had not been self-imposed but that he had been placed under official custody until he was granted an audience by the Emperor.

But let us consider the use to which he put this enforced confinement. Instead of brooding over his own precarious situation, and his separation from his wife and children, he actually rejoiced that after the noisy commotion of the Diet of Augsburg, he was given the peace and quiet of a solitary chamber in which to meditate on the ways of God and seek to understand the nature of his calling.

The Holy Path has been lost. By a strange quirk of fate, none of Josel's literary works are known to us. While state and communal archives are filled to excess with his political memoranda, his religious and apologetic writings, with few exceptions, have been either lost entirely or preserved in fragments only. Yuspa Hahn of Frankfort, to cite one instance, incorporated several passages from *The Holy Path* into his own work, *Yosif Ometz* ("Increase Strength"), which he wrote in the seventeenth century, quoting these passages as "sayings of the great Mediator and Prince Joselmann of Rosheim" which he had taken from a manuscript.[5]

In Augsburg, Josel had made an attempt to improve the social situation of the Jews and to render their position in the State and in their immediate environment more secure. However, he was aware that human beings as such could not be changed by either commandments or prohibitions. Even if the threat of excommunication, the harshest punishment in Jewish law, might keep some from satisfying their personal greed, that decision would be motivated not by a deep-felt spiritual need but by fear alone.

This was not what Josel had in mind. His aim, like that of the "Brethren of Common Life" and some of the Anabaptists, was to bring about a religious and moral rebirth that would involve the whole man, a true *renascentia* and reformation from within.

A renaissance of this sort could not be brought about merely by studying the Talmud and conscientiously observing the laws of Judaism. The Jew had to discover his origins anew for himself, renew the covenant that God had made with His people, emulate and relive the lives and the martyrdom of the prophets, the saints and the pious of the past, and pursue the paths of the Eternal in every thought and action. Only when each individual decided to accept the sovereignty of God of his own free will would he be able to experience his great regeneration. Only by testing and judging his own soul, by passing judgement and sentence upon it, and by becoming again what he was meant to be at the beginning, "by being holy," would he be able to guarantee the survival of the world and "to prepare the ground for the Kingdom of God."

But how could the individual attain this goal? How could he transport his soul into that state of bliss,[6] and experience that "exultation of inner joy and the ardent glow of love within the heart" which overwhelm him who is aware of his nearness to the blessed presence of the Deity?

According to Josel, there are two ways in which the individual can reach this goal: prayer and martyrdom.

"If you aspire to the good fortune of accepting for yourself in its entirety the yoke of the Kingdom of God, you must make your heart free for a little while from all ordinary concerns until you have achieved the proper devotion. To begin with, read the biblical verse 'Hear O Israel . . .' time and time again until it is entirely within your power to bring the proper devotion to your reading. Then employ this same procedure for all the verses that follow until you have completed the first paragraph of the *Shema* prayer. After that, continue in the same manner, completing with devotion first the entire *Shema* and, thereafter, everything you may read and study. Once you have achieved this, you should turn your heart to God at all times . . ."

These instructions for prayer did not by any means originate with Josel.

The great devotional thinkers of all times and the pious teachers of his people had always been aware of the significance of prayer in the purification, cleansing, and repentance of the human soul. They had experienced the solitude and the seclusion in which the sinful, guilt-laden creature, struggling and desperate, "gives expression to its distress before the countenance of God." They also instructed the worshipper how, by dint of long practice, patient self-preparation, self-denial and abstinence, he would transport himself into a state of calm devotion, profound concentration, ecstasy and bliss. Like Judah the Pious and his spiritual heirs, these men described the far-reaching effect of prayer, which is "capable of opening and closing the gates of destiny."

The other message which Josel made known to his brethren—that of the "Sanctification of the Name"—had also not merely been proclaimed verbally [or in writing] but had been demonstrated in action again and again throughout the centuries that had gone before.

"If a man should be led into temptation because of some sin, he may be confident that God will give strength to his heart so that he will be able to bear tortures worse than death for the glory of his Creator. . . . After all, it is known that for many a day now they have delivered themselves up to fire and death for the sanctification of God, and they do not cry alas and alack. And oh, how many of them have been hanged, as I have seen with my own eyes. I was there, too, when they went forth to be executed. They accepted the yoke of the Kingdom of God with great love, even when they endured great tortures and still lived on for ten days and ten nights, and they could not relieve themselves of it until their souls fled in purity. And that I have seen, I have faithfully recorded. . . . That is what our Sages meant when they said: 'He who has resolved in his heart to sanctify the Name of God will not feel the pain of torture.' "

It was not Josel's intention to have his treatise reveal some new wisdom to his people. His aim was simply, in an extraordinary period of history, to extricate his brethren from their petty troubles and humiliating conflicts and bring them directly before the countenance of God—so that a little of the light and bliss of the World Above might be injected into their dreary lives. At a time when Carben, Pfefferkorn, Margaritha and their like were seeking to undermine Judaism from within, Josel endeavored to rouse the Jews to offer moral resistance and to reinforce their religious strength. In an era when the Renaissance, humanism and sectarianism threatened to blur the boundary lines between the religions, Josel sought to make known to the Jews, in simple and easily understood language, the things that made their faith singular and unique. He wanted them to realize that each and every one of them bore upon his shoulders the responsibility for the future of the world; that every individual could help insure the survival of the world by his personal conduct and attitude; that morality and righteousness insured the survival of the world, while immorality and injustice would bring about its destruction. And he wanted them to know, too, that he who would love God "with all his soul and with all his life" and suffer a martyr's death for the sake of this love would not only thereby elevate his own insignificant life, but also bear witness to the might and the glory of God and thus actually serve to "increase the power of the Lord."[7]

While he was in Brussels, Charles received news of dangerous developments. The Protestant Estates, which had united to form the Schmalkald Confederation, in order to prevent the enforcement of the resolutions passed at Augsburg, were engaged in treasonable negotiations with powers hostile to the House of Habsburg. Meanwhile, Sultan Suleiman was preparing to make a new attack on the *Reich,* and was determined not to rest until he "would have laid waste all of Germany with fire and the sword and conquered all of Italy."

The Emperor, sorely pressed on all sides, opened negotiations with the "Evangelicals" so that, in return for certain concessions in religious matters, he might gain their assistance in the war against the Turks. Finally, in April 1532, he convened a Diet in Regensburg, at which he promised the members of the Schmalkald Confederation that he would grant them an armistice if they would place their troops and funds at his disposal.

One month later, on May 20, 1532, Josel received a letter of safe-conduct addressed by the Imperial Hereditary Marshal Joerg von Pappenheim to "the Chief of Jewry in the German Lands," calling on him to "wait upon the Emperor in connection with his business and concerns" at the Diet of Regensburg by order of His Imperial Majesty.[8]

This free letter of safe-conduct is the earliest piece of written evidence that Josel's position had been accorded official recognition by the Emperor and the authorities. It was the first official invitation extended to an individual to attend an Imperial Diet in the interest of the Jews of Germany. Josel himself records that he had come to Regensburg to wait upon the Emperor at the Imperial Diet of 1532 in order to stand guard for Israel.[9]

It appears that his presence was requested so that a solution might finally be found for the problem of Jews engaged in moneylending, a problem which the Final Decree passed by the Imperial Diet at Augsburg had been unable to resolve. Josel also reports in rather general terms that God saved the

Jews at that time from the accusations brought against them by princes and noblemen, and gave them a means of making a livelihood among the nations by permitting them to continue to lend out money at interest. Furthermore, it is known to us from other sources that Josel took the opportunity to have the Papal Nuncio, Campeggi, transcribe and notarize an important Imperial privilege dating back to the year 1216.[10]

Cardinal Campeggi had neither the right nor the authority to reconfirm an old Imperial privilege. But Josel, who enjoyed supporting the legality of his demands by means of official documents, felt it was important to gain possession of this historic patent which Frederick II, whose actions served as a model for Charles V's in many respects, had issued to the Jews of Regensburg. This privilege in itself represented the reconfirmation of an earlier letter of protection which had been issued by Frederick I in 1182, and extended permission to the Jews of Regensburg "to sell gold, silver and other metals and all manner of merchandise, and to procure these for themselves in the customary manner, to exchange their possessions and goods and to make a profit in the customary manner."[11]

It is interesting that Josel should have recognized the basic significance of this privilege in the controversy concerning the Jews engaged in banking and moneylending, for the document had been drawn up in Latin, its language was most difficult to understand, and it was not widely known. As a matter of fact, it was not until the end of the nineteenth and the beginning of the twentieth century that it was rediscovered by modern scholarship and deciphered and classed with other pertinent Imperial documents.

These Imperial privileges, issued in 1216 and 1182, respectively, had been conferred at a time when the Jews had not yet been forced out of the retail trade, but when the number of Jews in moneylending was already on the increase.

Therefore, this privilege of Regensburg was the first document to call attention to the significance of this development, and to draw inferences from it concerning the economy. If, therefore, this privilege gave the Jews permission to "make a profit in the customary manner," the intent was to permit the Jew to lend out money at interest and to accept security without legal restrictions. This meant that they could "enjoy earnings from moneylending which were determined not only by the rate of interest but also by the relation of the value of the pledge to the amount of money delivered."[12]

Josel's remark in his memoirs that at the Imperial Diet at Regensburg God had given the Jews a means of making a livelihood among the nations by permitting them to continue to lend money at interest, indicates that he used the Privilege of 1216 as a weapon against the Final Decree of the Diet of Augsburg, thus enabling the Jews to continue to engage in moneylending with certain limitations as set down in his "Articles and Regulations."

At any rate, the Imperial Police Regulations promulgated in 1532 provided for considerable modifications in the stringent decree that had been issued at the Diet of Augsburg in 1530. It was now left up to the local authorities having "usurers, Jews and monopolists" under their jurisdiction, to urge the latter to cease their "unseemly and unbecoming conduct."[13]

While he was in Regensburg, Josel had a strange experience which was to occupy his mind until old age, and which caused him great inner conflict.

In that era of conquests and discoveries of unknown continents, Jews and Christians alike listened with avid interest to tales of strange events and wondrous adventures. In the early twenties of that century especially, people were set agog by the appearance of a Jewish "emissary" who claimed to be the ambassador from some of the Ten Tribes of Israel which had been presumed lost.[14] In a strange-sounding Hebrew that was difficult to understand, this man related that he was the son of the late King Joseph and the younger brother of Solomon, of the tribe of Reuben. Solomon, he reported, was now king of a land called Chabor, in the Arabian Desert, not far from the Red Sea and beyond the legendary River Sambatyon. There he reigned over 300,000 subjects, all descendants of the ancient tribes of Reuben and Gad and of the half-tribe of Menasseh, a free, warlike and proud people. The King, he said, was assisted by seventy Elders, who conducted the affairs of the State after the manner of the Great Sanhedrin. Now they had sent him, David Reubeni, on a secret mission to Europe in order to bring help to his sorely oppressed brethren there.

After an adventurous journey through Nubia, Ethiopia, Egypt and Palestine, of which his personal record has survived, Reubeni arrived in Italy in 1524, a short, robust, suntanned man whose austere features were marked by privation, fasting and suffering. After being received with honors by the Jews of Italy and particularly by the Jewish refugees from Spain, he succeeded in obtaining several audiences with Pope Clement VII and in enlisting the Pope's support for his secret plan: namely, to arm the Jews of Europe so that, together with the warriors from the tribes of Reuben and Gad and from the half-tribe of Menasseh, and aided by the mercenaries of the Emperor, they might be able to wrest the Holy Land from the Turks.

Armed with a letter of introduction from the Pope and bearing an ample supply of money and gifts from the Jews of Italy, Reubeni, accompanied by a great entourage and proudly displaying the ancient banner of Judah the Maccabee, sailed for Portugal in order to request ships, guns and ammunition from King John III. In gratitude for these services, Reubeni was to offer to the Portuguese king a proposal of alliance with his brother, King Solomon of Chabor. The taciturn and unapproachable ambassador might have succeeded in his bold venture, had not the Marranos greeted their redeemer with such extravagant rejoicing as to arouse the suspicions of the authorities. When the Marranos actually mutinied and "New Christians" were liberated from their prison cells, the emissary from the land of Chabor was politely requested to leave Portugal.

Diogo Pires, Secretary to Portugal's High Court of Justice, a noble, talented and handsome youth of a well-known family, and friend and confidant to the King's household, had been transported into a state of ecstasy by Reubeni's appearance. As one chronicler reports it, "God touched his heart, he returned to the Eternal, the God of our fathers, and underwent circumcision." Pires then fled from the land that had forced him to deny the faith of his ancestors. He spent several years in Turkey and in Safed, where he joined the circles of those apocalyptics from Spain who led lives of penitence and abstinence. Brooding over the great calamity of their existence, they believed the bitter pain of their exile to be the birth pangs of the Messiah whose coming had been foretold by the prophets and the psalmists verse by verse, and indeed, almost word by word.[15]

It is likely that Solomon Molcho, as Diogo Pires now called himself, had received secret instruction in rabbinic and cabbalistic literature during his childhood. Now, his zeal aroused by the new turn his life had taken, emaciated by intensive study, fasting and self-castigation, and spurred on by the love that was lavished upon him wherever he went, he began to be troubled by dreams and visions in which a *maggid* revealed to him the future of his people, and told him that the Messiah would appear in 1540. Moreover, the destruction of Rome by German mercenaries in 1527 seemed to him the long-promised sign that Edom was doomed and that Israel's hour of redemption was approaching. He hurried to Italy, where as a herald of the Messiah and an instrument of God, saint and penitent, prophet and miracle worker, he announced the coming of the hour of judgment and the Kingdom of God.

In Italy, Molcho met David Reubeni once again. It is not known whose idea it was that the two should journey to Regensburg to see the Emperor, and to appeal to him to organize a joint crusade of Jews and Christians against the Turks.

"At that time," Josel records in his memoirs,[16] "that foreigner called Solomon Molcho, of blessed memory, who had converted to Judaism, had the extraordinary idea to stir up the Emperor by telling him that he had come to summon all the Jews to fight against the Turks. When I learned of his plans, I warned him by letter against stirring up the heart of the Emperor, lest he be destroyed by the great fire. I left Regensburg so that the Emperor could not say that I had a hand in this scheme. As soon as Solomon reached the Emperor he was put into chains and brought to Bologna [Josel must have meant Mantua], where he was burned at the stake for the sanctification of the Name of God and of the faith of Israel. He delivered many people from sin. May his soul rest in the Garden of Eden."

Why does Josel's account contain no mention of David Reubeni, whose journey to Regensburg is an established historical fact? Did he not find it necessary to warn Reubeni as he had warned Molcho, since Reubeni was a Jew and therefore neither subject to the laws of the Inquisition nor liable to the death penalty for apostasy or heresy? Or did he know that the kingdom of the two-and-one half tribes existed only in this man's imagination? In 1530, it became known in Venice that David, who had claimed to be a brother of King Solomon of Chabor and a son of King Joseph, and who had traveled throughout Europe to enlist the support of the reigning princes in the liberation of the Jews, had been unmasked as a fraud. It was said that while he was in Venice, the Senate of the city had sent the famed traveler, J. S. Ramusio to inquire of him whence he had come and what he did for a living; in the course of this interview, Reubeni's statements had been found out to be untrue. He was thereupon requested to leave the city.

Be that as it may, it was quite clear to Josel, the circumspect politician, that even if there had indeed been such a place as the Kingdom of Chabor, plans for a joint Christian-Jewish crusade against the Turks would have spelled grave peril for Jews the world over. What reason was there for the Emperor to assume that the Jews of the *Reich* would fight against the Turks, who had just extended their hospitality to the Jewish refugees from Spain? Was not Charles, whose suspicions against the Jews in this respect Josel had managed to dispel only two years before at Innsbruck, bound to regard the plan of Reubeni and Molcho as a devilish trick to betray the *Reich's* military secrets to the Mussulmen?

And moreover, if Sultan Suleiman were to learn that the Jews of Europe were out to snatch Palestine from his hands, would it not stand to reason that he would expel all his Jewish subjects as enemies and traitors?

Josel the politician has indicated in his memoirs the reasons why he left the Imperial Diet of Regensburg. But Josel the mystic fails to tell us how he felt about the Messianic notions that were rife in the century in which he lived, and that found their most outstanding advocate in the person of Solomon Molcho.

Should not a pious man like Josel, who had written a book just a year before about the sanctification of the Name of God, have rejoiced at the thought that a distinguished Jew, who had been accorded all the honors of this world, had voluntarily chosen to give up his position, repute, wealth and power in order to die as a witness to the glory of God?

Did not all signs point to the fulfillment of Molcho's prophecy? Were not the footprints of the Messiah apparent everywhere in the calamities, afflictions, war and ruin that had come into the world? Was theirs not a generation upon which "many troubles were poured out like a torrent?" Were not all the nations of the world warring with each other, and was it not explicitly set down in the *Zohar* that the dead of Palestine would rise again in that very year 1532?

Messianic notions and millennarian hopes had no less power over men in Josel's environment than in Italy, Turkey and the Holy Land. It was true, of course, that in Josel's country there were no thinkers, scholars, philosophers or scientists who were skilled in the art of foretelling the coming of the Kingdom of God for a given year, on the basis of exacting studies and computations. But the masses in the *Reich* were no less in a mood of suspenseful expectancy than those of the southern countries. Asher Laemmlein, who had predicted in Istria that the Messiah would appear in the year 1502, and had decreed a year of penitence and fasting in order to hasten His coming, had been an Ashkenazi Jew and may have come from Germany. So firmly had the Jews of the *Reich* believed in his mission that they actually made preparations to leave for the Holy Land, and felt that their own sins were to blame when the prophecy failed to materialize.[17]

Margaritha claimed that the Jews had in their writings "many excellent sayings about redemption and the future of the *Mashiach*," and that they hopefully awaited liberation by the Ten Tribes which had been dispersed by the King of Assyria.

In Pamphilius Gengenbach's *Nollhart,* there is a Jewish character whose sole desire is that God send the Messiah to his people the very next day and thus put an end to their troubles. In *Entchrist Vasnacht* the Jews exultantly hail their Messiah, "our gentle God," whom they had anxiously awaited ever since the fall of Jerusalem, and implore him to restore to them their former power, glory and chosenness, promising that they would "live and die with Him until they would attain the everlasting kingdom."

Like his brethren, Josel believed that the Messiah would appear on the Day of Judgment and create a new heaven and earth. But he was wary of attempting to calculate when that day would come and when the "measure would be full." He did not, in any of his exhortations and devotional tracts, attempt to cheer his readers with the thought that the end of their sufferings might be close at hand, and the Kingdom of God about to begin. Like Maimonides, Judah the Pious, and Lipmann Muehlhausen, Josel felt it was presumptuous to seek to penetrate the mystery of the Eternal and to "awaken love prematurely."

Thus a great many human, political and religious considerations motivated Josel in his effort to keep Solomon Molcho from broaching his plans for a crusade to the Emperor.

There also were considerations of a purely practical nature. The Jews of Germany were already in a state of agitation. Josel was concerned lest the appearance of the Messianic emissary might further encourage their hopes and dreams, and that the disillusionment which was bound to follow would result in a weakening of their moral fiber. He feared, too, that the Government would regard an open Messianic movement as revolution and rebellion, as an attempt to undermine the class and the social orders, and that it would suppress such a movement by force as it had but recently done with the Anabaptist movement, which it charged with "Judaization."

During those years, Josel had ample opportunity to witness

the tragedy of the Anabaptists at close range. By rejecting any intermediary between God and man, denying the Divinity of Christ, and adhering to the original Christian doctrine of love, the sect had come into a dangerous conflict not only with the ruling Catholic Church and the new Protestant faith, but also with the historic State.

Strasbourg, which has been described as the "haven of the persecuted," was then the home of the leaders of the Anabaptist movement: the erudite and pensive Hans Denk, the distinguished Silesian nobleman Caspar von Schwenckfeld, and the historian Sebastian Franck, whose history texts relate the sufferings of those people who devoted their lives to the dissemination of the doctrine of "love, faith and the Cross."

In 1529, these men were joined by Melchior Hoffmann, a furrier from Schwäbisch-Hall who believed that he had found the ultimate truth and wisdom in the book of Daniel. This pensive imaginative man had ecstatic visions, according to which the millennium of the faithful, the time when the rulers would be humbled and the poor raised on high, was close at hand. Finally he requested the Magistrate of Strasbourg to arrest him, in keeping with the prophecy which had been revealed to him. The members of the Magistrate complied with his wish. But he lived to see the seed he had sown bear fruit in the Low Countries and particularly in the city of Munster, where his followers laid the foundations for the Kingdom of God not with silent suffering and faithful waiting, as he required of them, but with violence and bloodshed.

The Evangelical Reform had already been introduced into Munster and the Episcopal government driven out of power as early as 1531. This peaceful reformation was followed by a bloody revolution after the arrival from the Low Countries of a group of fanatical Melchiorites, among them the personable and masterful Jan Bockelson of Leyden, and Jan Matthys of Harlem, who was known as the latter-day

"Prophet Henoch." Those Protestants and Catholics who resisted baptism were driven out, and all institutions which had not existed originally but had been "introduced only as a result of man's sin" were abolished. Accordingly, all the regulations established by the State, society, the economy and the Church were set aside, domestic privacy was forbidden and polygamy permitted.

While the Bishop of Munster was laying siege to the city, adults were baptized, gatherings were held, court sentences pronounced, rebels beheaded and Communion services conducted in the marketplace, which was renamed "Mount Zion."

When Jan Matthys was killed in a raid, Jan van Leyden took over. He appointed a Council of twelve elders, who were to draw up a code of laws in keeping with "the commandments and prohibitions in the Holy Scriptures." As "John the Just," the fanatical, eloquent and despotic demagogue was proclaimed King of "New Israel," to rule the City of Munster, the "New Jerusalem," and to reign supreme over all the kingdoms and empires of the world. Enveloped in sumptuous robes, with a crown upon his head, and attended by a huge retinue and his beautiful wives, he set out to restore "that which God had uttered through the mouth of all the prophets of the world."

In the face of this imminent danger, Catholics and Protestants joined together as they had done at the time of the Peasants' War and hurried to the aid of the Bishop of Munster. The city, by now literally starved out, was taken, the prophets were executed and all the Anabaptists were either killed or put to flight.

Luther and the Reformers sought to place the blame for the millennarian movement, which had led to the excesses in Munster, on the "false doctrine of Judaism."[18]

It is not easy to investigate scientifically the degree of interaction that took place between these two parallel religious movements [Anabaptism and Messianism] which were both rooted in the same causes—distress and persecution. Both based their doctrines on the same sources, the Book of Daniel and the apocalyptic writings, and both hoped to find deliverance from the troubles of their own day in visions of a Messianic future, free from all sin.

Historical sources readily reveal that the rebellion of Munster posed a serious threat to Josel's political mission, and that attempts were made to prove some connection between Jan van Leyden, the "King of New Zion" and Josel of Rosheim, the "Regent (*Regierer*) of German Jewry."

It was as "Regent" of all the Jewry of the *Reich* that Josel had signed his "Articles and Regulations" of 1530. He himself, as well as the *parnassim* of the communities, who had drawn up the statutes jointly with him in Augsburg, had submitted the documents to most of the Estates of the *Reich* and to the municipal magistrates without encountering any objections to the title he had adopted. He had signed subsequent petitions in the same manner, and on July 5, 1535, he still referred to himself as "Regent of All Jewry in the *Reich*" in a memorandum addressed to the Imperial High Court of Justice.

On July 6, eleven days after the fall of Munster, a grave charge was brought against Josel by Wolfgang Weidner, Imperial Fiscal Agent and Procurator at the Supreme Court of Justice *(Kammergericht)* in Speyer.[19]

It was charged that "in those difficult, swiftly moving times," when a tradesman of base birth had pretended to the title of "King," Josel, too, in a false, fraudulent, unlawful and unseemly manner, contrary to all law and authorization had passed himself off as a Regent of the Jews of the *Reich*. In view of the fact that this presumption on his part had not only brought slander, ridicule and derision upon His Imperial Majesty, the rightful Regent of the Jews, but also set a bad example for evil and seditious men, Josel was commanded, after the passage of three weeks, either to appear in person before the Supreme Court of Justice to explain his conduct, or else to have an authorized attorney represent him there in his defense.

Josel, who was then staying in Speyer, acknowledged receipt of the summons in a communication dated July 7.[20] In this letter, he stated that since he would be unable to appear in person before the Supreme Court of Justice at the specified date, he had authorized Dr. Christoff Hoss, a lawyer, to conduct the case against the Imperial Fiscal Agent in his behalf. On August 20, Weidner already proposed[21] that Josel be convicted as charged and severely penalized.

It was not until almost a year later, on July 5, 1536,[22] that Josel's lawyer submitted his defense. He categorically denied that the defendant had assumed an unlawful title with fraudulent, scornful and deceitful intent in order to ridicule and disparage the Emperor's Majesty and to foment insurrection and unrest. The fact was that the highest authorities of the Realm, the Imperial Counselors, the Hereditary Marshal von Pappenheim, the Austrian Government at Ensisheim, the Chief Burgrave of Prague, and many other officials all had made it a practice to address him in no other form but as "Regent of All Jewry," "Chief of all the Jews of the German Nation," and "Chief Rabbi of All Jewry," because they recognized Josel as the official representative of the Jews, in whose behalf he had had to appear at all Imperial Diets for the past three decades. Furthermore, Hoss pointed out, the title of "Regent" which Josel used was simply the German translation of the "Hebraic-Chaldean" term *parnas* and of *manhig,* a designation common in biblical and prophetic literature, titles which the heads of the great Talmudical Academies of Frankfort, Worms, Esslingen and Friedberg also used in addressing him. Seeing that it would be contrary to the dictates of justice and fairness to sentence a man to punishment on account of a title which had been accorded him by the high-born and lowly alike, Hoss moved that his client be acquitted and compensated for his expenses.

To this Weidner[23] replied on November 4, 1536 that even if Josel had not intended to revile the Emperor by the title which he had assumed, the consideration in this case was not the *animus,* the intention, of the defendant, but the *factum ipsum,* which in itself was *intolerabile, enorme, arrogans et seditiosum.* Also militating against him was the fact that, even as the Imperial laws said of the Jews, he, too, was *feralis secte et nativus Christiani nominis hostis,* and as such was concerned solely with the gain and welfare of the Jews and aimed at the destruction and total annihilation of the Christians. Even as one could easily expect fraudulent intentions and conduct in a slave, so it could be presumed also in the case of Josel that he had assumed an unlawful title with the plain intent to defraud.

Nor did the Fiscal Agent accept the plea that the title "Regent" corresponded to the Hebrew terms *manhig* and *parnas,* terms which could also have been rendered as "advocate," "commander" or "administrator." Besides, if Josel had wanted to use a Hebrew title he should have written his petition in the Hebrew language and signed himself as "*parnas*" and "*manhig.*" In view of the foregoing, the Fiscal Agent felt compelled to insist that the defendant had deliberately sought to diminish the Emperor's prestige and he should therefore be called to account for his action.

We have no record of the subsequent hearings in the case. In all probability it must have dragged on until 1540, because we know in that year Josel was sentenced to pay the heavy fine of two Marks in gold, and all the law costs. In 1536, however, he stopped using the title of "Regent" and, from that time on, referred to himself as "Commander" or "Advocate" of German Jewry.

The attacks that endangered his position and indeed his life during that period did not only come from the Christians. As his prestige grew, resistance to his outstanding leadership began to make itself felt in the ranks of his coreligionists as well, particularly among the *parnassim* and the elders of the large communities. These men, in many instances, exercised dictatorial powers over the members of their communities by virtue of their descent, wealth, scholarship, and their personal relationships with the reigning princes, and were not willing to submit to the orders of the new Commander of the Jews.

One such man who had acquired absolute authority over a Jewish community, in this case the Jewry of Prague, which had been the most renowned in all of Europe, was the Chief Elder (*Oberalteste*) Zalman Muncka, one of the wealthiest bankers in the city, who had received a writ of amnesty with many privileges from King Louis. The family name of Muncka has been identified with the surname Horowitz, which frequently occurs in Hebrew sources and the bearers of which combined in their personalities the opposing qualities of impulsiveness, lack of discipline and obstinacy with erudition, piety and a predilection for the Cabbala.[24]

Under the rule of the weak Jagellonian dynasty, the Bohemian Jews, who were a royal possession of the Kings of Bohemia and hence subject to them and to the Royal Chamber, had become a bone of contention between the princes and the Estates, who were then locked in a struggle for supremacy. The Magistrate of the united townships of Prague, in particular, had succeeded, at the beginning of the sixteenth century, in acquiring jurisdiction over the Jews and the right to appoint their judges and elders.

When the lands of Bohemia and Moravia fell to Ferdinand

of Habsburg in 1526, and he attempted to recoup the royal prerogative over the Jews (*Judenregal*), the Magistrate of Prague came into open conflict with the Royal Chamber, which complained bitterly about the city's encroachment upon the rights of the sovereign.

The Chamber charged, in particular, that Zalman Muncka, the "Chief" of the Jews there, whom it described as an overbearing, crafty and ambitious man, had sought, "in order to conceal and disguise unseemly and evil acts," to free himself of its authority and to place his party under the jurisdiction of the Magistrate of Prague, who was "backing him up" to the full. Muncka, it was alleged, wielded such coercive authority that the other officials of the Jewish community could not "act, behave or speak in any manner contrary to his wishes but had to do his bidding in all things."

Josel tells[25] us that when the other elders rebelled against the despotic rule of Muncka and his clique, and placed themselves under the protection of the Royal Chamber, the two factions began to quarrel with one another so violently "that they lunged at each other like the feuding sects in the various communities of Bohemia."

The rabbis of Poland and Germany, who watched the undignified spectacle with dismay, made an effort to persuade the Jewish community of Prague to entrust the settlement of its disputes to reliable arbitrators. Finally, Abraham ben Avigdor, a respected rabbi in Prague, turned to Josel and requested him "to repair the damage" and to draw up new by-laws for the community. Since the rabbis of Germany also importuned him to "give assistance to this great rabbi," Josel journeyed to Prague on horseback in the late fall of 1534. There he drew up a twenty-three point reform program, "which more than four hundred adult, responsible men were ready to sign." But the followers of Horowitz (Muncka), led by a man by the name of Scheftel,[26] were not willing to cede their authority to a foreign "commander." "They were out to hand him over to murderers, and made three attempts on his life," so that he was forced to seek protection from them within the walls of the Royal Castle. However, a majority in the community appreciated the by-laws he had drawn up for them and sided with him. In addition, he had the support of outstanding men from Austria and Italy, so that he was able to carry his point and help truth win the final victory.[27]

At that same time, the Bohemian Chamber reported to the King that the Jewish community of Prague had sent for a foreign Jew from Germany, who had come and enacted many Jewish regulations and statutes and had set them down in a special booklet.

Josel, who had undertaken the long and arduous journey from the Alsace to Bohemia "with much toil and trouble" in order to bring about a reconciliation between the quarelling factions, has no bitter words to say about his enemies in his memoirs. He attributed his rescue from danger of death to God, even as he was convinced that the cause for which he had labored had been the cause of the Lord. In his broad religious view of all the events of world history, he interpreted the gradual decline of the ancient Jewish community of Prague and the subsequent persecution it suffered from without as consequences of such recurring internal disputes, "as is proven by the occurrence of calamity upon calamity."

Only a few months after Josel had returned to Rosheim from Prague he had to make another horseback journey through the *Reich.* This time "judgment had gone forth"[28] upon the Jews of Silesia and they were in need of help.

In 1535 bloody riots broke out against the Jews in the Duchy of Jaegerndorf, which had been purchased together with the Duchies of Oppeln and Ratibor by Margrave

George of Ansbach, but was subject to the sovereignty of King Ferdinand.

In 1534, Abraham Hirsch of Leobschuetz, the Senior Elder of Jaegerndorf, had obtained from the Margrave a decree permitting the Jews to engage in the spice trade, which had been forbidden to them by the guilds.

Shortly thereafter, a young woman who had been convicted of witchcraft and procuring and sentenced to death, testified in court that Abraham Hirsch had requested her one day to get milk from a Christian woman for him, so that he might derive from it magical powers with which to kill all the Christian women in the land. However, she said, she had brought him milk from a sow instead. Hirsch had then poured it into the cloven skull of a criminal who had died on the gallows. "When there came forth a great squealing from the skull, as if there had been little piglets therein," the woman related, Abraham became very angry at the fraud, for now he had power to kill only pigs, not the women.

Although the Chief Elder (*Landesaelteste*) emphatically denied that he had committed the crime, he was thrown into prison and tortured. Under torture he pleaded guilty to witchcraft and named several other Jews as his accomplices. Thereupon all the adult Jewish males in the Duchy of Jaegerndorf were likewise arrested. They were more steadfast than their elder, who vacillated between denying and admitting his guilt. These Jews could not be coerced into making a confession. It was only when he stood tied to the stake that Abraham Hirsch finally "retracted everything in a loud voice, and allowed the sentence to be carried out on his body as atonement for all of Israel."

The martyrdom of this respected personality and the arrest of the Jews of Jaegerndorf caused great consternation among the Jews of Silesia, Bohemia, Moravia and Franconia. Their anxiety was increased when it became known at the same time that the Margrave George, under pressure from the Silesian Estates, was seeking to secure from King Ferdinand a decree calling for their expulsion.

The elders of the Jewish communities of Oels-Munsterberg importuned their sovereign, Duke Charles, father-in-law of George of Ansbach, to influence the Margrave in behalf of their brethren, two of whom had already succumbed to their sufferings in prison. While the Jews of Moravia were appealing to Ferdinand for help, the deputies of the Jews of the Margraviate of Silesia attempted to bribe George's representative, the Governor, with gifts; however, for their actions they, too, were put in prison.

The deputies of the Jewish community of Frankenstein then tried their luck at the Court of Ansbach itself. There, at that time, several Silesian noblemen and the Town Clerk of Leobschuetz were seeking a personal audience with the Margrave to persuade him to expel all his Jewish subjects from Silesia.

George of Ansbach, to whom his contemporaries gave the name "the Pious," because of his sincere espousal of the New Doctrine, had no hatred for the Jews. He valued their services as taxpayers and bankers. Like many of the princes of his epoch, he was an enterprising ruler, eager to stimulate trade and commerce in his Frankish territories. He also lived in great luxury, and secured the funds he needed to pay his debts wherever he could obtain them. Therefore, despite opposition from the Provincial Estates and the Protestant clergy, he had permitted Jews to settle in many of the cities in his Margraviate, because he intended to avail himself of their loans and tax payments. On the other hand, he was not averse to yielding to the demands of the Silesian Estates when the latter promised to reimburse the Margravian treasury for the loss of the Jewish tax payments.

Thus, at the Court of Ansbach, the Silesian noblemen and

the Town Clerk of Leobschuetz on one hand, and the deputies of the Jewish community of Frankenstein on the other, each sought to outbid the other in offers of money to the vacillating prince in order to win him to their cause. One party endeavored to have him expel the Jews, while the other attempted to persuade him to free the prisoners and not issue the expulsion edict.

"Twice the expulsion was practically settled on," the deputies from Frankenstein reported in a letter to their brethren in Silesia. It was only their pleas and importunings, they said, that had been capable of moving the Margrave, who, after all, was a God-fearing man at heart. However, they pointed out, immense amounts of money were being swallowed up in their endeavors, and they were already becoming acutely embarrassed for lack of funds because people were no longer willing to give them loans.

It must have been at this crucial time that Josel, bearing a generous supply of money and accompained by Rabbi Liebermann of Pfersee, appeared at the Court of Ansbach in order to open the Margrave's eyes to the lies and slander that had been spread about the Jews and to prove the innocence of the prisoners.[29] "With the help of God," as he put it, and for a consideration of six hundred florins, Josel succeeded in getting the "Margrave Joergel" to change his mind so that he recalled the expulsion edict and said to him: "Let the prisoners go free."

Throughout those years that he was engaged in defending his brethren in Innsbruck, Augsburg, Brabant, Regensburg, Prague and Ansbach, Josel continued to conscientiously discharge his duties as Leader of Alsatian Jewry.

Now that the Jews of the Alsace had been expelled from nearly all the Imperial cities, many had settled in rural areas. In many instances, they were also prevented from doing business in their former places of residence. In these difficult times, Josel persistently endeavored to maintain at least their good relations with the city of Strasbourg, the most important political and economic center of the Alsace region.

Unlike Augsburg and Nuremberg, Strasbourg was not ruled by big and enterprising capitalists. Ever since the time of the Black Death, when the guilds had first taken over the government of the city, the economy of Strasbourg had been molded by the politics of the artisans. But the middle class, which included the greatest humanists, historians and educators of the time, and which for years had given shelter to the persecuted Anabaptists and to the leaders of the French Reformation, was free of all partisan prejudice. After a series of hard struggles between the crafts and the patricians, the burghers of Strasbourg had succeeded in drawing up a constitution which "was extolled as a masterpiece even at that time because it seemed to have established a harmonious equilibrium, on a democratic foundation, between the patricians and the middle-class elements, between the permanent authority on the one hand, and the administration which changed each year on the other."

Of course, this ideally constituted republic had expelled the Jews from the Strasbourg area in 1388. They had been allowed only one day a week to attend to their business in the city, during which time they had to be accompanied by either a gaoler or a soldier, and the citizens were not permitted to transact money loans with them.

However, these regulations had not kept the Jews from continuing to engage in money trade with the people of Strasbourg. Unlike his counterparts in Colmar or Oberehnheim, the Magistrate of Strasbourg showed no hostility toward them. Indeed, Josel repeatedly spoke highly of him, declaring that he had accorded the same fair and "honorable" treatment to the Jews as he had to the Christians, and that he had given them shelter within the walls of the city during the

Peasants' War.[30] Upon his return from the Low Countries in the early summer of 1531, he was therefore greatly dismayed to learn from his brethren that the safe-conduct of all the Alsatian Jews had been revoked because a man from Dangolsheim named Mennel had purchased stolen goods, and had also assaulted a Christian woman.

Josel immediately put Mennel on oath, questioned him, and then called a judicial inquiry before two of the Councillors of Strasbourg. The inquiry revealed that the defendant was not as guilty as it had appeared. Josel therefore requested the Magistrate to allow the continuation of the time-honored custom, and not to prohibit the Jews from doing business in the city—for, as he pointed out, people the world over had no other alternative but to engage in buying and selling and to ply their trade in order to make a living. He recommended, however, that if any one of his fellow-Jews should be found guilty of an offense, he should receive that penalty which had been decreed for such offenders in the "Articles" of Augsburg.[31]

Three years after this incident, Josel found it necessary to amend the "Articles" in order to preserve the trade relationships between the Jews and the city of Strasbourg.

In response to many complaints from the Christians that the Jews were evading the local courts of justice, Josel had stipulated in the Augsburg code that Jewish creditors should not be rash in instituting legal proceedings against a Christian debtor at a non-resident court, but should first seek to arrive at an amicable settlement with him. However, the Jews had not always followed these regulations, and many burghers complained bitterly that their creditors had sued them at the Imperial Court of Rottweil.

It was not solely his concern for the welfare of his constituents that motivated the Magistrate of Strasbourg to look after the interests of the Christians involved in such proceedings. The city of Strasbourg had never lost its traditional privilege of *non appellando,* the right to insist that any litigation involving one of its citizens be conducted before a local judge only. The city retained this right even when, in 1495, the High Court of Justice (*Kammergericht*) had been established as the supreme judicial authority of the *Reich.* From that time on, Strasbourg had "its own *Reich* Court of Justice." The Magistrate firmly insisted on this special privilege, and regarded any circumvention of the local court of justice as a serious infringement on his juridical rights.

Josel, with his sense for legal problems, was aware that the Councillors of Strasbourg would be displeased if the Jews sued subjects of the city at out-of-town courts and inflicted "still other hardships" on them. By "other hardships," Josel meant engaging in forbidden categories of business and charging "exorbitant rates of interest."[32]

In order to put an end to these constant complaints, Josel decided to enact a new law, which would impart a more stringent interpretation to Paragraph Three of the "Articles" of Augsburg.

In his capacity of "Commander of all the Jews in German Lands," he issued a decree on June 25, 1534, enjoining all Jews making application for a safe-conduct from Strasbourg not to sue citizens of Strasbourg at out-of-town courts.[33] He ordered all those compelled to institute legal proceedings against burghers of the city to do so only at the regular court binding for Strasbourg. Any violation of this new ordinance was to be reported immediately either to Josel himself or to the corporate body of Provincial Jewry. The offender was to be excommunicated forthwith, and no one was to give him food or shelter or to associate with him until such time as he would have given satisfaction to the Magistrate of the city of Strasbourg.

Josel submitted this ordinance to the Magistrate of Strasbourg with the explicit request that he show it to every Jew making application for safe-conduct, and obligate him by oath to comply with it in every respect. Thus in the future offenders would receive their just deserts, and the innocent would not have to suffer on account of the guilty.

However, by 1536 the Councillors of Strasbourg sent indignant reports to Rosheim once again to the effect that a number of Jews, including one Samuel von Eschbach and one Bluemel von Pfaffenhofen, had cited subjects of the city of Strasbourg before the Imperial Court of Justice in Rottweil, causing the defendants excessive expense. The Councillors threatened that unless the Jews ceased and desisted from this practice once and for all, the Magistrate would not permit Jews from either the Upper or the Lower Alsace to enter the city.

Finally, in July 1536, Josel, who, at great personal expense, had sought to cancel the Rottweil lawsuits, called a conference of Alsatian Jewry *(Landjudenschaft)* at Rosheim.[34] There he drew up an agreement by which the entire corporate body of Provincial Jewry solemnly bound itself to cite citizens of Strasbourg only before the regular court of justice in that city, and to use as a court of appeals only the court of justice there, consisting of the thirteen Imperial Supreme Court Justices.

In Article Four of the "Articles" of Augsburg, Josel had decreed that a Jew who unknowingly had accepted stolen goods as security must never again have dealings with such "thievish and pilfering" individuals. The Rosheim Agreement went one step further. It stipulated that any merchandise stolen from a citizen of Strasbourg and then sold to a Jew had to be restored to the rightful owner without any claim to compensation. Josel felt that he had to impose this severe obligation on his brethren out of gratitude to the city of Strasbourg, which had always dealt kindly with them in times of war and distress and had given them shelter within its walls.

He forwarded this agreement to the "gracious, noble, wise and honorable Councillors," in the hope that they would continue to grant safe-conduct and protection to the Jews as of old. For, as he put it, he knew very well that men of such great intelligence would not wish to deal unfairly with either Christians or Jews.

CHAPTER SIX

THE COMFORTER

ALMOST simultaneously with the conference at Rosheim on August 6, 1536,[1] John Frederick, Elector of Saxony, enacted a mandate which strictly forbade Jews to settle, sojourn or do business in his country or to travel through it.

The original mandate has been lost, but its contents are clearly indicated in a printed circular which the Elector sent to his bailiffs at the time, and they are reiterated, too, in an even more stringent decree enacted in 1543.

Faithful to the tradition of the Electors of Saxony, John Frederick was an ardent follower of Luther and was bound to the reformer by ties of close personal friendship. As the leader of the Evangelicals, the head of the Schmalkald Confederation, and sovereign of a state of major importance, he was able to exert a strong influence on political and religious developments in the *Reich*.

His motives in issuing this unexpected edict of expulsion are not known. Some contemporaries suspected that the wrath of the short-tempered prince had been provoked by the involvement of Jews in an ore theft in the Ore Mountains. Josel was of the opinion that John Frederick had been led by the "heretic tracts" of the priest Martin Luther to outlaw the Jews and not to allow them even one foot's breadth of space in his country."[2] However, this assumption of Josel's is one of the very few that is not borne out by established facts.[3] The "heretic tracts" of Luther which "were out to stir up princes and peoples until Israel should be laid low"[4] did not appear until 1543. Josel seems to have confused the mandate of 1536 with the decree of 1543, in which the "deceitful calumnies and lies spread by the Jews against the true Messiah" were cited as a motivation for the anti-Jewish attitude of the government. These words had been taken, almost verbatim, from Luther's tracts which appeared at that time.

In 1536, Josel was still not aware that Luther's attitude toward the Jews had undergone a fundamental change. Had he known this, he would not have so eagerly sought an opportunity to make the reformer's personal acquaintance in order to avert the evil decree concerning the Jews of Saxony, and to secure a personal audience with John Frederick. Nor would he have requested a letter of introduction to the Elector of Saxony from the Magistrate of Strasbourg, or asked Wolfgang Capito and Martin Butzer, the two outstanding leaders of the Reformation in Southern Germany, to prepare Luther for a visit from him at Wittenberg.

Wolfgang Capito had been bound to Josel for some time by ties of warm friendship. He had come from Hagenau, a city of tolerance, where Josel, too, had spent his youth. A "mild, warm personality, tending to melancholy in his undogmatic way [he was] the most broadminded of all the German reformers, the protector of the persecuted and the oppressed." Wolfgang had remained true to the ideals of the early years of the Reformation at a time when sectarian bickerings had splintered the movement and turned what originally had been the search of the individual soul for direct communion with God into an authoritarian Church Establishment.[5] He was a friend of Erasmus and a mystic, close to the Anabaptists and their millennarian hopes. He both knew and loved the Hebrew language, which he taught at the newly founded College in Strasbourg, and he was an avid collector of Hebrew books and manuscripts, whose contents he would often discuss with Josel.

In a letter dated July 11, 1543,[6] Josel wrote to the Magistrate of Strasbourg that Capito had reproachfully informed him, in the presence of the most learned printer Eyl, that among certain Hebrew literature which he had received from Constantinople, there had been a Hebrew book in which the author "had spoken of the Messiah in such insulting terms that I will neither repeat it nor set it down in writing." However, he added, Capito had told him that he had studied all the books and commentaries of the Jews as well as their prayerbooks. Had he found vicious language in any of those writings such as that recorded in this book, he would not have taken so great an interest in the Jews or had pity on them. But since he had nowhere found such statements in this other literature, he could only assume that in the olden days people had been permitted to write as they pleased.

This was the man who, on April 26, 1537, wrote Martin Luther a letter which not only reflects Capito's own character but gives some indication of the impact of Josel's personality on his contemporaries.[7]

In this letter, Capito stated that a distinguished leader among the Jews, one Josephus, a man of piety and good repute after the manner of his people, whom they regarded and respected as their patron, had complained to him that John Frederick of Saxony wished to expel all the Jews from his country, and to refuse them permission even to travel through the Electorate. Capito asked Luther either to give Josel a personal hearing, or to pass on his petition to the

Elector so that the Jews would understand that the Christians were ready to deal kindly not only with strangers, but also with their enemies.

He himself, Capito continued, had compassion on this people, which had been so long despised by all. The Christians should deal more kindly with them, if for no other reason than that they sprung from the blessed race. True, the Jews now represented only branches severed from the true olive tree, onto which the Christians originally had been grafted as wild growths, but there had been a time when they were the guarantors of the promise and the covenant of God. In closing, Capito stressed that he had written the letter in agreement with Martin Butzer, who had left for Basel that very day.

The Magistrate of Strasbourg wrote in a similar vein to John Frederick,[8] requesting that the Elector grant safe-conduct to Josel, who was undertaking the journey "for the sake of his own people," and give him a gracious hearing. For Josel had always "acted in fairness and honesty" in the interest of his fellow-believers, and had "proven himself and labored diligently after the manner and the spirit of his faith in God." Besides, it was pointed out, the Christians were duty-bound, according to the teachings of St. Paul, to have mercy and compassion on these unfortunate people.

Armed with these letters of recommendation, Josel, who had written to Luther several times himself,[9] set out on his journey "to the high-born Prince, the Duke John Frederick."[10]

As he traveled along the banks of the Rhine and the Main in those early summer days of 1537, and the forests of Thuringia enclosed him in their first fresh green, his heart was filled with joyous expectations. For the man whom he was going to visit was a "wise and good man" such as God had sent from time to time to come to the aid of His oppressed people.

Had not this man courageously taken Reuchlin's side when he had begun his defense of the Jewish books? And had he not spoken out against the ritual-murder libel and cautioned against forcing Jews to accept baptism against their wills?

Had he not expressed his pain and sorrow at the fact that so great and glorious a people, which had produced such illustrious personalities as Abraham, Isaac, Jacob, Samuel, David, Daniel and St. Paul,[11] a people which God had chosen and set apart from all the other nations, was now compelled to live and suffer in slavery?

Finally, had he not, in 1523, in his booklet "That Jesus Christ Was Born a Jew," boldly placed "Christ" and "Jew," the most illustrious and the most despised of names, side by side on the same title page in order to proclaim to the world that the two were kinsmen and brothers? Josel well remembered the excitement with which the Jews at that time had read, studied and discussed this revolutionary tract, line by line. The Marranos in Antwerp had even sent it covertly to their oppressed brethren in Spain to give them comfort and encouragement.

Of course, Josel was aware that the reformer had not written this book merely out of fairness and mercy. When he recommended that the Jews should be treated kindly, he did so in the hope that such kindness might "attract some of them to the Christian faith." When he exhorted the reigning princes to permit the Jews to engage in a trade and to work side by side with the other citizens, he did so with the thought that non-Christians would not want to become Christians so long as it was evident that "the Christians were dealing with other men in such an un-Christian manner."

Even Reuchlin, much as he had fallen under the mysterious spell of the language of the Jews, had put his own Christianity far above Judaism and carried on his toilsome studies in the Cabbala only in so far as they might help him discover the true plans of salvation and grasp the greatest ideal of all—the Messianic prophecy.

It was therefore no surprise to Josel that Luther, too, believing as he did that all non-Christians and heathens were lost and damned forever, should feel that he had found in his own doctrine the sole true path to salvation. But then, the purpose of Josel's journey to Saxony was not to engage the reformer in a debate on questions of Jewish and Christian belief. All he sought to do was to request Luther to translate into action what he had proclaimed in theory in his tracts concerning the Jews, and not to permit the "kinsmen, cousins and brothers of the Lord" to perish in misery.

Thus deeply immersed in his thoughts, and "with great effort,"[12] Josel finally approached the Electorate of Saxony, only seven miles away from the border. In all probability he had advised Luther in advance of his visit and had informed him also of the letters of introduction from Strasbourg. "However," Josel relates, "He [Luther] did not admit me into his presence but only wrote me a letter."[13]

This letter, addressed by Luther to his "good friend," his "dear Josel,"[14] has been a subject of repeated debate and commentary. It has been quoted for decades by students of Lutherania because it reflects some of the reformer's basic views on the Jewish problem of his day, and on Christian-Jewish relations during a critical phase of his own personal religious quest.

In his letter to Josel, Luther wrote that he would have been most happy to intercede with the Elector in behalf of the Jews both orally and in writing, even as he had done service to all Jewry by his tract ("That Jesus Christ Was Born a Jew"). However, since the Jews had so shamefully abused his services and displayed conduct that the Christians could not tolerate, they had only themselves to blame if he ceased to speak for them before rulers and princes.

In his heart, he said, he had always been well disposed toward them, and he still would wish that people might deal kindly with them, and that God should look upon them with favor some day and bring them near to their Messiah. However, he had no intention of strengthening them in their ways of error through his favor. If God should grant him the time, he wished to write a book to convert some from the seed of the holy Prophets to their promised Messiah, although it seemed strange to him that the Christians were given the task of leading the Jews back to their rightful sovereign. He asked the Jews to remember that, in view of the deadly enmity existing between the two religions, the Christians certainly would have considered it beneath them to worship even the best king if he were a Jew, let alone such an accursed and crucified Hebrew, had not the power and the might of the true God compelled them to do so. Furthermore, he urged them to satisfy themselves that God would never free them from their misery, which had already lasted over 1,500 years, unless they would accept their kinsman and Lord, the dear Crucified One, as their Messiah. For his part, he continued, he had read the writings of their rabbis, and had he found some truth in them he would have been open to persuasion, for he was not so "callous and hard" in his views. But their rabbis could only clamor that Jesus had been crucified and condemned by the Jews, even as their ancestors had condemned, stoned, and tortured all the holy Prophets of the past. Even the heathens, whom the Jews regarded as their worst enemies, had been willing and prepared to give them aid and advice, for they could not bear to see the Jews curse and blaspheme their own flesh and blood, Jesus of Nazareth. But he, Luther, predicted that their beliefs would come to nought, for the date which had been foretold by Daniel for the coming of the Messiah had long since passed.

This letter, which is couched in friendly and serious terms, reflects the ambivalent attitude of the reformer to the Jewish problem. It mirrors the tragic inner conflict which tortured him as long as he lived: his love for "ancient, pious Israel to whom the mystery of God had been revealed,"[15] on the one hand, and his aversion to this self-righteous and obdurate people who did not understand God's promise and His revelation, on the other. But, contrary to his past attitude, his approach to them in this letter to Josel was no longer one of love and solicitude. He no longer held up to them Jesus, the man, for their emulation, but sought to bind them to Christ, the Deity, instead. For if the Jews would refuse to accept the fact that the Savior was indeed the Messiah—as Luther had ceaselessly sought to prove by word and pen, by commentary and interpretation, by discussion and disputation—then the Law would remain in force, severe and implacable, for one segment of mankind, and the time "when all things would be fulfilled" would not come to pass.

This was the reason, too, why he so heatedly attacked the Jewish scholars who, adhering to the exegesis of their own rabbis, sought to disprove his Christological interpretation of Old Testament texts with all the weapons of ingenuity and knowledge at their command. The Jews, he declared in despair in one of his after-dinner speeches[16] were incapable of tolerating even the most trivial arguments; to debate with them was like striking an anvil with a blade of straw. How, then, could one discuss great things with them if they would neither admit nor accept the validity of even these few arguments?

But the main reason why Luther refused Josel's request was his agitation at the thought that "this people which had been driven, chased and hunted down from place to place without a lasting home of their own,"[17] this "vine which now is good for burning only,"[18] still had the strength to bear fruit, and that the Law, which in fact he felt had ceased to exist, could still hold such irresistible fascination for Christians. Luther had already charged the Anabaptists with "Judaization," and asserted that "the spirit of Muenzer was out to turn Christians into Jews."[19]

Moreover, at the very time when Josel turned to him for help, Luther received confirmation of a rumor that had cropped up from time to time in the past; namely, that a certain sect in Moravia, the Sabbatarians, led astray by the Jews, had turned away from Christianity. They observed the Jewish Sabbath, and circumcised their males; further, they believed that the Messiah had not yet appeared, and openly declared themselves adherents of Jewish Law.

"What should one grant to the Jews, who harm the people with regard to life and property, and entice so many Christians away with their false beliefs and superstitions?", Luther angrily demanded of some friends in a discussion of his correspondence with Josel of Rosheim.[20] "For they have circumcised many Christians in Moravia and now call them by a new name: the Sabbatarians."

Josel's accounts do not indicate whether he made further attempts to secure an audience with John Frederick even without the help of Luther. He only relates that he was not able to present the Strasbourg letter of introduction to the Elector of Saxony at that time, and that he had to wait until he met him, some years later, in Frankfort on the Main.

Of all the reigning princes of Germany, the one to espouse the new doctrine most intensely and passionately was the Landgrave Philip of Hesse.[21] Philip possessed the most eminent political mind among the princely families of his day. But his was a complicated personality, pensive and pious and yet given without restraint to all the urges and passions of the flesh. Tortured by the pangs of conscience, he sought to resolve his inner conflict by means of assiduous Bible study and the independent investigation of religious problems. He was a friend of Zwingli, the humanist and republican, whose broad-minded doctrine he sought to reconcile with the inflexible creed of Luther. But for all his theological cogitations, Philip was an enterprising politician, and believed that with the help of intrigue and armed might, alliances and treaties, he would be able to satisfy his personal ambitions and at the same time win over the entire *Reich* to the Gospel.

His contemporaries referred to him as "Philip the Magnanimous" and described him as "mighty in counsel and wisdom," for despite his moral failings, and his conduct (which was ambiguous and at times even perfidious), he was more broadminded in matters of religion than most of his peers.

"One cannot in good conscience kill another because he is in error in matters of faith," he once said. "For faith, after all, is a thing that is beyond the control of the individual. It is entirely a gift from God, and he to whom God has not granted the gift of faith can never acquire it on his own."

It is true that Philip had decreed in 1524 that in the future Jews were not to be permitted to reside in an administrative district, or to set foot on Hessian territory, and that he had revoked their safe-conduct and right to protection. However, this order had been issued shortly before the outbreak of the Peasants' War and therefore, in all likelihood, solely for the purpose of appeasing the excited populace. Moreover, it is not known whether the expulsion actually took place. At any rate, it remains that in 1532, the permission to reside in the Hessian territory was extended to the Jews for a period of six years.

When, some time thereafter, the structure of the established Church of the district was altered on the basis of the Protestant doctrine, and the sovereign was authorized to reign over his subjects not only as head of the State but also as head of the Church, and guardian of the faith, there was lively debate concerning the position to be occupied by the Jews in this new *"res publica Christiana."* The question was raised as to what place there would be for an alien national and religious entity within this commonwealth, where society was to dwell together as a Protestant Christian community in love, faith and the fear of the Lord.

In December 1538, almost coincidentally with the promulgation of the disciplinary regulations and the statutes of the Elders of the Protestant Church at the Synod of Ziegenhayn, the Councillors of Hessia submitted to the Landgrave a "proposal for tolerating the Jews."[22]

In this proposal, which had been drawn up in seven articles, they laid the foundations for a Jewry Law which was meant to permit the Jews to earn a living and, at the same time, to prevent them from engaging in business practices which would discomfit the population, and which would serve to effect the gradual integration of the Jewish element into the Christian State.[23]

The Councillors proposed that in such cities where there were no guilds, the Jews should be permitted to buy and sell and also to do some "honest" business. It was recommended that they should not be allowed to engage in financial operations or usury, but that they should have the right to lend out their money at rates of interest from two to three per cent, provided that such transactions would be made in the presence of a bailiff or with the knowledge of one of the Councillors. Furthermore, they were to be obliged, as of old, to pay protection monies to the reigning prince. Finally, the Jews should be made to attend sermons by members of the

Protestant clergy, but not permitted to engage in religious debates with Christians.

Philip submitted these recommendations to his theologians so that they might give their opinion in principle and, in view of the close relationship then existing between Church and State, discuss from the religious viewpoint the future policy to be adopted vis-à-vis the Jews. Philip addressed himself primarily to Martin Butzer, the reformer from Strasbourg, who for years had been his advisor on theological, organizational and educational changes. Philip had called Butzer to Cassel at that time so that he might find ways to employ leniency rather than force in quelling the Anabaptist movement which had flared up again in Hessia.

Martin Butzer of Schlettstadt was to play a crucial role in the life of Josel and in the lives of the Jews of Hessia. Originally a Dominican friar, he had never outgrown the missionary zeal to which he had been stirred in his monastery days.

This active and versatile dialectician, a born politician and organizer, has been described as the "prototype of the conciliatory theologian," because he knew how to bring together even the most diametrically opposed religious tendencies such as Biblicism and humanism, early Christianity and Thomism, Baptism and Lutheranism, and the doctrines of justification by faith alone and the sanctification of the individual by active morality and good works.

This flexibility and versatility enabled him again and again to effect reconciliations between the quarreling Protestant factions, and to preserve the oft-threatened unity of the Evangelical movement. However, despite his purity of conviction, these qualities also frequently brought upon him charges of ambiguity, insincerity, and desultoriness.

Butzer's attitude toward the Jews was marked by the same vagueness and lack of consistency. Like Luther, Butzer still looked upon the Jews as the descendants of the pious patriarchs, as the people who once had received the Divine revelation and promise and who had assumed the yoke of the Commandments in order to educate the rest of mankind. They represented the remnant which the Lord had set apart and preserved in life, so that, at the end of time, it might be converted and "Christianity implanted into it even as the wildling into the olive tree."

Butzer had both admiration and respect for this people of the Messianic mission. He berated the reigning princes for dealing with them in a harsh and godless manner, for compelling them to engage in barter and usury by barring them from all honorable occupations, and for expelling them from their territories. He called on all Christians to embrace the Jews in a spirit of sincere love, and thereby to lead them to Christianity.

On the other hand, he believed that even as God had chosen the Jews and set them apart from the other nations, He had also rejected and condemned them in His wrath because they had not heeded His Word and had not done His will. It was not permissible to have sentiments of affection or pity for these people, who had so stubbornly resisted the dominion of Christ. Butzer felt that "they should be considered enemies and combatted as friends," and that they should be disciplined with severity and "rigorous mercy."

This inconsistent attitude is reflected also in the "Advice" which the Hessian preachers, counseled and influenced by Butzer, submitted to the Landgrave in December, 1538.

According to this "Advice," it was the task of every Christian sovereign, by means of good laws and proper government, to train his subjects to become pious and honest people. It was pointed out, however, that the piety and salvation of the people was dependent on the predominance within the State of a true faith, meaning of one religion only. It was for this reason that God had commanded the people of Israel to uproot those who would violate the laws of this true religion. He had forbidden them to associate with unbelievers and commanded that even the strangers who dwelt in their midst be made to observe the Sabbath and other Jewish ceremonial laws.

In view of the foregoing, it would seem that the Jews and the heathens had been justified in "persecuting the Prophets, Christ, yea, the Apostles, and all the Christians so cruelly," for they had only felt it proper to make use of all the means at their command to prevent the desecration of their religion, the greatest and most precious possession of men. To accord official tolerance to a false religion would have been wickedness. It was for this same reason that, in the olden days, kings, princes, cities and the Church had barred the Jews from their territories. True, the ancient Christian emperors of the Holy Roman Empire and also the bishops had tolerated Jews in their territories, but only under the condition that they did not cause harm to the Christian religion.

The preachers, therefore, were of the opinion that the Jews might be permitted to reside in Hessia for the present, under the following conditions: they were to promise under oath to build no new synagogues; not to insult Christianity; to discuss their religion with theologians specifically appointed for this purpose; to attend sermons of Christians; and, finally, to obey the Law of Moses and the Prophets only, and not "those talmudic, godless fabrications" (meaning the teachings of the Talmud).

The preachers categorically rejected the recommendation of the Councillors that the Jews be permitted to engage in certain types of commerce and in a limited amount of money-lending, asserting that "the Jews had no scruples about defrauding people of other faiths." There was no necessity for the authorities, the preachers said, to seek to be more merciful than the Lord God Himself and to protect the wolves at the expense of the sheep. They therefore recommended that, in order to protect the poor people, the Jews should be barred from all business activity, moneylending and even from clean, profitable crafts, and allowed to do only such work as would be most toilsome and degrading.

This "Advice" from the preachers, which represents a strange mixture of ideas borrowed from canon law, the late Middle Ages, and the Reformation, was answered by Philip in a letter[24] which he addressed to the Governor and the Councillors bearing the date of December 23, 1538.

He categorically rejected all the Articles, since, as he put it, he could not "see why the Jews should be treated so harshly and kept within such narrow confines as suggested in the counsel from the learned gentlemen." He said that he had been unable to find, either in the Old Testament or in the New, anything to suggest that it was mandatory to deal cruelly and unkindly with the Jews. This circumstance, he pointed out, was the real reason why the early Christian emperors and bishops had always given them preference over the other unbelievers. Even if the Jews were the enemies of Christ as stated in the Gospels, it was still only right to love them for the sake of their forefathers. "For it is a splendid race from which Christ, our Savior, too, was born. The Apostles also came forth from this race that is familiar with the words which were uttered by God." Quoting from St. Paul's "Epistle to the Romans," Philip questioned whether the Lord could indeed have rejected His people after having chosen it as His own. And like St. Paul, Philip, too, cautioned against looking down with disdain upon the Jews, the branches of the true olive tree. "But if you should look down upon them, know that you have not begotten the root; it is the root that has begotten you."

Philip also felt compelled to reject the economic proposals made by the theologians. He explained his action by stating that "the Jews had shown more goodness and kindness to his subjects in matters of loans and money advances, and also had been less guilty of usury, than the Christians." He asserted that the recommendations of the learned gentlemen had been "formulated and constructed in such a narrow fashion" that if they were to be carried out the Jews would not be able to subsist in the country. "Therefore," he said, "if opinion is such, it would be more proper to tell them immediately and publicly to leave the country."

Philip sent to the Councillors ten articles he had drawn up as a basis for his "Laws Governing the Jewish Status" *(Judenordnung)*, which was published that same year (1539). According to these regulations, the Jews of Hessia were permitted to engage in "fair trade" and, under the supervision of a duly constituted authority, to lend money at an interest rate of five per cent. Severe penalties were instituted for usury, bribery, the purchase of stolen goods, and for sexual relations with Christians. The religious stipulations of the preachers were, in part, incorporated into the new *Judenordnung*. Jews were forbidden to build new synagogues, and it was further ordained that in the future, the Jews, together with their wives and children, were to attend sermons delivered by Protestant ministers.

Josel followed the developments in Hessia with close attention. In view of the fact that the two heads of the Schmalkald Confederation had set out to deal with the Jewish problem in the spirit of the "Christian State," Josel feared that the other Protestant Estates would be inspired to follow suit.

Since the time of his futile journey to Saxony, Josel had searched for ways and means to make personal contact with the leaders of the Protestant movement. It was not expected that an Imperial Diet would be held in the near future, for Charles was away from the *Reich* during those years. At such a gathering, Josel might have been able to influence public opinion as the advocate of his people under the auspices of the Emperor.

It was then, however, at this most crucial point, that an unexpected opportunity offered itself.

In February, 1539, the emissaries of the Emperor met with the Protestant Estates in Frankfort on the Main in a final attempt to arrive at an amicable settlement of the religious controversy.

Josel was also in attendance at this conference, which has been referred to as the "Frankfort Convention" (*Frankfurter Anstand*) because it ended in a temporary settlement between the Catholics and the Protestants. There Josel met not only Philip Melanchthon, Martin Butzer, Philip of Hesse, and John Frederick of Saxony, but also Joachim II of Brandenburg who, Josel relates,[25] had "likewise intended to expel all the Jews from his country."

Actually, it was not possible at that time to expel the Jews from the March of Brandenburg, since they already had been banished from there "for all time" in 1510. It was during the reign of Joachim I, the father of the Elector whom Josel met at the conference, that the host desecration trial had taken place in the March. The elder Joachim had not dared to arouse the ire of his Estates by readmitting the Jews. Shortly before his death, however, he had permitted a large number of Jews to do business in the country and to visit the annual fairs (1532 and 1535).

The younger Joachim's approach to the religious problem was entirely different from his predecessor's. Joachim I had remained devoted to the old Church.[26] In his desire to act as mediator between the two faiths, Joachim II, much as Henry VIII had done in England, set up an official Church

Establishment which was independent of both faiths, accepting both the concept of justification by faith from Protestantism, and the ceremonial of the divine service from Catholicism. But this innovation only succeeded in making him unpopular with his Protestant as well as his Catholic subjects.

Josel therefore had cause to fear that, in an effort to conciliate the Territorial Estates of the old faith and the new, who were united only in their hatred of the Jews, Joachim II would revoke the privileges which his father had granted to the Jewish traders.

However, as Josel puts it, "miracle upon miracle"[27] came to pass in Frankfort. Philip Melanchthon, Luther's closest associate, "presented creditable evidence" to the entire conference and to the Elector Joachim II in particular that the thirty-eight Jews who had been charged with host desecration and executed in 1510 in the March had been innocent.[28] It seemed that shortly before his own execution, Fromm, who had made the accusation, had admitted to his father confessor that his accusation of the Jews had been "falsehood and calumny."[29] Melanchthon alleged that the priest, driven by his conscience, had reported this confession to his superior, Bishop Jerome of Brandenburg, in an effort to secure a last-minute reprieve for the Jews who had been sentenced to burn at the stake; but the Bishop had forbidden him to make Paul Fromm's confession known to the Elector.

Melanchthon's solemn declaration carried considerable weight with the assembly, especially since Fromm's father confessor was then living in nearby Wuerttemberg, and had revealed the whole story after his conversion to Protestantism.[30]

Noting the profound impact of this disclosure on the assembled delegates, Josel, with characteristic common sense, turned the agitation of the princes to good use: he attempted to right the wrongs done his people, and demanded the restoration of the privileges, which actually had been irrevocable because they had been issued under solemn oath. He succeeded in prevailing on both John Frederick of Saxony and Joachim II of Brandenburg "to grant a firm foothold once more to the Jews in their lands."[31]

Immediately after returning to his country, John Frederick issued a mandate granting Jews permission to travel through the Electorate, and to procure letters of safe-conduct there.[32]

In a personal audience in Frankfort, Joachim II gave Josel the promise that he would allow the Jews to engage in trade and traffic in his country again.[33] "And he has kept that promise to this day," Josel was to write years later with deep gratification.

Only two months after the end of the Frankfort Convention, Joachim enacted a decree dated June 25, 1539, permitting the Jews to travel through Brandenburg and to visit the free markets, in view of the fact that the Emperor and other Estates had also accorded them these privileges.[34] In the early 1540's, to the great chagrin of Luther and of the Estates of the Electoral March, he even permitted Jews to take up permanent residence in Kurbrandenburg and befriended such Court Jews as Michel von Derenburg[35] and Lippold, Warden of the Mint, in whom he placed full trust and confidence.

It may be presumed that it was not merely pangs of conscience, or even Josel's representations, that moved Joachim to have mercy on the Jews. It is likely that this spendthrift gentleman, who delighted in riding to hounds and giving sumptuous feasts, and who was consequently deep in debt, was persuaded also by the prospect of future taxes and loans which would be raised for him by his Jewish subjects and court agents.

At this memorable meeting in Frankfort, which centered around the theological inquiry into acute religious questions, the Jewish problem was discussed by "many non-Jewish scholars." Josel, who participated in these disputations, succeeded in "convincing them, in the light of the Holy Torah, that Luther, Butzer and their followers had been in error, so that they came to agree with him."[36] When one of the scholars attacked Josel in "heated, angry and threatening" language, he answered him calmly, convinced that the spirit of God could not dwell in an angry man. "Would you, a learned man, indeed, threaten us, unfortunate people that we are?" he demanded. "Know that the Lord God has kept us alive since the days of Abraham. Surely He will preserve us in His mercy even from the wrath of such as you."[37]

Butzer himself reports[38] that a Jew (who could have been none other than Josel) had tried to convince him at the Frankfort Convention that the Christians were wronging the Jews greatly by their accusations. He had also shown him a book in which it was written that the Jews were duty-bound to seek the welfare of the heathens among whom they dwelled. However, Butzer had retorted that while Jewish and Christian books alike contained much that was good, the trouble was that many people did not practice what was preached in these writings. The fact remained that the Jews had been profiteering from usurious trade to an outrageous degree.

Josel bitterly complains[39] that Martin Butzer did not rest content with the accusations he had hurled at the Jews in Frankfort, and with the harsh "Advice" he had given in Cassel. He went so far as to "insult all the Jews together with the other great Estates," and to deal with them even more severely than the preachers of Hessia "without need or constraint (which would have warranted such action)."

Early in 1539, the "proposals" of the Hessian Councillors, the "Advice" from the preachers, and the conciliatory letter in which Philip gently put his theologians in their place appeared in print. [40] The general public, as well as Martin Butzer, assumed that the Jews themselves had procured the documents and published them in this form, so that the letter of the Landgrave might vindicate them and expose the Protestant preachers. This assumption can be neither confirmed nor denied in the light of existing sources, and thus remains a matter for speculation.

A Hessian friend wrote to Martin Butzer in Strasbourg that the Jews, "exceeding wroth" at the proposals of the preachers, had published the Landgrave's letter. He felt that in their anger, they would now heap insults on the Evangelical doctrine, and sing the praises of the Pope and his followers.

Butzer was greatly annoyed that the profound differences of opinion existing between himself and the Landgrave, whose closest advisor he fancied himself to be, should have been made public. He therefore countered the challenge from the Jews with a heated reply of his own.

The resulting pamphlet, entitled "Of the Jews,"[41] reiterated the recommendations of the Councillors, the advice from the theologians, and also contained a letter addressed by Butzer to an unnamed "gentleman and friend," an open reply to the communication that had been sent him from Hessia.

Butzer acknowledged that Philip had found the economic aspects of the counsel of the clerics too harsh, and had viewed the proposed ban on trading by Jews as tantamount to expelling all the Jews from the country. However, Butzer said, Philip had agreed with the theologians on all the other points. He had not desired the Jews to practice usury and thereby cause harm to come to the Christian religion, and it was his will, too, that they should listen to Protestant sermons, so that God might perhaps guide at least a few of them to the truth.

It was not so strange, he said, that the Jews, as his friend had written to him, should be more partial to the abominations of the Papists than to the pure doctrine of the Gospel. For, apart from the fact that the Papists worshipped graven images and idols and paid lip service to Christ, Judaism and the Catholic faith actually were one and the same.

Because the Jews of the present day were of that rotten seed which was persecuting the blessed seed, Butzer continued, because they were the foes of the true faith, as were the obdurate Papists, Turks, and other infidels, it should not be surprising that they should hate and detest the Evangelicals and favor the evil Papists.[42]

The advice from the Hessian preachers and the pamphlet by Butzer who, as late as 1537, had still given warm support to Capito's letter to Luther, caused a great stir and confusion among the people, who had already been severely shaken by the religious schism. Thus a poor Jew unable to defend himself was beaten and robbed of his possessions on the highway near Friedberg, outside Frankfort on the Main. His assailants hooted at their victim: "Jew, go and read Butzer's book. He writes that it is permitted to strip you of your possessions and to distribute them among the poor."[43] They were not punished.

The Jews of Hessia were particularly afraid that Butzer's bitter words might incur them the disfavor of Philip, and cause them many indignities in the future. But most of all, they were disturbed by the decree in the *Judenordnung* that stated they would be forced to attend sermons delivered by the Protestant clerics.

In their distress they turned to Josel, asking him to advise them what stand to take toward the authorities and the Protestant preachers, without either acting contrary to their duty as loyal subjects or causing harm to their own souls.

In a treatise entitled "Letter of Consolation from Joseph (i) or Josel to His Brethren Against the Booklet by Butzer,"[44] which was meant to be read to the Hessian Jews in Hebrew at Sabbath services in their synagogues, Josel gave them "faithful advice from the holy biblical and prophetic writings."

He then had the pamphlet translated into German and sent it to the Magistrate of Strasbourg, who had become greatly incensed at the attacks of the Hessian Jews on the leading reformer of the city, so that he might satisfy himself that it contained no insults or defamatory remarks against any person or persons.[45]

Of this document, too, only fragments have survived, but these comprise two complementary texts. One is an excerpt written partly in Latin and partly in German by one of the Town Clerks for the Magistrate. The second text, which is more detailed, is in German, and obviously represents a word-for-word translation of Josel's original Hebrew letter. But due to the fact that entire pages are missing, it is not possible to understand the connection between many of the passages.

What is certain, however, is that this document, as its title implies, was meant to be a "letter of consolation," and at the same time a religious tract and hortatory message. As opposed to the formal tone and pathos that characterizes the language of *The Holy Path,* the style of this letter, like that of the didactic poems and dialogues of that period, is simple and colloquial, lucid and timely. True, Josel drew upon the Scriptures, and on prophetic literature in particular, for his parables and allegories. But he relied to an equal extent on the historical events of his own time and on his own experiences in political life to help him point out to his brethren the deeper import of the catastrophe that had befallen them—a catastrophe such as had come to them again and again in their past history and which they had been able to overcome each time because they were filled with imperturbable faith in the profound and unfathomable ways of their God.

With heartfelt words and deep compassion, he addresses himself directly to his "dear and good friends and brethren in Israel." It is as if his every word echoed the lament of that suffering prophet of the Babylonian exile: "Comfort ye, comfort ye, my people."

He allayed the fears of the Hessian Jews that the Landgrave, provoked by Butzer, might turn against them, pointing out that God had endowed the leaders of the nations with sufficient intelligence so that they would not be swayed by the malicious clamor of the mobs but would, instead, protect the Jewish people from its accusers. The greater the sovereigns, he said, the greater the grace they received from God, the deeper their understanding of the Holy Scriptures, and the more conciliatory their attitude. He recalled to his brethren the protection which the city of Strasbourg had given them at the time of the Peasants' War; the expulsion of Margaritha, the accuser, from Augsburg by Charles V; Capito's good letter to Martin Luther; Philip Melanchthon's disclosure of the innocence of the Jews from Brandenburg; and the freedoms which the Electors of Brandenburg and Saxony had conferred upon them. Indeed, Josel asserted, even Butzer's vicious tract had a point in its favor, for it had clearly given the lie to a rumor which Josel himself had already sought to combat at the Augsburg Diet; namely, that the Jews were to blame for the rise of Protestantism.

As to the question of whether or not the Jews should attend sermons by Protestant ministers as required by the *Judenordnung,* Josel pointed out that each individual should be free to make his own decision. Whoever deemed the ordinance to represent religious coercion, and felt that to comply with it would be equivalent to "casting some doubts on his faith," should follow the dictates of his heart and disregard the law. On the other hand, this ordinance did not pose a threat to pious and learned Jews, whom nothing could sway from their religious convictions. In fact, he, himself, had attended several lectures by Wolfgang Capito "because of his great scholarship," and left only when he began to preach matters of faith, since that had been unpleasant for him.

Josel suggested that if the authorities should demand a confession of faith from the Jews, they should answer in the words of the Prophet Malachi: that they loved and worshipped only the One God Who was the Lord and Who would never change, and that they remembered the Law of Moses, the servant of the Lord, which Yahweh had commanded to him for all Israel, "even statutes and ordinances."

He requested his brethren not to engage in debates with Christians about their faith, and cautioned them against making derogatory statements about Martin Butzer. For he maintained that if Butzer's attacks on the Jews had been motivated by no other consideration but love and faith and zeal for his God, they were not evil. On the other hand, if the "rash judgments" which that man had passed on the Jewish people did not find favor in the eyes of the Lord, the Lord Himself would reveal His displeasure in due time, and make known whether the man had acted for the sake of God or out of a "poisoned mind."

In view of the fact that the question of whether Jews should be permitted to continue moneylending had been discussed in the recommendations of the Councillors, in the "Advice" of the preachers, and in the Ten Articles of the Landgrave Philip, Josel, too, felt called upon to give his opinion on the problem.

He pointed out that God had given them permission to accept interest from strangers. Therefore, in view of the fact that the nations in whose midst they dwelt had imposed on them greater financial burdens in the form of tolls, safe-conduct, annual tribute and other imposts than on any other people on earth, the Jews were compelled to regard these nations as strangers and to charge them interest so that they might procure the necessities of life. "But if this heavy burden were to be removed from us," Josel declared, "we would more readily desist from this practice than many other peoples who have no such justification for usury."

However, he continued angrily, there were among the Jews many ignorant and foolish men who did not rest content with the small earnings allowed them, but were taking greater profit than was permitted by their law. These were the people whose selfishness had given rise to "such disputations and letters against all the Jews." Dispersed among the peoples of the earth, these Jews had been infected with greed, pride, disloyalty and all the other vices which had caused mankind to stray from the paths of God ever since the Fall of Adam. Like their Christian contemporaries, the Jews, too, had come to worship money, wealth and worldly possessions, and envy and discord were rampant in their midst because they lacked the wisdom to study the Holy Scriptures.

Josel admonished his brethren impressively not to put the blame for the misfortune that had befallen them as much on the machinations of their enemies as on their own sinful ways; to take stock of their own shortcomings before pronouncing the Christians guilty, and to do their penance quietly and in solitude, so that they might find a way to repentance, purification and moral rebirth.

However, Josel's final admonition and message of consolation said: "Be pious and suffer; then you will be saved from the scheming of Martin Butzer."

By this he meant to imply that, in addition to deserved sufferings, God also imposed undeserved troubles on His people. Suffering was the means through which men whom

God had favored and chosen would become aware of their mission. Suffering, bravely and gladly borne, would not cast a pall on their existence; rather it would elevate their lives and bring them nearer to perfection. "For just as the olive yields up its oil only in the press, so Israel, too, must suffer in order that it may be restored to goodness."

Josel's serene confidence, as proclaimed in his letter of consolation, that God had endowed the great men of the nations with the ability to understand the Holy Scriptures and thus to save the Jews from the superstitions of the populace, was borne out sooner than could have been expected.

It happened at this time that a young peasant boy disappeared without a trace from the village of Sappenfeld, near Eichstaett. After a long search, his decomposed body was found in Weissenburg Forest. The Jews of the nearby town of Tittingen, which was in the territory of the Count Palatine Otto Heinrich of Neuburg, were accused of having murdered the child and were placed under arrest.[46] Josel went through a great deal of trouble until he finally succeeded, with the help of the Supreme Court of Justice, in convincing the Count Palatine of Neuburg and the Masters of Pappenheim, who owned the Weissenburg Forest, that the accused were innocent and in obtaining their release.

What Josel fails to indicate in his rather sketchy report of the incident is that Jews outside of Tittingen were also implicated in the accusation. Moritz von Hutten, the Bishop of Eichstaett, of whose diocese the village of Sappenfeld was evidently a part, had the boy's corpse, which had been mangled, circumcised, and branded with a cross,[47] taken to Eichstaett—probably with the intention of making the boy another St. Simon of Trent, and establishing a new place of pilgrimage in his bishopric.

With this purpose in mind, he summoned the Jews of the neighboring Franconian domains to the Episcopal Court, in order to convict them of ritual murder. But neither the ordeal through which they were put nor the judicial investigation yielded the hoped-for results, and the judges were forced to acquit the defendants.

In view of the fact that Josel makes no mention of the Bishop of Eichstaett, it may be assumed that he intervened in behalf of the prisoners from Tittingen only. The other accused Jews were aided by a courageous statement made in their defense by a Protestant cleric at a time when another Protestant, Martin Butzer, was persecuting the Jews of Hessia in the name of the Evangel.

While the investigation was taking place in Eichstaett, two Jews from Sulzbach, in the Upper Palatinate, submitted to the Episcopal Counselors a "timely tract," an anonymous treatise which was printed without place or date of publication. It "submitted to the judgment of all and sundry whether it is true and believable that the Jews were secretly strangling the children of the Christians and making use of their blood," and bore the motto "he who sheds the blood of another, his blood shall also be shed."[48]

Originally, this tract had been a confidential communication in letter form, written by the author shortly after the ritual murder trial of Poesing in 1529, to a gentleman, apparently one of high rank. The questioner had asked him for his views on blood libel in general and on the burning of the victims of the Poesing accusation in particular.

While the name of the addressee is unknown to this day, the contemporaries of the writer already suspected that he was none other than Andreas Osiander, pastor of the Church of St. Lawrence in Nuremberg, who lived in the area of Eichstaett and Neuburg. Osiander was the first to defend the Jews against the blood libel. His independent and upright conduct even toward Luther had made him unpopular with the unbending followers of the reformer. It was known that

Osiander, under the influence of Reuchlin, was engaged in the study of the Cabbala, that he was corresponding with Elijah Levita, the noted Hebraist, and that he had a thorough knowledge of rabbinic literature, Jewish laws and customs, the Talmud, and the Jewish privileges. It was no secret that he had a command of the Hebrew language, which he had studied under Johann Boeschenstein in Ingolstadt, and that he had brought to Nuremberg Woelfflein of Schnaittach, a Jewish schoolmaster, for the express purpose of obtaining additional instruction in the "Chaldean" tongue.

In his statement, Osiander declared it inconceivable that the Jews should murder children and make use of their blood. For their own law, which they had received from God Himself and which was binding upon them for all time, not only forbade them to kill a human being, but even prohibited them from making use of the blood of animals which was, after all, entirely harmless. It had never come to pass, he pointed out, that baptized Jews, no matter how much they might have detested their former co-religionists, had accused Jews of ritual murder. If Jews from time to time had pleaded guilty to these charges, he wrote, they had done so only under the agonies of torture in a state of temporary insanity.

Osiander listed the following seven causes for the recurrent accusations of ritual murder:

1. Poor, debt-ridden or despotic rulers who would avail themselves of the blood-libel charge as a means of ridding themselves of their Jewish creditors.

2. Senators, judges and jurymen near the sovereign whose negative attitude toward the Jews reflected that of their ruler.

3. Priests and monks who hoped to acquire an aura of great sanctity and to set up new places of pilgrimage by doing away with the Jews.

4. Heavily indebted citizens who hoped to rid themselves of their obligations by way of such accusations.

5. Magicians and exorcists who used the bodies of murdered children for their black arts and then blamed their crimes on the Jews.

6. The death of children from unknown causes, for which there was no other explanation but that they had been murdered by the Jews.

7. The death of children due to parental neglect. Parents of such children placed the blame on the Jews in order to escape prosecution by the law.

The counselors of the Bishop of Eichstaett assigned to Professor Johannes Eck of Ingolstadt the task of composing a rebuttal to Osiander's statement on the ritual-murder libel, a practice which Osiander said "imparted an evil smell to the name of Christianity." Eck, the most learned and vociferous advocate of Catholicism in Germany, the most dangerous opponent of Luther, and the most implacable exponent of medieval ecclesiasticism, framed his reply in a tract entitled *Ains Judenbuechlins Verlegung* ("On the Publication of a Jew Book").[49] In this tract, which was to acquire widespread notoriety, Eck revived all the accusations that had been made against the "cunning, false, perjured, thievish, vindictive and traitorous Jews" through the centuries, defended the true Christian faith by openly branding the "Lutheran corrupter as a braggart, a bearer of tales, a miserable slanderer, a bribed protector of the Jews," and "a villainous defamer of Christianity," and called for new and more stringent laws to combat the Jewish vermin.

Josel might have had an opportunity to present a public refutation of Eck's tract, the most abusive to have been written against the Jews even in that "Age of Grobianism." For in the spring of 1541, he traveled "on official business" to the Imperial Diet of Regensburg,[50] where Eck carried on his heated debates with the Protestants Butzer, Melanchthon, and Pistorius on such questions as personal justification, original sin, the sacraments, and the priesthood.[51]

Perhaps it was due to Eck's serious indisposition during that session that the disputation did not take place. Or it may have been that Josel was wary of attacking the leader of the Catholics in the presence of the Emperor, who reconfirmed the privileges of Innsbruck and Augsburg at this Diet[52] and forbade the Estates, on pain of severe penalty, to force their Jewish subjects to wear Jewish badges outside their places of residence.[53]

Again "on business," Josel was on hand also at the next Imperial Diet which King Ferdinand, representing the Emperor who was then abroad, convened at Speyer in 1542.

This "business" was related to Josel's efforts on behalf of the Jews of Prague, who had suffered "a disastrous fate" at that time.[54]

During the reign of Ferdinand, the heated struggle between the Estates of Bohemia, who had proposed the expulsion of the Jews at every Provincial Diet, and the King, who wanted to retain his prerogative over the Jews *(Judenregal)*, came to a head. As late as 1534, Ferdinand himself, who was in need of the Jewish tribute, had given his protection to the Jews of Kremsier, and in 1535 he had advised the Margrave of Ansbach against expelling the Jews from the Duchies of Silesia.

So too, in 1538, when the Bohemian Chamber proposed that the Jews be given notice to leave the country, so as to put an end to the exhausting disputes with the Estates and particularly with the Magistrate of Prague, the King could not be prevailed upon to abandon his political principles.

Only after the complaints had taken on increasingly strong implications, when the Jews were being accused of spying and of divulging military secrets to the Turks, and when they were actually blamed for the terrible fires that swept through the forests of Bohemia during the severe winter of 1541-42, did Ferdinand, who was sorely pressed by the Turks and dependent upon his subjects for financial assistance, yield to the widespread demands.

Early in 1542, he opened negotiations with the Jews of Bohemia. On January 22 of that year, he decreed that the homes of the expelled Jews, particularly those in the Jewish section of Prague, be turned over to the craftsmen of the city. The mass emigration, for which he gave official permission at the Imperial Diet of Speyer, took place that April. However, Ferdinand permitted some of the most distinguished and wealthy Jews to remain in Prague for a time in order to settle the affairs of the Jewish community, to collect outstanding debts, and to sell immovables. In addition, he guaranteed safe-conduct and Royal protection to the emigrés who were departing for Poland, Turkey and the border territories.

Actually, the expulsion of the Jews from Prague was never completed. Those who remained, together with their families, kinsfolk, schoolmasters, religious functionaries and servants, still represented a sizeable community. Eventually, in 1546, Ferdinand issued to them a "free and unlimited safe-conduct" since he wanted to enable a limited number of Jews to remain in Prague in peace and safety.

Josel believed that this favorable outcome was due to his own endeavors at the Diet of Speyer, and to the influence of certain Jews in Prague.

"At the urging of the public, I hurried to the aid of our brethren, together with other influential persons in Prague, in order to plead with the King. And God beheld the great fast, the mortification, the penitence, the prayer and the charity and permitted a remnant to stay behind until, in the end, I lived to see the inhabitants return to their former homes, increase and multiply, and rebuild what had been destroyed."[55]

CHAPTER SEVEN

THE APOLOGIST

IN the letter he sent to Josel in 1537, Martin Luther announced his intention to discuss the Jewish problem in a more detailed work. But six years were to pass before he carried out his plan, and revealed to all the world that his attitude toward the People of the Book had undergone a radical change.

In his work, *Against the Sabbatarians,*[1] which was published in 1538, he had already argued controversially with the Jews, who, as the corrupters of the Christians, having been led astray by their rabbis, no longer received comfort from the prophets and no longer perceived either signs or miracles. He sought to make it clear to them that their fifteen centuries of exile, bereft of Temple and Priests, should be ample proof that God had turned His countenance from them and had abandoned them. Nevertheless, he had still made this one final, though resigned, attempt to convert them and to show them, by the example of their own history, and by the misery which they had experienced, that the time of their chosenhood was at an end.

During the years that followed, he delivered his famous lectures on the Book of Genesis and particularly on the

"Covenant of Circumcision." At that time, he delved deeply into the works of the medieval biblical exegetes, Nicolaus Lyranus and Petrus Burgensis, of the rabbinical commentators of the Middle Ages and of his own day, and of Hebraists such as Servet and Sebastian Muenster, who had been taught by Jews. But he also studied anti-Jewish tracts such as Lyra's *Pulcherrimae quaestiones Judaicam perfidiam in catholica fide improbantes,* Burgos' *Scrutinium Scripturarum,* Salvatus Porchetus' *Victoria adversus impios Hebraeos*[2] and Margaritha's *The Whole Jewish Faith.*

The effect of these works on his thinking; his profound disagreement with the Jewish interpreters of the Holy Scriptures and those non-Jewish scholars who adhered to their views; his fury at what he assumed to be missionary activity on the part of the Jews in Moravia; his concern with the acute problem of usury in his own day; his anger at individual Jews whom he felt had deceived, ridiculed or menaced him; his irritability and excitability which increased with advancing age; his intolerance to opposition and his hypersensitivity to criticism; and his growing depression, which vented itself in increasingly reckless attacks even on his own followers—all prepared the ground for his tract entitled *Of the Jews and Their Lies,* which he published in 1543.[3]

The immediate purpose of this work was to answer a sharp critique, probably written by a Jew, of his "Letter Against the Sabbatarians." The tract, which has been lost, was framed in the form of a dialogue between a Jew and a Christian and, according to Luther, presumed to "distort the sayings of the Scriptures and to overthrow the foundations of the Christian faith."

In his work, Luther asserted that he had no intention of writing anything either about or against the Jews, for in view of their obduracy he felt that there was no chance for their conversion. Yet, his conscience impelled him to warn the German people against their arts of seduction, to counteract their vile intentions, and to expose their lies.

These were the four "lies" which he sought to disprove:

1. The Jews gloried in their noble descent from Abraham, Sarah, Isaac, Rebekkah, Jacob, the twelve Patriarchs and the holy people of Israel. They praised the Lord for having set them apart from the heathens, and for not having made them *goyim,* and they demanded that, on account of their noble lineage, the Lord should make them masters over all the world. However, they failed to realize that the heathens, as descendants of Noah's son Japhet, had claim to the same nobility, glory and honor as the seed of Shem. The Jews did not know that all men who are conceived in sin are subject to God's wrath and damnation—so that they could not be the people or the children of God, either by birth or by nature.

2. They boasted that the Lord had set them apart from all other nations and sanctified them by the covenant of circumcision. But they failed to grasp the actual meaning of the scriptural passage in which Abraham was commanded to circumcise all those born in his household—not only his sons, but his servants and slaves as well. Thus the Ishmaelites and the Edomites, who were also of the seed of Abraham, had likewise accepted the law of circumcision and passed it on to their children and grandchildren. Moreover, God had made the covenant of circumcision with them only in order that they might observe His word in spirit, deep within their "circumcised hearts." But the Jews had disregarded this commandment, for they had failed to circumcise their hearts. They had dissociated the law from the symbol, and this had done away with the spirit that the ancient covenant had symbolized.

3. They further boasted that God had given them the Law on Mount Sinai and had spoken to them Himself; indeed, they claimed that He had entered into a marriage with them

as a bridegroom would with his bride. But the woman whom God had taken as His bride had become a vile hussy, a whore, full of envy and greed, malice and wrath. She had become disobedient and obstinate and even less worthy of belonging to God than the Devil in Hell. True, she possessed the Commandments, but she did not observe them. The Word of God might have gone forth to her, but she no longer heard it.

4. They gloried in having received the land of Canaan, the city of Jerusalem, their laws and their ritual from none other than God Himself, but "they are not mindful of the reason why they received them."

God had allowed the kings of Babylonia and Assyria to take them away from their country, and He had let the Romans destroy their Holy City. Thus God had not cared for their Temple, their priests and their princes. Yet their necks had remained unbowed, and their brazen brows had not blushed with shame. For fifteen centuries they had been banished and rejected, but they still clung to the foolish belief that God would lead them back into their land "because of their merits."

But far worse than their arrogant boastings, was their belief that the Messiah was yet to come, a belief in which they would stubbornly persist even if God Himself were to proclaim atop Mount Sinai or from the Temple of Jerusalem that the Messiah had come long ago. Jacob and Moses, David and Daniel, the Prophets and the Psalmists had foretold the coming of the Son of God in countless sayings and indeed, the "true Jews of the ancient days" had still known that this Messiah would inherit the scepter and realm after the fall of Judah. But the Jews of the present day were no longer aware of this Divine promise. Their accursed rabbis were deliberately and willfully poisoning their youth with their lame and blasphemous subterfuges, and they corrupted, distorted and defiled the clear and unambiguous meaning of the Holy

Scriptures with their cunning and delusions. They even dared teach that God would fulfill His promise not for the sake of His mercy and compassion, but because of their own merits.

Even as the Sadducees in the olden days had taught that there were neither angels nor devils, and that there was no Heaven or Hell, so the Jews now claimed that it was not a sin to break a vow or to rob or kill a heathen. They cursed the Christians in their synagogues and called down every conceivable calamity on the heads of the Gentiles. Furthermore, they practiced idolatry with signs and figures, and they referred to Christ as a sorcerer, as the Prince of Devils, and as the son of a whore who had committed adultery with a blacksmith.

Save for the Devil, the heathens had no enemy more evil, poisonous, and violent than those bloodthirsty dogs, the murderers of Christianity. It was for this reason that history texts had so often blamed them for the poisoning of wells and the murder of children.

Their complaint to God that they were being held prisoner by the Christians, to whom they referred as Haman and Edom, was also an unmitigated lie. It was rather the unfortunate Christians who were being tortured, persecuted and held captive in their own country by the Jews, who wanted to seize all the wealth and power of the world, and who did nothing but sit by the fire, loafing, roasting pears, guzzling and boozing.

How, Luther asked, could the Christians atone for their guilt, make amends for still not having avenged the blood of Christ, for protecting the synagogues, the homes, the lives and the wealth of the Jews, for permitting them to dwell unmolested in their countries, despite all the murder and rape which these people had committed?

Luther's answer to his own question was that "in addition to prayer and the fear of God," the Christians would have to "practice rigorous mercy, and see whether they might be able to save at least a few of them from the flames and the fire."

Luther had the following "sincere advice" to give as to the practical application of this "rigorous mercy."

1. Their synagogues should be set on fire. Pitch and brimstone should be added to the flames, and whatever will not burn should be buried, so that not even a stone may be seen, forever and ever.

2. Their houses should be destroyed, and they should be herded into a stable like gypsies, so that they may know that they are not masters of the land but prisoners in exile.

3. Their prayerbooks, the Talmud, and the Bible, should be taken from them, so that they should no longer have the power to curse God and Christ.

4. Rabbis should be forbidden, on pain of death, to give religious instruction, to praise God and to worship Him in public, so that they will no longer be able to commit blasphemy.

5. Their safe-conduct and the right to travel on the highways of the Empire should be revoked.

6. They should be forbidden to practice usury, and their money, their jewels, their gold and their silver should be confiscated, because everything they possess has been unlawfully acquired by theft and usury. Although they claim that Moses permitted them to charge interest on loans, this commandment was applicable only to the Jews in Moses' time who dwelt in Canaan, and not to the Jews of the Emperor who live dispersed among the nations. In their case, the law of Moses no longer applies, since the Imperial law is binding upon them.

7. Jewish men and women who are young and strong should be given flails, axes, spades, distaff and spindle so that they may earn their living by the sweat of their brow, though it would be far better for the welfare of the citizens if the

Jews were to be driven from the country, even as they were expelled from Spain, France, Bohemia and the Imperial cities.

In the concluding passages of the work, which is replete with countless quotations from the Bible and learned textual commentaries, Luther again reminded the Christians of the great difference between their Messiah, who was immortal, and the worldly Messiah of the Jews.

The Messiah of the Christians, he said, was the Resurrection and the Life, the intermediary between man and God. While he did not bring his followers worldly riches, he gave them happiness and good cheer, and far from making them vindictive and bitter, he made them kind and merciful, even in their dealings with their enemies.

The Messiah for whom the Jews waited, on the other hand, would come from the Fool's Paradise. He would fill their bellies with food and would secure for them the gold, the silver, the goods and the wealth, the land and the people of the heathens. The kingdom of the Jewish Messiah would be a kingdom of this world, of earthly joys and earthly pleasures, and the Jews would rejoice in their Messiah like sows which "have not eaten of the Apple and know not the difference between good and evil."

Luther's book, *Of the Jews and Their Lies,* was published in January 1543. Four months later, Josel addressed a memorial to the Magistrate of Strasbourg.[4] He stated that he could not understand how a man who had bowed in fear and humility before the infinite majesty of God could have been capable of publishing "such a crude, inhuman book full of abuse and slander." At the time he still thought that Luther, torn by inner conflicts, was suffering from a temporary spell of insanity, or that he had been under the influence of "Mameluke, apostate Jews," when he had written the book. He still felt that it might be possible to open Luther's eyes by appealing to his reason, or by discussing the controversial biblical texts with him, or at least to convince the public of the absurd character of the accusations which "truly do not apply to our faith and to all Jewry."

Josel brought his request before the Magistrate of Strasbourg rather than directly to Luther because the reformer had refused to grant him a personal interview in 1537. Josel offered to engage in debate, either verbally or in writing, with Luther or anyone else "who would be willing to undertake such a task," or to refute the book *Of the Jews and Their Lies* "with all sincerity and impartiality" in the presence of all the scholars in the Empire with quotations from prophetic literature, even as he had disproved the accusations of Margaritha at the Imperial Diet of Augsburg. For it was neither just nor fair, he declared, to allow honest and pious people to be insulted or condemned without a hearing on the basis of slanderous statements made by one man.

Moreover, he asked the Magistrate not to permit a new edition of this dangerous tract to be distributed in the Strasbourg area, since the population, already goaded on by Luther's threats, was insulting and cursing the Jews, saying, "they will kill us."

In their reply, the Councillors did not even deign to consider Josel's proposal of a disputation. But since it had been reported to them that the pastor of Hochfelden had called on his congregation from the pulpit to attack and kill the Jews, they, too, doubted the wisdom of permitting the publication of a second edition of the tract. They promised Josel that they would prohibit the publication in the area of their jurisdiction, and that they would urge the ministers "not to preach turmoil from the pulpit," for "the authorities knew what to do."

In the conclusion of his tract, Luther prayed to God to relent in His wrath and to put an end to the sufferings of the Jews "for His dear Son's sake."

But Luther's own anger still continued unabated. Only two months later, he published a book entitled *Of the Shem Hamphoras and the Race of Christ.*[5] This work, too, was intended to open the eyes of the Germans to the Jewish peril. Its avowed purpose was to demonstrate, especially to those who had let themselves be drawn into the Jewish religion, what their attitude should be toward this diabolic creed. He no longer desired to convert the Jews, since, after all, it was impossible to turn the Devil into an angel, Hell into Heaven, death into life, and sin into holiness.

The first half of the work is a translation of Chapter 11 of Porchetus' *Victoria adversus impios Hebraeos,* which asserted that the Jews had always been a vicious people, and accused them of having written a disgraceful and blasphemous book against Christ. In their book, the Jews had attributed all the miracles wrought by the Savior to the fact that he had fraudulently gained possession of the *Shem Hamphoras* [the Tetragrammaton], which had been graven on a rock and carefully guarded in the Temple of Jerusalem.

According to Luther, this *Shem Hamphoras,* or "Expounded Name," was a secret magic formula, composed of the letters of verses 19-21 of the fourteenth chapter of the Book of Exodus, and containing "the great Name of the God Jehovah, which is called the Tetragrammaton."

Even at the present time, Luther told his readers, the Jews still believed that their knowledge of this Name conferred supernatural powers upon them, and that, by cabbalistic arts and magic incantations, by juggling numbers and making combinations of insignificant, lifeless, and meaningless letters, they would be able to gain control over the angels and even to do the work of God Himself.

These raving, stupid fools not only showed their contempt of the true and everlasting God by their disobedience and blasphemy, but also sought to make of Him a slave far beneath all the Devils, so that He and His wondrous Divine power might bear testimony for evil and serve the purposes of the Devil's lies and calumnies.

It would not be surprising if the Christians were plunged into the depths of Hell in punishment for having tolerated these accursed slanderers in their midst. Their only excuse could be that they had known nothing of their monstrous deeds before this time. "However, dear Princes and Lords," Luther declared, "Know that if in the future you will give protection to Jews, I beg to be absolved from guilt. They heap insult not only upon Christ, our Lord, and hence also upon His Father, but upon the Divine Majesty of God the Father Himself even more than upon Christ."

Luther's proposal to the authorities that the synagogues of the Jews should be burned, their prayerbooks and copies of the Talmud confiscated, their rabbis prohibited from giving religious instruction and conducting services, and that the Jews be forced to perform hard physical labor was not carried out anywhere in the *Reich.* However, some of the Protestant princes accepted his recommendation that the Jews be expelled. Johann von Kuestrin, Margrave of the New March (*Neumark*), a zealous follower of the new doctrine, revoked the safe-conduct of the Jews under his jurisdiction soon after the publication of Luther's tracts. But his brother, the Elector Joachim II of Brandenburg, took pity on the Jews. That tolerant sovereign had no intention of breaking the promise he had given Josel in 1539 by doing the bidding of the zealous reformer. He merely calmly rejected Luther's evil slurs on the Jewish alchemists he had befriended. John Agricola, Joachim's court chaplain, whom some even accused of having taken bribes from the Jews, openly spoke out against George Buchholzer, the Dean of Berlin, when the latter held forth from his pulpit on the perfidy of the Jews.

John Frederick of Saxony, on the other hand, issued a mandate in May 1543, revoking the concessions he had made to the Jews in 1539, and forbidding them to travel through the country on pain of severe penalty. He explicitly gave as the reason for his change of heart the fact that the works of Martin Luther had made it clear to him that the Jews had been spreading false doctrines.

But a threat even greater than that posed to the Jews by official decrees and trading restrictions was the hostile mood of the populace, which had been stirred up by these publications, and the widespread opinion that "one can obtain forgiveness by destroying a Jew or his property."[6]

Josel dealt with this new danger in a long memorial addressed to the Magistrate of Strasbourg, which he had written "for the sake of myself and my brethren on the tenth day of the eleventh month of the year, five thousand three hundred and three years after the Creation of the World according to the reckoning of the Jews" (July 11, 1543). He pointed out that the Jews in various localities of Saxony and Brunswick had already been "sorely beset, robbed and driven away." He therefore begged the Councillors to intercede with the reigning princes of those provinces on behalf of his brethren, and to convince the members of the Schmalkald Confederation that "in these swiftly moving times" it was imperative to keep the King's peace and not to revoke the royal right to protect the Jews.

In contrast to Luther's crude *Shem Hamphoras,* Josel's memorial is couched in the language of quiet, inner emotion and dignified composure. His letter reflects the superiority of a wise man, sure of his cause, who construes the wild polemics of his opponent as a tumult of unconscious and uncontrollable forces. Knowing this, he makes no attempt to refute Luther's accusations point by point, even as it is of no avail to use words or reason in fighting the fires of a volcano, the raging of the storm, or the roaring of the waves.

In his memorial Josel merely drew comparisons, with subtle irony, between his own ancient faith and the new faith of Luther. He made mention once again of his futile journey to Saxony, where he had gone to plead the cause of his people, and where Luther had refused to receive him. For he had fancied himself to be above God and the Prophets, even as he now did as he sought to destroy the Jews and deprive them even of their hope for a better world to come. For God, for His part, had never thought it beneath Him to prepare sinful men for the imminent judgment, and to give a gracious hearing to those who would intercede in their behalf. Thus He had warned Abraham of His intention to destroy Sodom and Gomorrah, and He had listened with forbearance and compassion to Abraham's plea that He have mercy on these sinful cities. The Prophets, too, stern and inexorable though they had been with the people, had never deprived them of the tidings of comfort that God still loved them despite their sins, and would eventually turn His countenance toward them once more.

For this reason, Josel declared, it was inconceivable that a man of scholarship should deal with them in such a despotic and violent fashion, and so burden their consciences. If the intent was to outlaw them and to deprive them of their rights simply because they did not share Martin Luther's beliefs, such action could have dire consequences. For Luther was also defaming persons much greater and mightier than the unfortunate oppressed Jews, accusing them of worshipping the Golden Calf of Aaron. He, Josel, had no intention of laboring the point of what Luther meant by this, for he had no desire to become involved in all these controversies and disputations.

His only purpose was to offer strenuous opposition to

Luther's accusation that his forefathers had written "insulting things" about the Messiah and the faith of the Christians. The Jews of his own day, Josel asserted, knew nothing of such libelous writings, and he himself, an old man, had never read a book of that kind. Moreover, Wolfgang Capito, who was well-versed in Jewish texts and commentaries and also in the Talmud, had told him that he had never found such remarks in the books of the Jews. And, even assuming that the Jews in ancient times might have written ill of the Messiah, the Jews of the present day could not be blamed for that.

The contents of the Holy Books were entirely different from Luther's insinuations. The belief of the Jews was the belief in the Ten Commandments, in the message of the Prophets, and in the Law. Since the text of the Holy Scriptures was not easy to understand, the seventy Elders of the Temple, and holy men such as Daniel and Ezra, and other great teachers after them had explained and expounded the biblical texts, and it was from these commentaries that the Talmud had evolved.

The Talmud explained how the Holy Covenant, the holidays, the commandments and the ceremonies of Judaism should be observed; it was a compendium of judicial procedure and civil law which bade the Jews to live in humility, honesty and piety. The Talmud contained no attacks on anyone; indeed, the study of the Talmud contributed to the understanding of the true character of the Messiah.

By these allusions, Josel meant to reveal the contrast between Luther's notion that there was no value in observing the Law, and the Jewish concept of devotion to the laws and precepts which God had given to His people.

Josel contrasted Luther's doctrine that "whatever man fulfills of his own free will is sin" with the Jewish tenet that man may atone for his sins only by good deeds, performed of his own free will, and by lofty tasks deliberately undertaken. And while Luther proclaimed that only the grace of God could cause the believer in Christ to become a righteous man, Josel maintained that only he could be righteous who toiled and strove, who pursued the paths of God and assisted Him in His work.

In *Of the Jews and Their Lies,* Luther had admonished the Protestant preachers to have no mercy on the people which had been condemned by its own God. Josel, however, reminded the Magistrate of Strasbourg in his letter that God had vowed to take revenge on the King of Babylonia because that ruler had shown no mercy to the prisoners committed to his keeping.

Luther had called upon the reigning princes to refuse all protection to the Jews and to drive them away like mad dogs. Josel countered with a reference to God's promise to the Prophet Jeremiah that His wrath would strike the tyrants who had carried off His flock.

Luther was convinced that the Jews were deserving of more severe punishment than even the peoples of Sodom and Gomorrah, that physical destruction alone was not sufficient atonement for their sins. To this, Josel remarked that according to the Book of Daniel, Darius, the King of Persia and Media, had stood so greatly in awe of the power of the living God that he had caused the men who had slandered the prophet to be thrown to the lions in the pit.

In his answer,[7] the Magistrate of Strasbourg promised that he would prohibit the printing of Luther's works in his territory, but he refused to intercede with his allied reigning princes and cities in behalf of their imperiled Jewish subjects.

Unlike Saxony, with which he was on friendly terms, Philip, the Landgrave of Hesse, was not ready to expel his Jews. However, he now felt compelled to add several restrictions to the *Judenordnung* of 1539. In a new decree, he forbade the Jews of Hessia to engage in moneylending, discounting and coining transactions, and commanded all Jewish men, women and children regularly to attend the sermons delivered by the Protestant clergy.

In an attempt to prevail on Philip to revoke or at least to modify this new mandate, Josel once again requested a letter of introduction of the Magistrate of Strasbourg to that "kind and righteous prince, a man great in the understanding of the Holy Scriptures."[8] Every God-fearing individual, he pointed out, was bidden by natural as well as Divine law to guard his fellow-man from all trouble and hurt. If he, Josel, were ever in a position to render aid to a stranger, even one who was not of his religion, he would help him even at the risk of his own life. How much more so, then, was he obligated not to shirk the task of standing by his own brethren in their distress.

However, his request was again refused, this time on the grounds that "one is not certain of his meaning." He was instructed to appeal to his immediate superior, the *Unterlandvogt,* or, as a last resort, to the Elector Palatine.

In his tract *Of the Jews and Their Lies,* Luther had written of reports in history texts that Jews had murdered children in order to use their blood for ceremonial purposes. But these charges were not confined to the history books of the past. As Josel well knew, they were very much a part of his own day and he was dealing with harsh reality.

That very year in which Luther's writings were published, Josel was called to Wuerzburg to aid a man, three women and a young girl who had been charged with having murdered a child who had been found dead.[9] By the time Josel and the two men who traveled with him arrived at the Episcopal residence, the suspects were already in prison and had been "tortured almost to death."

He was told that a scoundrel[10] had attempted to seduce the girl, but that all his powers of persuasion had failed owing to her innocence and courage. It was due to her stubborn resistance that the charge of ritual murder had been made against these four people.

Throughout the four weeks (December 30, 1543 - January 28, 1544) which he spent in Wuerzburg, plying the Bishop with offers of huge sums of money in an effort to persuade him to revoke the death sentence, Josel gave comfort and cheer to the prisoners and explained to them the deeper meaning of their martyrdom. He told them of the countless martyrs among their people who had proudly gone to their deaths with their heads held high, because they had deemed it a great privilege to be permitted to die bearing witness to the unity of God.

Josel reports with pride that the brave young girl, for whom he had felt particular compassion, had "sanctified the Name of the Lord by bearing up under tortures for over thirty-two weeks." The other prisoners, too, had borne their terrible sufferings with superhuman endurance, and their torturers had been unable to wrest a confession from them.

Since all his efforts to change the Bishop's mind had been to no avail, Josel left Wuerzburg at the end of January. Several days later, he appeared at Speyer, where the Emperor had convened a new Imperial Diet.

At this Diet, Charles was not primarily seeking to adjust the religious differences in his realm. He wished rather to obtain increased political support from the reigning princes, or, as one author puts it, "to become the leader of an aristocracy of German princes."

He believed that his cherished dream of the restoration of the medieval Emperorship to its former splendor and holy purpose, and of the re-establishment of the union between the Empire and the Church, even in opposition to the Pope, was about to be fulfilled. Those around him, including his enemies, realized that they were no longer dealing with the shy, retiring King of Spain, but with the mightiest sovereign in Christendom, a ruler who was willing and ready to suppress the revolt of the Evangelicals and to translate his plans for his Empire and the world into reality.

In his personal account of the Imperial Diet of Speyer, Charles himself writes that he "realized at that time that it was not only no longer beyond the bounds of possibility, but that, indeed, given the proper circumstances and suitable means, it should be an easy thing to crush the arrogance of the apostates by force."

However, the hour of decision had not yet come for Charles. The Turks had taken Gran and Stuhlweissenburg, and their navy was already sailing on the Tyrrhenian Sea. Francis I, in league with the Ottomans and the pirates of Algiers, had embarked on his third war against the House of Habsburg, and it was to be expected that some of the princes of the Schmalkald Confederation would ally with him.

Charles gave his promise to the Protestants that he would stop the lawsuits pending against them at the Supreme Court of Justice (*Kammergericht*) and revoke all the Final Decrees enacted by the Diet against them if the Estates of the *Reich* would agree to give him substantial assistance in money, arms, and troops for his defensive war.

While the Emperor was engaged in these momentous negotiations, Josel appeared in Speyer in order to register his complaint with the "rightful sovereign lord" of German Jewry with regard to the new ritual-murder accusation at Wuerzburg, the restrictions placed on money trade by Jews, the venomous writings of Luther, the expulsion of Jews from various territories, the constant danger to their lives and their arrest and torture "without lawful judgment."

In a privilege that has since become famous,[11] under

date of April 3, 1544, Charles declared that he had given a favorable hearing to the appeal of the German Jews and reconfirmed all the freedoms and privileges which his ancestors and he himself had issued to them. He granted them safe-conduct, and guaranteed them the right to engage in trade and traffic on land and at sea unmolested, and he forbade the closing of synagogues and the expulsion of Jews from the principalities, counties and other territories of the realm, particularly from the Imperial towns where they had been residing at the time of his accession. He reiterated the provision which he had already made in his decree of 1541 that no Jew should be forced to wear the Jews' badge outside his place of residence, and he vowed that he would inflict unusual and severe punishment on anyone who dared to attack them.

"Whereas the Jews and Jewesses in most of the territories of the *Reich* have been burdened and taxed much more heavily than the Christians with regard to life, assets and property, and whereas they have neither landed property nor other respectable occupations, offices or crafts among the Christians which would enable them to make capital payments and support themselves, except for such sustenance as they can attain by means of their cash assets; now therefore do We permit and allow said Jews once again to . . . invest and employ their cash assets for their needs and profit at interest and at rates proportionately higher . . . than those allowed the Christians and that such practices on their part be tolerated."

Charles further mentioned in his privilege that the Jews were being accused of using the blood of Christians "for their needs," and that they were being taken to court on unsubstantiated charges made against them by slanderers or envious antagonists, all despite the fact that the Popes had strictly forbidden such dealings, and his own beloved ancestor, the Emperor Frederick II, had taken severe and drastic steps against this injustice.

As "sovereign lord and judge" of the Jews, Charles therefore decreed that no Jewish man or woman, irrespective of station, should in the future be arrested, tormented, tortured, stripped of his or her possessions or put to death unless adequate evidence and proof of his or her guilt could be furnished by reliable witnesses. In the future, all such accusations made against Jews first had to be reported to the Emperor as the "supreme authority" over the Jews, and all action against the accused had to await the Emperor's sentence.

This privilege, issued by Charles V in April 1544, the most liberal and generous ever to have been granted to the Jews, corresponded article for article with the demands and the wishes which Josel had made for years. The article pertaining to moneylending at interest was practically a word-for-word restatement of the thoughts which Josel had expressed in his "letter of consolation to his brethren,"[12] and the protests of the Popes and of Frederick II against blood libel had been mentioned in Josel's memorial to King Ferdinand after the Poesing ritual murder of 1529.

The Emperor explicitly declared that he had deemed it necessary to issue this privilege after hearing the grievances of the Jews in Speyer. Josel was therefore right when he exultantly asserted that at this particular Imperial Diet, Charles had granted to the Jews freedoms and privileges the like of which no Emperor or King had ever granted them before.[13]

While it may be said that Josel was the real author of this "Magna Carta," there were other determining factors behind the issuance of this document.

As we have already pointed out, Charles considered himself the rightful heir of the emperors of the Middle Ages. Thus, as he had always deemed it binding upon the sovereign "to adhere closely to the exact terms of all agreements, even those made with unbelievers, never to act in violation of letters and contracts at the expense of others, and not to waive any privilege which he had inherited,"[14] as the guardian of a great tradition he was duty-bound to follow in the footsteps of his ancestors in their policy toward the Jews, and to preserve for the serfs of the Imperial Chamber all the privileges which had been conferred upon them in the past. Hence, in the article of the Privilege of Speyer in which he rejected the blood libel as a lie, he expressly referred to the decree enacted by his "beloved ancestor" Frederick II of the House of Hohenstaufen.

However, Charles considered himself not only the lawful descendant of the Salic and Hohenstaufen dynasties, but also the true heir of the Caesars of ancient Rome. He was the autocratic bearer of absolute authority. If, as the German Emperor, he was duty-bound to preserve time-honored customs, he was also authorized as *"princeps legibus solutus"* to "make changes in the ancient law."

Like the medieval rulers, he, too, still regarded the Jews as serfs of his Imperial Chamber, as a prerogative of the Crown which was his to protect and defend against the pretensions of the princes and the cities. But now he referred to himself also as their "supreme lord and judge," and as their "highest authority." This meant that he now considered them subjects of the *Reich* according to ancient Roman law, by virtue of which they had enjoyed—although with some limitations—the rights of citizenship in the old *Imperium Romanum.*

Hence it would be wronging Charles to regard the Privilege of Speyer as a sort of reward for the assistance which the Jews had been ready to supply at the time to help carry on the campaign against France. Unlike his predecessors, Charles never regarded the Jews of the *Reich* as an asset which he could exploit, mortgage, or give away at will. Even in the worst financial crises, and at times when he himself was in need of funds, and despite constant warfare at home and abroad, he required the Jews to pay a special tax on only one occasion, at the Imperial Diet of Speyer.

He did not even demand the customary Crown Tax, and it seems that the golden tribute penny *(Goldene Opferpfennig)*, which the *Reichsrabbiner* Samuel had been empowered to collect for the Imperial Treasury, was very rarely levied.[15]

The war against Francis I, which had been declared at the Diet of Speyer, was waged in person by Charles in the summer of 1544. He invaded France with his troops, laid siege to St. Dizier, and by September he had reached Chateau Thierry, just twenty hours away from Paris. In that month Francis was forced to sign the Peace of Crépy with the Emperor, thus putting an end to the struggle for Burgundy and Italy and for supremacy in Europe, which the Houses of Habsburg and Valois had carried on for decades. Francis agreed to make no further alliances with the Protestants and, in case of armed conflict between the rebellious Estates and the Emperor, to make his troops available to the latter.

"In the year 1545,"[16] Josel records in his memoirs,[17] "the Emperor set out with a mighty army to do battle with the King of France, and he pushed forward until he came to a place near Paris. (On this account) authorized officials went about the country to obtain pledges of war contributions from the Jews of Germany." Eventually, Josel relates, German Jewry agreed to raise a total of three thousand florins, of which four hundred were earmarked for the Emperor's personal use, and they had made donations of gifts in the value of an additional one thousand florins.

At the Diet of Worms in 1545, Charles acknowledged that "Our Jew, Josel of Rosheim, Commander of all Our Jewry in the Holy Empire . . . paid in cash the sum of three thousand Rhenish florins in behalf of Our said Jewry at Our request, which sum We have graciously accepted from him."[18] However, he explicitly declared that this financial assistance for his defensive war did not represent a change in his policy, and that it was not to be construed as prejudicial in any manner to the privileges and freedoms which he was reconfirming for the Jews in appreciation for the help they had given him.

But even while Charles, at that Diet of Worms, was assuring the Jews of his Imperial grace and favor, a commission of the united Estates, which had been appointed to "deliberate on good and permanent police regulations" was proposing that the Jews be expelled from the entire *Reich.* Thus the subjects of the Empire would no longer suffer untold damage from their usury, and they would no longer inform the Turks of developments within the *Reich.*

"At that time, while I was in Worms," Josel relates,[19] "all the princes and potentates decided to expel the Jews and to have the Emperor grant them a permit to do so. However, a good man—may his memory be a blessing—came forth and explained to them that this could not be done, for, according to the laws and precepts, they had to be retained within the domain of the Roman Emperor and King." Thereupon, Josel records, the Estates decided unanimously not to expel the Jews, in view of the fact that they had enjoyed protection, shelter and safe-conduct in the *Reich* from of old.

Josel does not mention the name of the "good man" who had objected to the planned expulsion. But in all likelihood this protector of the Jews was a devout Catholic, for, according the Josel's report, he had alluded in his argument to that early medieval Christian doctrine which stated that the Jews, though they were doomed to eternal servitude, must never be entirely wiped out. A remnant had to be saved until the end of days so that, by their very existence and sufferings, they might bear witness to the eternal truths of the prophecies contained in the Bible.

The decision which the Emperor had not felt ready to make at the Imperial Diets in Speyer and Worms because he had not judged the political situation to be sufficiently secure at the time was finally made at the Diet of Regensburg in 1546.

By that time a five-year armistice had been signed with the Turks, Charles had been victorious in France, and the disturbances in the Low Countries had been quelled. For the first time since Charles had come to the throne, the borders of the *Reich,* in the east as well as in the west, were secure. The Duke of Bavaria, whose chancellor, Leonhard von Eck, had for years allied with the enemies of Charles both at home and abroad, now openly took the Emperor's side for the sake of the unity and the preservation of the Catholic faith.

The youthful Duke Maurice of Saxe-Meissen, the Albertine, a son-in-law of Philip of Hesse, the most ambitious and unscrupulous prince in the Protestant movement, was lured away from his allies by the promise that he would be given the Electorate of Saxony, formerly held by his cousin John Frederick, and the protectorate over the Episcopal sees of Magdeburg and Halberstadt.

The Emperor's advisors were convinced that the Schmalkald princes were divided and lacked outstanding leadership, and that the younger generation had lost its faith in the Evangel after the rulers had used it as an excuse for secularizing bishoprics and annexing whole territories to their own domains.

Although the "rebellious and insubordinate princes of Saxony and their followers stayed away,"[20] and Charles was determined "to draw the sword for the preservation of his holy Catholic faith and in the interest of Christianity,"[21] the

Diet, at least to all outer appearances, adhered to the traditional forms. The mood of the Emperor seemed to be one of peace and, contrary to his usual habit, he participated in the colorful courtly festivities and entertainments.

Josel had come to Regensburg for the purpose of receiving the great Privilege which the Emperor had promised him in Speyer in 1544, but which he still had not confirmed at that time [1546].

"At that Diet, in Regensburg," Josel relates, "I made a public appeal to the Emperor to keep his promise and thus, with the help of God, the agreements were written down and sealed by the Emperor with his own hand."[22]

The war was officially begun on June 16. Charles had made known throughout the land that it was not his wish to take action against the new religion. His intention, he declared, was merely to mete out punishment to the disobedient elements who had insulted and injured the Emperor's majesty and authority and had sought to wreck the entire *Reich.* On July 20, the disloyal, perjured instigators and rebels—the Landgrave of Hesse and the Elector of Saxony—were put under the ban of the *Reich.*

Throughout those weeks of suspense and excitement, while the Schmalkald troops, well-armed and superior in numbers to the opposition, massed in Augsburg under the command of Schaertlin von Burtenbach, the military commander of the cities of Upper Germany, and while the Imperial mercenaries still were stationed in the Low Countries, Hungary and Italy, Josel remained in Regensburg near the Emperor.

It was not without some personal risk that Josel remained in this open and unprotected city where the Diet was held. The majority of the Regensburg population had embraced the new faith and loathed "Charles of Ghent," the "Spaniolish Emperor" and "destroyer of the Gospels," who sought to "bring the free Germans under his yoke and had perjured himself against the German land."[23]

In addition, Schaertlin von Burtenbach had occupied Fuessen in the meanwhile, and was planning to march on Regensburg with his troops, capture the city and take the Emperor captive. He probably would have been able to carry out this plan at the time, if the Protestant leaders of the Confederation had not imprudently called him back to Swabia to join forces with the troops of the Elector of Saxony and the Landgrave of Hesse.

Josel had good reason for persevering in this precarious position. The Spanish mercenaries, whom the Emperor had imported into Germany to fight against the Schmalkaldians, were notorious for their violence and cruelty. Reports circulated to the effect that they looted people's homes and that women and maidens were not safe from defilement and rape. Josel might well have recalled the conduct of the Swiss mercenaries who had imperiled the lives of the Jews in the Alsace during the Burgundian War.

He therefore turned to Nicholas Perrenet, Master of Granvelle, the shrewd, worldly wise and amiable Burgundian minister to the Emperor[24] who was known to be responsive to flattery, who was not disinclined to accept gifts, and who played an influential part in the decisions made by Charles.

Josel, who probably spared neither money nor gifts, turned Perrenet's influence to good advantage in behalf of his brethren.

"Then the Emperor decided to muster an army and to march against those two princes (the Elector of Saxony and the Landgrave of Hesse)," Josel relates in his memoirs.[25] "Thus there came into the country foreign troops, the Spaniards, who fell upon the Jews. But God was at my side when I came to the great ruler, who was known as the Lord of

Granvelle, and who was second only to the Emperor, to ask him to request the Emperor to protect us. He stood by us, saying to the Emperor: 'Behold, the Jews have suffered so much at the hands of the apostate Lutherans, and now your own people, the *Sephardim* (Spaniards) have come to deliver them up (to death) in spite of the new privileges which you have issued to them yesterday and the day before.' And the Emperor agreed to make a proclamation as follows: 'It is not right to kill the Jews. Let it therefore be decreed and sealed on pain of punishment that no man from any of Our armies may lift up either his hand or his foot to injure or harm any Jew whatsoever.' And messengers sped through all of Germany forthwith, proclaiming that anyone who would violate this prohibition would be liable to the death penalty. All at once, the mercenaries became well-disposed toward the Jews, and when the Emperor and his army went forth into battle, the Jews supplied the mercenaries with bread and wine."

The Emperor, satisfied that the Jews were supplying his troops with provisions, issued a mandate ordering "the troops, German and foreign alike" of all the nations to spare the Jews of the entire *Reich,* and not to violate either the King's peace of the land or the right of safe-conduct.[26]

In the first weeks of August, Charles left Regensburg and, after his troops joined him on August 12, he took shelter in a permanent camp near Ingolstadt.

At that same time Josel set out on the homeward journey to Rosheim, where he arrived on August 20.

But the return journey, made on horseback, did not go smoothly. The Schmalkald troops, who had taken up positions near Donauwoerth and other places in Swabia, and who sat idle while waiting for the Emperor's men, ate and drank their fill, gambled, quarrelled and uttered blasphemies. One of the chaplains recorded that they were "robbing and plundering the poor, our friends—and this is not natural at all—even as much as the enemies."

The Jews met with the same fate. During his journey, Josel received the news that the captains and the troopers of the Schmalkald army had taken several Jews prisoner and had broken into their homes and looted or destroyed their possessions so that "many poor widows and orphans had been despoiled and driven from their homes."

Particularly grim was the news from Ries on the Danube and from the town of Wallerstein in the County of Oettingen, where the Jews had been forced to give a large amount of money to the captains and the mercenaries. Those who were in no position to make such payments or who could not furnish receipts for monies paid were ruthlessly turned over to the barbarous troopers.

No one had dared to bring up the Emperor's mandate, which was said to be valid for the entire *Reich,* to the enemy captains in the service of the outlawed princes, "because they were not under the protection of the Emperor and the *Reich.*"[27]

No sooner had Josel arrived at Rosheim after an arduous journey on horseback than he set out again, this time for Strasbourg, in order to appeal to the Magistrate to protect the victims of persecution there. But now, for the first time in all the years of his activity, he was denied admittance to the city and was asked to submit his petition in writing.[28] Several days later, however, the Magistrate decided to make an exception in his case, and to allow him entry, saying that they were now ready to give ear to his request. But all other Jews were forbidden to set foot in the city.[29]

The meeting took place on September 1. Josel made a forceful and impassioned appeal to the Magistrate to have mercy on the Jews, even as he had taken pity on them at the time of the Peasants' War, and to prevail upon his Schmalkaldic allies to spare the Jews from compulsory war contributions, looting and murder.[30]

However, the Councillors refused his request, giving Josel to understand that they were unwilling to admit strangers to the city in "these dangerous and troubled times." "Therefore," he was told, "let things remain as they are with the Jews for the time being." With regard to his pillaged co-religionists in Swabia, it was suggested that he communicate with those who caused the damage, for they would know how to best answer him.[31]

The Magistrate had good cause to speak of "troubled times" and to view the future with foreboding. For just then, despite their great numerical superiority over the opposing forces, the Schmalkaldic troops which had laid siege to Ingolstadt had to retreat without storming the walls of the fortress. Josel mentions that the princes of Saxony and Hesse, together with the free Imperial cities, had mustered over one hundred thousand men in infantry and armored cavalry, while the Emperor's army numbered only forty thousand.[32]

Charles slowly followed the Schmalkaldians into Swabia. Without an open battle, he managed to seize all the permanent positions of the enemy. Due to the failure of the promised French and Danish support to materialize, the Schmalkaldians had lost the confidence of the early days of the war, when public opinion had extolled the Protestants as the saviors of the imperiled German freedom and as the proud heirs of Ariovist and Arminius.

In the fall and winter months of that year, all the cities of Swabia and Franconia fell to the Emperor. They were forced to prostrate themselves before him as a sign of degradation and to pay the heavy fine imposed by the conqueror. Strasbourg, throughout that period, had been negotiating with Francis I of France. Now, Francis having failed her, Strasbourg, too, was forced to surrender to the victorious Emperor in February 1547.

In December, 1546, after only a brief siege, the Protestant city of Frankfort surrendered to the Emperor's commander, Count Maximilian von Bueren. Since the unruly Spanish mercenaries were terrorizing the populace of the city, the Jews, fearing that they would meet with the same disaster as their Christian fellow-citizens, asked Josel "to put in a good word for them with the commander-in-chief, Count von Bueren."[33]

Josel relates[34] that originally the Emperor had not intended to lay siege to Frankfort at all, but that when the enemy army was sighted near the city, the populace was seized with such panic that the Councillors went forth to the city gates in abject humility to meet the commander and beg his forgiveness for having rebelled against the sovereign head of the *Reich.* Count von Bueren accepted their surrender on behalf of the Emperor, but insisted that it be unconditional and that he be allowed to deal with the burghers as he saw fit.

As for Josel, he was very kindly received by the Count when he conferred with him in behalf of the Jews of Frankfort and presented him with a gift of eight hundred gold florins. "But the Jews," Josel relates, "were safe in the streets of the city. The mercenaries sold to them the loot they had captured at Feuchtwangen and Darmstadt, so that they made a goodly amount of money. Thus our mourning was turned into joy."[35]

Charles had been able to conquer Southern and Western Germany with such ease because John Frederick of Saxony had been forced to leave the Swabian theater of operations in order to come to the rescue of his own country, which had been invaded by Duke Maurice, his cousin and the ally of the Emperor.

Charles, crippled by gout, his strength sapped by unremitting toil and worry, had grown old before his time. But with the courage typical of him, he shook off his sufferings of body and mind. Against the advice of his physicians, he followed his troops from the south to the north of the *Reich* in order "to hunt down" John Frederick, leader of the heretical princes and his long-time enemy. In April, 1547, Charles came upon him near Muehlberg on the Elbe. Helped by the Hussite Bohemians in Magdeburg or Wittenberg, he was all but in retreat to defend himself against Alba, the Emperor's general.

In shining armor, helmet and plumes, a long spear in his hand, the Emperor himself took part in the battle in which John Frederick lost his freedom, his Electoral title, and his Electorate.

Shortly thereafter, Philip of Hesse also capitulated, his surrender symbolized by the act of prostration. Like John Frederick, he, too, had to march as prisoner with the Emperor's Court. Exulting in his victory over religious and political opposition, Charles declared that he "came, he saw, and God conquered."

In his petition of 1546 to the Magistrate of Strasbourg, Josel had stressed that the Jews, living dispersed throughout the world and having neither land nor troops, and therefore giving no cause for war, would remain neutral in the struggle between the two opposing powers. However, deep in his heart, Josel's feelings were not neutral. Although he sensed something of the great and solemn tragedy of this historic event, in which "for the first time in history there was open battle on German soil over the paramount problems of religious life as well as the social order," he could not forget that Luther had threatened his brethren with death and destruction, that John Frederick had expelled them from his country, that Butzer had spoken out against them in his

"Advice," and that the city of Strasbourg had closed its gates to them. Nor was he willing or able to forget that it was the Emperor who had safeguarded their right to engage in commerce, had protected their lives and possessions, set free the prisoners of Wuerzburg, and had testified to their innocence for all the world to hear.

"But we, the Jewish people," he records in his account of the temper of German Jewry during the Schmalkald War, "uttered fervent prayers in Frankfort on the Main in the morning and in the evening, calling on our Father and King in Heaven, on the one Almighty God Whose power would be able to help even the smaller of the armies win the victory, beseeching Him to protect our Emperor and thus also us Jews. . . . The victory which the Emperor won came to pass in the year 1546. The All-merciful God in His compassion wrought great miracles for us as well, in that no Jew suffered harm in this terrible civil war in which Germans fought against Germans in bitter hatred."[36]

At that point Josel openly took the side of the Imperial Sovereign, opposing the various powers whose good will and favor he had labored so long to obtain.

His action was not motivated merely by considerations of political expediency. He did not simply take advantage of the political situation with detachment and common sense, or decide to act as he did after a practical consideration of the events of those fateful years. Vaguely and unconsciously, there still lived within his memory that legend which he had heard long ago in the "Alsatian Land": the legend of the return of an Emperor of Peace, a crowned Messiah, who would come forth from the mountain "in garments white as snow, riding on a white horse, with bow and sword in his hand" to sit in judgment over the corruption of men, to raise up the poor and the oppressed, and to restore justice and right "in deliverance and liberty before God."

CHAPTER EIGHT

HISTORIAN, PHILOSOPHER, EDUCATOR

JOSEL'S memoirs end with the year 1547, with the account of the Emperor's victory over his Protestant adversary, who had also been the fiercest enemy of the Jews. At that time when Josel, proud and exultant, could consider the struggle of his life at an end, he felt called upon to record the happenings of his eventful past and to render an account to himself of all the experiences that had come his way during those forty years of indefatigable and extraordinary activity.

He was influenced in this decision by any number of motivations. He took an almost childlike pleasure in storytelling, and he was greatly interested in recounting events of interest, describing dramatic scenes, instructing his contemporaries by means of parables and allegories, and gaining a realistic grasp of historic moments. He had an innate sense of history which impelled him to seek the causes and effects of events, and to attempt to relate them to one another.

Josel was like the humanists of his day who, inspired by their studies of the great historians of antiquity, assiduously gathered the legal material, documents, writs and inscriptions of the Middle Ages in order to throw new light on the history of their own people, and to gain a better understanding of their own era through knowledge of the past. He diligently studied Imperial and Royal privileges, papal bulls, and the minute books of city councils in order to establish the legal position of his people, to utilize the historical testimonials as authoritative evidence in his apologetic writings, and to preserve the documents as such for posterity.[1]

Even as many of his contemporaries wrote down their memoirs, autobiographies, diaries and family chronicles[2] in order to give an account of political and military events in which they had been actively involved, or to tell of economic attainments which had led them from obscure anonymity into the light of a life of wealth and contentment, or in order to describe the perils and adventures they had experienced in strange and newly discovered lands, so Josel, too, felt it his duty to preserve the story of his life for posterity.

But unlike Schaertlin von Burtenbach, Goetz von Berlichingen, Hermann von Weinsberg, Bartholomew Sastrow or Thomas Platter, Josel did not write his memoirs in order to erect a memorial to his own person, to vindicate himself, or to present the story of his own bravery in the face of severe trials as an example for his descendants to emulate.

Josel's aim was not to give an account of his personal experiences and recollections, but to record for posterity the memory of the "severe afflictions," and "to relate the great and fearful things over which his soul weeps in secret."[3]

A direct inducement for writing his memoirs was provided by an experience Josel had during his attempt in Wuerzburg in 1544 to save the Jews who had been accused of ritual murder from execution. At that time he was most painfully upset by the recollection of the fate which had befallen his great-uncles at Endingen long before, and which in many respects was similar to that of the prisoners whom he had now come to defend, and also by the memory of the sufferings of his own parents, who had been in such a precarious situation during the Burgundian War. The past and the present merged before his eyes, and the indissoluble tie between consecutive generations, which now seemed bound together forever by a common link of tragic fate, came to him as a new revelation.

In those days a prayerbook was brought to him, on the first page of which one Jacob ben Yitzhak of Nuremberg had recorded the history of the persecution of the Jews of the Alsace during the Burgundian War.[4] When the Jews had been driven from their homes in the Alsace, this prayerbook had fallen into the hands of a clergyman of Colmar, who in turn had sold it to Jacob ben Yitzhak of Nuremberg and on that occasion had told him of the "terrible fate that had befallen the Jews of the Alsace."[5]

"And when I came here," we read in Josel's memoirs for the year 1544,[6] "I told myself: It is proper that I should write down now that which I have heard from my father and my mother."

But he did not deem the notes of Jacob ben Yitzhak and the accounts of his parents as sufficient historical source material for the events that had taken place before his birth. He made inquiries of old people who had lived through the persecutions, and of his own mother-in-law, whose nephew had been among those forcibly baptized. It seems that he also studied the memorial books of the Jewish communities of the Alsace, for a pertinent entry in the memorial book of Niederehnheim conforms to Josel's own account.[7] Thus Josel was in a position not only to give a dramatic account of the persecutions, even to the point of reporting how cold it had been at the time, but also to state the numbers of those rescued, killed, and baptized, and to record for posterity the names of the cities where the Jews were forced to take refuge, the name of the rescuer, and even the name of the servant who had brought the ransom money.

For the events in which he himself had been actively involved, he needed no "true and accurate documentation" to cite as supporting evidence. But he must have availed himself of personal notes and copies of his petitions to the Emperor, to the *Landvoegte* and to the city Magistrates as aids to his memory.

Nevertheless, as methodically and accurately as Josel expresses himself, and as objective as he is with regard to his personal experiences, it is not possible to gain an understanding of Josel's extensive political activity from his memoirs without the aid of other historical sources.

For instance, he tells us nothing of the "Articles and Ordinances" which he drew up for the Jews in 1530, and he speaks of his disputation with Margaritha and his relations with Luther only in passing. His memoirs contain no information on the contents of the privileges which he obtained from the Emperor, or on his activities on behalf of the Hessian Jews, his work as *parnas* of Lower Alsatian Jewry, his relations with German Jewry, or the litigation which he was forced to carry on at the Imperial Supreme Court of Justice *(Reichskammergericht)*.

By contrast, Isaac Abrabanel, the Spanish diplomat and courtier, and a contemporary of Josel, begins his own reminiscences with an account of his personal career.[8] He acquaints his readers with his father, his grandfather and his illustrious forebears, who traced their descent to King David. He gives a vivid description of his spacious home in Lisbon, which was a meeting place for scholars, and a "hall of justice and learning," as he put it. He tells of his pleasant relations with King Alfonso V, of the great honors conferred upon him, and finally of the bitter fate of exile that befell him and tore the soul from his body so that, like Job, he became as dust and ashes.

Josel's memoirs, however, begin with an account of the ritual murder of Endingen. When he tells the story of his great-uncles, he does so not because they were his relatives, but because they had suffered martyrdom. When he writes of his parents, he mentions them not as his closest kin but as witnesses of the persecution of 1477. He reports to us that his sister was married to one Isaac ben Yehiel of Pamseh, who was a son or grandson of the man from Colmar who saved the Jews at the time of the Burgundian War; but he is not out to boast of this distinguished family connection. His purpose simply is to demonstrate, by the example of the "humble" descendants of this "good man," who "all attained honor and wealth," that "he who devotes his life and property to save the lives of others will enjoy the fruits in this world, while the principal will remain for him and his descendants in the world to come."[9]

He fails to mention the date and place of his birth, the cities in which he lived, the names of his teachers, and the people and influences that helped to shape his character. He does not even record the name of the woman he married and the number of children she bore him. This was not due to false modesty, or lack of self-confidence and self-assurance. Nor was Josel a stranger to introspection or to the emotions of the soul. The very fact that he was the first German Jew to write down his life reminiscences shows how profoundly he had been influenced by the spirit of his times, which had "placed man in the center of the world so that he may freely look around on all sides and choose his own position in it," as Erasmus put it.

It was not the story of his own life but the history of the German Jews that Josel quite deliberately made the theme of his memoirs. This is the reason why he set them down in the stern, almost impersonal form of annals, in which he recorded the events as they happened, year by year. His own personality figures in these accounts only because he had been actively involved in the happenings he discusses.

In his circumspect manner, Josel sought to relate the events of Jewish history in his own day to the developments of history in general. Thus he linked the persecution of the Jews in 1477 with the war of Charles the Bold, Duke of Burgundy and with the deeds of the "evil" Swiss, the loss of his pledges and securities with the Landshut War of Succession, the expulsion of the Jews from Regensburg with the death of Maximilian in 1519, their perilous situation in 1525 with the Peasants' War, and their deliverance in 1547 with the victory of the Catholics over the Protestant party.

But the prudent politician and the retrospective historian were at variance in both theory and practice. Josel's interpretation of history, like that of his predecessors who had reflected on the course of the history of their people,[10] was strongly colored by theological and metaphysical concepts. In everyday life, Josel could establish a connection between cause and effect, and trace the unwholesome position of the Jews in society to the unhealthy conditions that prevailed in the society and economy of his day. But Josel the theorist viewed the era in which he lived simply as another manifestation of the will and the workings of God, by which He had always revealed Himself to His people.

According to this latter view, the concept of natural evolution is alien to Jewish history, for the history of the Jews is unlike that of all other peoples. Even as the Jewish people is not led by a king of flesh and blood but by God Himself, and even as "a wondrous Providence is the foundation and bedrock of the very existence of the Jews,"[11] so, too, every individual who is charged with the task of leading this people acts only as an instrument in the hands of this all-knowing and all-merciful God. Miracles such as those which came to pass on Mount Sinai and in the land of Israel long ago still occur in the present day. Again and again, we see God's great mercy revealed in miraculous ways. Over and over again in history He avenges the insult offered His people and the blood of His servants that is shed, and proves that He has not cast aside His children even though they now dwell in the lands of their foes.

Thus, again and again, as Josel points out, He wreaked His vengeance on the Swiss for the Jews who had been murdered in the Burgundian War. He sent angels of destruction to the manorial lords in the Alsace who had wanted to expel the Jews in 1528 so that three of the plotters of evil succumbed to sudden illness, and the fourth was slain by his enemies at his own residence. The Elector of Saxony, who did not keep his promise and had done them harm, suffered defeat and ignominious captivity at the hands of the Emperor.

When Pfefferkorn had planned to burn the books of the Jews, God had mercy on His people in their distress and wrought miracle after miracle, sending a Gentile scholar to save them from the heretic's schemes. And when Martin Butzer debased and endangered the Jews of Hessia, the Lord revealed the innocence of the martyrs in the March of Brandenburg who had been accused of host desecration and burned at the stake.

"This profound and unfathomable secret is revealed in the infinite and various mercies which God has vouchsafed unto us at all times.[12] Indeed, we have now beheld it with our own eyes. A nation which founded a new faith with all sorts of modifications and attempted to cast off every yoke, plotted to attack us and to destroy the Israelite nation by many oppressive decrees and abuses so that it might cease to be a people. But God saw the distress of His people and He sent His angel in the persons of compassionate kings, who gave power and strength to the Emperor Charles to defeat the enemies over and over again, to frustrate their alliances and conspiracies, to subdue them and to conquer their cities and provinces without effort. He (the Emperor Charles) won the battle in a miraculous manner and saved the Israelite nation from the might of this new faith, which had been founded by a monk called Martin Luther, who is impure,[13] and who planned to wipe out all the Jews, young and old, and to slay them."

However, it was Josel's opinion that the miracles wrought by God would not have come to pass without the cooperation of pious and righteous men.

He attributed the success of his own mission in 1528 to his arduous pilgrimage on foot from Rosheim to Prague, because he believed that by much toil and hardship, prayer and fasting, he had been able to bring about a change for the better in the situation of his brethren.

He believed, too, that the Jewish community of Frankfort had been spared in the Schmalkaldic War through the merits of its pious men, who devoted themselves with sacred zeal to the study of the Torah.

When the Jews were about to be expelled from Prague in 1542, "God permitted a remnant to stay behind because He had beheld the great fast, the mortification, the penitence, the prayer and the charity. . . ."

But the singular and distressing fate that had befallen them during the decades in which he had been their leader had not been caused solely by the malice of others. Even as the Spanish Jews, after their expulsion from Spain, attributed their misfortunes to their own sins and transgressions, so Josel, too, was not content to place the blame for the misery of the Jews in Germany on external circumstances.

In his negotiations with the Imperial authorities and the municipal magistrates, he had uncovered in a most realistic manner the factors that had led to the expulsion of the Jews, and in his "Articles and Regulations," he had endeavored to improve the position of his people in society so as not to endanger their right to reside in the cities. But in his theoretical interpretation of history, he viewed the persecution of his people as a punishment inflicted by God because his brethren had become envious and grasping, thirsty for power, quarrelsome, greedy and avaricious, disunited and insubordinate, and because they had forsaken the faith of their fathers.

Josel discussed these problems in greater detail in his classic work, entitled *Sefer Ha-Mikneh* (The Book of Acquisitions).[14]

The *Sefer Ha-Mikneh,* which has not survived in its entirety (the extant manuscript begins on page 62, chapter seven), is a strange *mixtum compositum.* It seems that Josel took it with him on all his long journeys, and that whenever he had a leisure hour, he confided to it his thoughts and recollections, his doubts and hopes. At the end of Part One,[15] he writes that he completed this section "on the day before the New Moon of Elul 306 according to the lesser reckoning (1546) at the Court of the Emperor in the city of Regensburg."

The manuscript consists of several ethical and religio-philosophical treatises, commentaries on biblical passages, interpretations of "the words of the sages and more recent scholars," explanations of Aggadic texts and Midrashim, copies of excerpts from the works of medieval philosophers and cabbalists, accounts of historical events, and personal reminiscences.

On superficial examination, the work would appear to be a random and haphazard miscellany of scholarly notes, accumulated over many years by a hungry mind striving for knowledge and understanding.

The fact is, however, that the author had intended to write a moral and educational book or, as he himself put it, to set down "words of instruction and words of wisdom." It was his intention to enlighten the reader and to admonish him, to teach and to caution him, so that he might profit in his daily life from the writings of the Fathers "which are more precious than gold and pearls."

The first chapter which has survived consists of nine "pillars" or sections. It begins with an "enumeration of the infamous deeds of the apostates and notorious slanderers which are recorded in the Talmud and in the Aggadah."[16]

Josel then cites a great number of illustrations from his own time to show what great trouble informers and converts have brought upon the Jewish people throughout its history.[17]

Thus he traces the expulsion of the Jews from the Lower Bavaria-Landshut region in the middle of the fifteenth century to the slander of evil men, who had carried a rumor to Duke Ludwig that the very wealthy Jews of his country possessed more gold than the Exchequer, and that they were not paying sufficient taxes. Investigation did reveal that one Eliezer Landshut had in his possession whole sacks filled with gold florins. Although he had originally intended to decree the death penalty for such a crime, the Duke contented himself with confiscating the money of Eliezer and the others and ordering them to leave his territory within a week. As for the informers, they became converts to Christianity and so were able to remain in the country.

The expulsion of the Jews from Augsburg in 1438, too, had been brought about by a Jewish informer who had persuaded two Christians to attempt to blackmail a Jewish trader for a thousand florins. When the Burgomaster of Augsburg learned of these fraudulent dealings, he said to himself: "If the Jews are capable of dealing in this manner with their own, how will they deal with strangers?" He therefore had the two Christians arrested, but expelled the Jews from the city. The Jewish schemer managed to get away.[18]

The ancient Jewish community of Nuremberg likewise

owed its sad fate to the action of another Jew. This man had at first intended no harm. Originally from Aubin, he had desired to move to Nuremberg. As a man of means, he believed that his wealth would open all doors for him and that he would be able to come and go as he pleased. He therefore did not consider it necessary to ask admittance of the community of Nuremberg. When the officials and elders objected to his settling in their city, he became so enraged that he persuaded the Magistrate of Nuremberg to follow the lead of Ulm and to expel its Jews.

At the time of the expulsion of the Jews from Ulm and Nuremberg[19] Josel had been an innocent youth, and in all probability he believed the story that the expulsion had been brought about by informers. But when he wrote his *Sefer Ha-Mikneh,* he was a leader of his people, wise and rich in political experience. He had dealt with Imperial and municipal authorities for many years. He knew that although there had been no Jewish informers either in Colmar or in Oberehnheim, the fate of the Jews had been the same everywhere.

Whether Josel realized that his political statements and his views as expressed in the *Sefer Ha-Mikneh* were contradictory is open to debate. But it is certain that his moral sense was at variance with his sense of history, and that the former generally won out.

Aventin of Bavaria, the outstanding historian of that period, said that "indignation had unclosed his mouth" when he asserted that it was the moral duty of the historian to guide men to inner contemplation and to a regeneration of their entire being.

The historian and theologian, Sebastian Franck, who regarded the religious schism as the work of the devil, compared the fate of empires with that of individuals. Even as men who sinned would be destroyed, he believed, so too, he was convinced "that if empires do wrong, they will crumble. Wherever evil is done and whenever entire nations turn evil, the punishment will be destruction."

In the same vein, Josel viewed historical developments as parables. The informer or the apostate who endangered the community was the visible symbol of all evil, the incarnation of sin itself.

The acrimonious and bitter terms in which he warned his brethren against the apostates, and drew for them an ugly picture of the bad end that would come to the wicked, derived from something more than mere "indignation" on his part.

In the course of his own life, Josel had seen what terrible harm Pfefferkorn, Margaritha, Carben and their like had caused his people. On one occasion, he branded Luther's bitter change of heart toward the Jews as the work of "Mameluke, apostate Jews," thinking primarily of Margaritha, who had become "as thorns in our flesh."

Even though the incidence of apostasy continued to be moderate, it was undeniable that the many religious debates, the disputations on the Messianic character of Christ, the intimate contacts between learned Jews and Christian Hebraists, the Christological interpretation of the Bible by Catholics as well as Protestants, and the missionary activities of Luther, Butzer and other reformers caused many a Jew, and not only the worst among them, to become perplexed, to waver and thus to become easy prey to attempts at conversion.

Stephen Isaac, one of the converts of that period, left an autobiographical account[20] in which he explains how his father, Isaac the Elder, came to abandon Judaism and embrace Christianity in 1546.

"While he was a teacher among the Jews," Stephen relates, "my father—after first invoking the favor of God—began to read and to study most assiduously the Fifty-Third

Chapter of the Book of Isaiah, in which the sufferings of Christ Jesus, our Savior, are plainly described. And after he had pondered all the facts and seen that the contents of said book could not be taken to refer to anyone else but Christ Jesus, he gave honor to God and betook himself to several theologians, conferred with them in greater detail, and was also comforted and strengthened by them in Christ."

Another convert, Gerhard Veltwyk, a highly respected counselor at the court of Charles V, acquired fame through his Hebrew work entitled *Wandering Through the Wilderness,* and his sincere zeal for Christianity, which he earnestly sought to propagate among his former co-religionists.[21]

Rabbi Jacob Gipher of Goeppingen was converted to Protestantism under the influence of Martin Luther and, as a "Doctor in the Hebrew Language," assumed the name Bernhard. Luther, who had honored him with the gift of a copy of his book *That Jesus Christ Was Born A Jew,* had expected that Bernhard would persuade his co-religionists to return to David their King. Although neither Bernhard nor Matthew Adrianus, a most scholarly convert from Spain who lived in Germany, could be moved to accede to Luther's importunings, Josel had good reason to stand on guard for his people.

However, Josel wished to do more than merely remonstrate, instruct, and warn his people against those who abandoned their faith and brought trouble upon the community. It was his purpose to "give them to drink of the clear and pure waters of the commandments and the Torah,"[22] so that, perhaps, some of those who longed to bring their souls nearer to perfection might draw comfort and instruction, encouragement and inspiration from the precious words in his work.

For this reason he devoted the second part of his book, an ethical-philosophical treatise divided into six sections, to sayings of the philosophers and the cabbalists, from which he said that he had "tasted milk and honey as a dainty tidbit."

Josel was neither a speculative thinker nor a systematic philosopher. He was an eclectic, who pondered over what men more eminent than himself had thought before his time, and then attempted to communicate his findings to the more enlightened and open-minded among his people. Thus he took over several basic tenets from the philosophies of Maimonides, Nachmanides, Gersonides and other thinkers of the past without completely identifying with them himself, and at times interpolating a comment or rebuttal of his own. For instance, he based his own interpretation of the words of Elihu, in which the latter had "answered the weighty arguments of Job against the Providence of God,"[23] on the explanation supplied by Gersonides, and in his treatise on *Hakhmah,* or "Wisdom," he followed the reasoning of Maimonides, whom he revered.

Of greater significance than these clumsy ventures into philosophy is the fact that this extremely busy politician, who was constantly traveling, so often felt the desire to retreat into quiet and solitude, in order to meditate on the Divine emanation, on Divine Providence, Divine revelation, communion with the Supreme Being, on the imitation of God, the meaning of prophecy, and on the qualities that characterized a perfect leader and a perfect nation. "For it is thought, not gold, that is food for the intellect."[24]

This pursuit of things Divine gave him the strength to maintain the equilibrium of his soul and the serenity of his spirit amidst the loud tumult at the Imperial Diets, and throughout his difficult negotiations with the authorities. It imparted to him that imperturbable calm which confounded his adversaries, that unshakeable faith and trust which won him the heart of the Emperor and the steadfast conviction that the cause which he championed was the cause of the

God of his fathers, Who had said to Moses: "My presence shall go before thee, and I will lead thee."[25]

Josel has frequently been described as a cabbalist, because he wrote commentaries on cabbalist writings, meditated on the "profundity of the mystery of the Heavenly Chariot,"[26] and delved into the "mystery of the Unity of God."[27] Actually, however, he was neither a cabbalist nor a rationalist, or perhaps, indeed, he was both, for at that time sharp boundaries still had not been drawn between the sphere of reason and the world of the emotions, between philosophical inquiry and religious restraint, and between law and mystical vision.[28]

The first chapter of the ethical-philosophical treatise begins as follows: "When the Scriptures say: 'Acquire wisdom,' Solomon means to imply that one should strive to acquire wisdom in whatsoever one may do."[29]

Josel, true to the spirit of Maimonides,[30] defines "wisdom" as the education of the intellect to the highest possible level, so that man may perceive God and grasp the sense of human existence.

Maimonides taught that the ultimate and supreme degree of piety and hence supreme bliss is given only to him who has recognized God. Love for God is dependent upon man's progress in his perception of the Diety, and this love, which is kindled by the perception of God, gives rise in turn to that Divine service to which the sages refer as "the service of the heart." In this form of worship man concentrates all his thoughts and meditation on God, even while engaging in other pursuits, and centers his entire spirit and personality upon Him.

"Man should delve into the mysteries of the Torah with insight and understanding," Josel wrote.[31] "He should labor over it and meditate on it when he rises up, when he walks along the way, and when he sits down, every one according to the degree of his insight. Let man be understanding, and let him lay the words upon the tablet of the chamber of his heart so that he may have the good fortune to take possession of the wellspring of the mysteries of the Torah for himself and for his descendants."

It is the union of human intelligence with active reasoning—*deveikuth*—the "cleaving" of the human soul to the Divine, which is the essence of perfect devotion, devotion which enabled the prophet to strengthen his own mental powers and to foresee the events which could come to pass in the future as consequences of certain developments in the past and present.

But even he who finds prophecy beyond his reach is capable of grasping the cause-and-effect relationships of things by the strength of his wisdom, if he will turn to the perception of God. Guided by Divine Providence, he will then be given another kind of perception enabling him, with the help of his mental powers and his insight, to understand the causal links between events, and to foretell what the future will bring. Such a man will save his generation from disaster by his admonitions or compel it to listen to his words.

In his commentary on Elihu's speech to Job, Josel declares that reason, "that angel, an intercessor, one from out of a thousand," is the bond which links man with the world of the intellect. It is with the aid of his intelligence that man can survey the intermediate links of the concatenation of causality, and discern the interlocking ideas which will lead him onto the right path. Reason, which thinks out and grasps all things, can help even him who is laboring under some sickness of the mind, that is, one who has been defiled by sinful desires, to free himself from his animal lusts so that he may take courage with all his strength and find healing.

In order to make his brethren recognize the greatness and the almighty power of the One God, Josel incorporated part of the *Guide of the Perplexed* into his *Sefer Ha-Mikneh.* "I, the author of this compilation, have seen that great men before me have copied secret things from the *Moreh Nebukhim* in order to explain them to the people of their generation insofar as their intelligence was sufficient to grasp them. And so I said to myself that I, too, have a passion for extracting the secret things which might benefit the people of my generation, those who are living now, in the year 307 [1547]."[32]

But what Josel wanted to communicate to his own generation was not the way to reconcile philosophy with faith and free inquiry with religion. Unlike the challenge faced by the contemporaries of Moses Maimonides, the problem confronting the people of Josel's day was not the question of whether it was possible to resolve the conflict between science and revelation. Josel's generation vacillated between the truth of Judaism and the truth of Christianity, between a Messiah who had already come and the Messiah who had yet to appear. It was the task of Josel to lead those erring and perplexed souls back to the "God of the Commandments," the "God of the Bible," the "God of Creation," and the "God of Revelation" as the author of the *Guide of the Perplexed* had understood and experienced Him.

In the concluding chapter of his "Guide," Maimonides placed the perfection of knowledge above the perfection of virtue, because he believed that intellectual perfection made it possible for man to comprehend the ways and the workings of God, whereas moral perfection merely enabled him to be helpful to his fellow-men.

Josel did not accept this view. It was at variance with both his personality and all his work. Moreover, he was a German Jew, an heir of the *Hassidei Ashkenaz,* to whom piety in everyday life meant more than philosophical speculation, who deemed prayer and penitence more important than creative thought, and who valued sacrifice for one's fellowmen above intellectual attainments. Thus, despite all his admiration for Maimonides, Josel considered the value of penitence, prayer and good deeds equal to that of knowledge.

"Above all," Josel explains, "take note of this allegory: We perceive with our senses that one who is ill shows a weakening of his powers. But if he eats good food the weaknesses decrease and finally vanish altogether. In many illnesses the restoration of strength is due to the fact that strength has been supplied to that principal force which acts to eliminate the pains and the harmful elements."

In like manner the entire soul can gain strength by cleaving to the Divine through penitence and prayer. Penitence and prayer are the nourishment of the soul. It is only with the strength of his soul that man can fight his evil impulses, the animal lusts which give him pain. This victory over the enemies within him will impart to him the power and the strength of a prince and a sovereign, to whom all lesser things must bear obedience.

Once man, in prayer, penitence and good deeds, finds his way back to the purity of his youth and has propitiated God by his return, he will be granted a reward, as it is written: "He will recompense man according to his righteousness."

But while Josel followed the pattern of the German Hassidim of the Middle Ages in his conception of the value of prayer and penitential discipline, he could not accept their other tenet: namely, that the Jew should bear humiliation and contempt without defending himself.

The times, the spiritual climate, and the views on life in the world in which Josel had matured were not the same as the ones they had known. His brow felt the piercing, nipping blast of the winds of the Renaissance which made him see men in distinct and sharply defined outlines, rather than in the pale and insipid colors of the Middle Ages. In his proud bearing, his refined manners, and his frank relations with his fellow-men, he was no longer the humble scholar, the ascetic saint of an earlier age, but the patrician of the Imperial cities of Germany, erect, proud and fully conscious of his dignity. His type is depicted by Dürer in his portrait of Willibald Pirckheimer, the humanist of Nuremberg, and by Hans Holbein in his likeness of Boniface Amerbach, the printer of Basel.

Josel's personality reflected something of the *homo nobilis,* the *homo universale* of the humanists, who knew the meaning of human dignity and was able to defend it, one who "was his own master, his own molder, shaping himself out of that stuff which pleased him most."

If Josel asserted again and again that there was no difference between men on earth, and that God, the Creator of them all, had created Jews and Christians alike in His image and given the earth to all men for their gain, he simply taught a philosophy which he found written in the Holy Scriptures. But his words carry overtones also of the ideals and philosophies of some of the best and finest minds of his day, who imparted "an entirely new glory to the idea of man as such."

"All of us are equally dear to God," we read in the message of comfort from the great physician Paracelsus. "His mercy, too, is the same for all. And although it is true that he who loves greatly will be greatly rewarded, redemption will still be the same for all."[33]

Sebastian Franck, the most remarkable thinker of the period, was firmly convinced that God had set down the *lumen naturale,* the "light of nature," as a natural law for all men to enable them to distinguish between good and evil, to recognize His will and to accept His word.

Because the human heart and spirit, the human mind and will were thus the same everywhere, because there was only "one and the same life for all on earth," and because no one could be certain that he possessed the ultimate truth of religion, Franck insisted on equal rights and tolerance for all, Jews and Christians, heathens and Mohammedans, not merely for the sake of tolerance but because ethics, the love of one's neighbor and the respect for the dignity of one's fellow-man, demanded it.

"Therefore, while no one shall be master over my faith and no one shall force me to be a slave to his mind, he shall be my neighbor and dear brother to me, whether he be a Jew or a Samaritan, and I will give him goodness and mercy as much as I can. I will not throw down anyone who does not throw me down first. I am fair in my dealings, as one human being with another."

In a very similar vein, Josel on one occasion wrote to the Magistrate of Strasbourg that[34] "the law of God and nature commands every God-fearing man to allow neither harm nor wrong to be done to his fellow-men." If he, Josel, were ever to be in a position to help a stranger, even one not of his own faith, he would intercede for him even at the risk of his own life.

The religious philosophy of the Renaissance, and especially those followers of universal theism such as Pico della Mirandola, Marsiglio Ficino, Conrad Mutianus Rufus, the humanist in Erfurt, Johann Reuchlin and Sebastian Franck, taught that every religion held the same content of truth and the same ethical principle. God did not reveal Himself to any one people or individual at one specific moment, but sent His light to various individuals and nations in various centuries. The "wisdom which is the Divine heritage," the "Spirit of Christ," they maintained, had dwelt in Orpheus as well as in Seneca, in Socrates as well as in Moses, in Plato as well as in Christ, and in Graeco-Roman mythology as well as in the books of the Old and New Testaments. The "invisible Christ," the "true son of God" had been revealed, not only to the Jews in a small corner of Syria, but also to the Greeks, the Romans and the Teutons. All theistic religions and philosophies partook of this Divine wisdom; the moral law that was part of nature had been implanted by birth in all the great teachers of mankind and they, in turn, had transmitted it to the other mortals.

Josel's own religio-philosophical convictions remained unaffected by this universal brand of theism which prevailed in his day.

To him, "the profound and unfathomable mystery of God," the revelation which God had vouchsafed to Moses and to the entire Jewish people,[35] was not the same as that which other nations had experienced in the course of history. No prophet but Moses had been commanded by God: "Go, go forth, thou and thy people which thou hast led forth from the land of Egypt." To no other man had God ever said: "I know thee by name because thou hast found favor in My eyes." And no one else had striven like Moses to experience the name of God and to understand His ways. No one else had labored so mightily as he to "gain the level of an angel" so that he and his people with him might attain the highest degree of perfection. And to no one else had God ever replied, "That which thou hast now said I will do"; namely, "to grant perfection to thee and to thy people."

But although Josel rejected any syncretism which sought to lump together the ideas of Pythagoras with those of the Bible, those of Islam with those of ancient Greece, and those of Christianity with those of the Cabbala, he agreed with the philosophers of his day that Christians and Jews, heathens and Mohammedans, all had been created by the same God and also worshipped the same God, that God had given His laws and precepts to all men who dwelt on earth, and that "the same fate had been meted out in equal weight and measure to every people without exception."

Holding these convictions, Josel, unlike the generations that followed him, never viewed the contrast between Jewish existence and the Christian environment as a tragic conflict that poisoned his soul. Though he clearly saw that barriers of religion and morals, faith and custom, history and tradition, had raised a dividing wall between Judaism and Christianity, between the German nation and the Jewish nation, he still was able to perceive behind all these divisive factors the common values which linked them together as human beings created in the image of God, or as *Menschenbilder,* "human images," as he expressed it.

"Only he who finds his way to his own nature can find the path to truth and to God," said Paracelsus, Josel's great contemporary.[36] Only because he had found the way to his own nature was Josel able to understand the nature of others. Only because he had found his own God was he capable also of understanding the God of others, the God of Charles the Catholic as well as the God of Capito the Protestant. It was only because he "remained firm as a rock in his character"[37] that he was able to imbibe the ideas of his time without blurring the boundaries which divided the Christian *Weltanschauung* from the *Weltanschauung* of the Jews. It was only because he always remained his own self that he was able to adjust himself to an alien world without succumbing to it himself, and to preserve the independence of his thinking without closing his mind to the appreciation of the greatness of contributions of religions other than his own.

His tolerance was not the tolerance of Nathan the Wise, for the era in which he lived was far removed from the tolerance of the Age of Enlightenment.

Unlike the rationalists of the eighteenth century, this generation, deeply concerned as it was with such profound religious problems as sin and redemption, grace and guilt, freedom of conscience and the sanctity of the revealed Word,

Divine righteousness and Divine law, the inner light and the Last Judgment, could not view the Jewish problem as an abstract concept, a principle of humanity.

In an age when Faustus lived and plied his magic arts, when the Virgin Mary appeared to the piper of Niklashausen and the Devil met Luther in the flesh, when the horsemen of the Apocalypse galloped through the land and the Angel of Death danced with emperors, kings, popes and paupers alike, people were not able to approach the Jewish problem with the lucid wisdom of Lessing or the kindly sympathy of Dohm.

Therefore, Josel, too, did not consider the three rings of Nathan the Wise alike in any manner. Each one of them had for him a specific significance and a specific splendor, and he knew well which of the three was the genuine one.

However, this certainty did not bring him the smugness and satiety of ownership. It only drove him to acquire this possession anew for himself, to make it his own again and again by ever-increasing toil, and to fight and to suffer for it so that he might preserve it pure and whole for future generations.

In his own activities he fulfilled the instruction that was given to the heirs of that ring which he believed to be the genuine one: "The word is in thy mouth and in thy heart, to do it."

However, all his deeds would have been of little avail had not everything he did been pervaded, inspired and hallowed by that one trait of character which he probably would have called the "guiding force of the soul": namely, his loving compassion for all suffering creatures.

It was that "sacred sympathy" which shone forth from the altar paintings at Isenheim, that "balm dwelling within the heart" which healed the sick of Paracelsus; it was that never-failing love which the Hassidim believed was capable of "sensing the need of men and of bearing their suffering."[38]

CHAPTER NINE

THE ADVOCATE OF GERMAN JEWRY

IN September 1547, after the conclusion of the Schmalkaldic War, Charles traveled to Augsburg to hold an Imperial Diet at which he intended to submit to the conquered cities and rulers a plan for final clarification of the relationship between the Emperor and the Estates, for the establishment of religious unity, and for a reformation within the Catholic Church. He planned to reconstruct the rebellious and disintegrating Empire on firmer foundations, and to unite all the reigning princes, under his leadership, into one single Confederation, the *Reichsliga.* He hoped, too, to bring about religious peace throughout his Empire by means of a religious settlement, the "Interim," which entailed concessions to the Protestants with regard to problems of justification by faith, laymen's communion and marriage of clergy, and by means of a thorough purge and reformation within the Catholic Church itself.

The Diet of Augsburg has been described as the "armored" Diet,[1] because the Emperor had with him not only the captive rulers of Saxony and Hesse but one hundred thousand Spanish and Italian mercenaries to back his authority. Other historians have described this Diet as the most sumptuous and costly ever held, and bitter complaints were rife about the extravagance of the princes and noblemen who feasted and caroused there as if gold rained down from the skies and no one had ever even heard of war, misery, fire, distress, or of pillage and destruction.

At this Diet Josel, too, realized to his dismay that the end of the Schmalkaldic War did not mean the end of his own struggles, and that the mission which his brethren had entrusted to him was still not completed. Even as the Emperor, after each victory, found himself confronted again and again by the same coalition of enemies, so Josel, too, at the age of seventy, found himself facing the same adversaries whom he had so fearlessly fought in his youth: the Imperial cities of the Alsace.

In January 1548, he was compelled to present Charles, on behalf of the Jewry of the *Landvogtei,* with a lengthy bill of complaint.[2] He pointed out to the Emperor that the Jews of the town of Tuerckheim and of the Imperial town of Rosheim were being terrorized "in an inhuman, tyrannical manner." Jews from abroad were being prevented from entering these cities, rocks were hurled at them, and the homes, the doors, the windows and the shutters of the resident Jews were often demolished with axes during the night.

Orders from the *Landvogt* were of no avail, because the Councillors insisted that he had no right to inflict punishment on the burghers of the towns.

For this reason Josel begged the Emperor to forbid the two towns from engaging in such "disturbances" on pain of corporal punishment and to threaten that he would prefer charges against them before the *Reichskammergericht* if they did not meet their obligations.

On January 30, 1548, Charles issued an order to the towns of Rosheim and Tuerckheim to protect the Jews and to discipline the transgressors, so that he should have no cause in the future to take further action against them.[3]

On that same day, the Imperial Chancery issued a privilege to all the Jews of the *Reich,* in which Charles explicitly stated that he had been informed by the "Commander of Jewry in the Holy Roman Empire of the German Nation" that a deliberate infringement on their rights had taken place. He asked the Princes temporal and ecclesiastical, the knights, the manorial lords and the cities to safeguard the right of the Jews to engage in commerce on the Imperial highways and in the Imperial market places, to protect their lives and property, and neither to close nor to destroy their synagogues.[4]

Josel had laid particular stress on the synagogue problem because at that time the synagogue of the free Imperial village of Gochsheim, Franconia, which was subject to the jurisdiction of the Magistrate of Schweinfurt and under the protectorate of the Landgrave of Hesse, had been closed[5] so that the Jews could not "observe their ceremonies and recite their prayers to Almighty God together."[6] Since they had reason to fear that the closing of their synagogue was only a prelude to their expulsion, Josel requested the Emperor on behalf of the Jews of Gochsheim to protect their centuries-old community, which belonged to the *Reich.*

This time, too, Charles acceded to Josel's request. Referring to the Privilege of Speyer, Charles issued an order on January 17, 1548, commanding the Protector of the village of Gochsheim to reopen the synagogue, not to expel the Jews, and to put a stop to the terror.[7]

Josel followed up this Imperial mandate with a letter to the Burgomaster and the community of Gochsheim dated March 15, in which he admonished them, in terms which the Councillors of Schweinfurt described as "sharp and insolent," to obey the Emperor's order so that he, Josel, as Commander of Jewry, would not be forced to prefer charges against them before the Supreme Court of Justice *(Kammergericht)*.[8]

At this Imperial Diet at Augsburg, Josel, for the first time in forty years of official activity, asked the Emperor for a personal favor. The Emperor Maximilian, King Ferdinand after him, and Charles V thereafter had issued to him a letter of protection and safe conduct which held good also for his wife, his children and his sons-in-law. This letter certified that he was permitted to settle wherever he pleased in the *Reich,* to engage freely in trade and traffic everywhere, and to pass all customs stations safely and without payment.

In 1547, during a stay in Bohemia, he had misplaced this letter of protection, and without it he was seriously handicapped. The only legitimation he was thenceforth able to show on his long and often dangerous journeys was a transcript from the Imperial town of Oberehnheim.

Mindful of the "obedient services" which Josel had rendered to him and to the Holy Empire in the past, and in view of the reliable reports of his good conduct from several provincial governors, manorial lords, knights and renowned cities in the Alsace,[9] the Emperor immediately granted Josel's request for a duplicate letter of safe conduct. According to the reports, Josel had "conducted himself well and above reproach at all times in accordance with his character and station," had transacted the affairs of Jewry faithfully and diligently at the Imperial Diets and elsewhere, had supplied the troops with funds and provisions during the campaign against France and the Schmalkaldic War, and had "proven to be obedient to the best of his ability."[10]

For years Josel had lived in the midst of events of worldwide interest. He had followed developments in national and international politics with a watchful eye, and established close contacts at the Imperial Diets with the leading considerations of expediency, greed, ambition and avarice and dissolved again for the same motivations, and had seen, too, the manner in which the "Most Christian" King of France, who had brutally persecuted the followers of the new doctrine in his own country, had allied himself with the Protestants of the *Reich* against their own sovereign.

In such times of utter moral anarchy, when manners were loose and convention was violated at every turn, Josel often wondered if the mere favor of the Emperor would be sufficient protection for his brethren. Had he not often enough seen Charles compelled to compromise his political principles and religious convictions in order to preserve the Empire? What if the Emperor were to leave Germany for a period of years, as he had frequently done in the past? And indeed, what if Charles, who was said to be little more than a "heap of medicines," were to pass the crown on to his son Philip, a fanatical, cruel and rigidly Catholic prince who mercilessly persecuted every dissenter from his own faith?

Josel well knew that the decline of the princes after the defeat near Muehlberg was only temporary, and that they were not yet ready to submit to the Emperor's authority for any length of time. As a result of the subjection of the cities, the knights, and the peasants, and the abundant profits derived from the secularization of Church properties, their power had increased greatly. With the help of wars and inheritances, they had expanded their territories and had also consolidated their power within their own states by adept management of their domains, and by the introduction of Roman law and of police and municipal regulations.

Would these princes not find it expedient, Josel reasoned, to readmit the Jews in order to increase the volume of their trade and commerce? Several of the lesser ones, such as the Archbishops of Cologne, Mayence and Treves, the Duke of

Juelich-Berg, and the Margraves of Ansbach and Baden-Baden had already given them safe conduct. Should it not be possible to obtain for the Jews of these states the same privileges that Charles had conferred upon the Jews of the *Reich*? It should be remembered that the princes who had taken possession of the royal prerogative over the Jews (*Judenregal*), a privilege which was reconfirmed by the "reformation of good police regulations"[11] at that very Diet of Augsburg, were not bound by the Imperial laws concerning the Jews.

These same considerations led Josel to request letters of protection and safe-conduct for the Jews from the Estates of the *Reich*.

He turned first to King Ferdinand, the ruler of the greatest state within the Empire, whom Luther had once accused of giving better treatment to the Jews than to the Protestants. He asked him to follow the lead of his brother, the Emperor, and to permit the German Jews in his hereditary territories to engage in commerce and to "protect them from violence according to law."

On the last day of April, Ferdinand issued a gracious "Letter of Protection, Patronage and Safe-Conduct" to the Jews of the Holy Empire, entitling them to travel and to engage in trade and traffic in peace and safety in all the hereditary provinces of Austria, except Lower Austria and the County of Goerz.[12]

Two months later, on June 22, Josel, as "Advocate of All Jewry," presented a petition to all the Electors, reigning princes, prelates and Estates of the Empire.[13]

In this petition he pointed out that the small number of Jews who "still dwelt scattered hither and yon" in the Holy Empire were in great distress. All Imperial privileges and papal bulls notwithstanding, they were frequently arrested, robbed of their possessions, driven from their dwellings and deprived of their means of livelihood by trade restrictions. All this occurred despite the fact that it brought no advantage to the Christian population, since the Jews charged them lower rates of interest than did their own co-religionists. Moreover, he stated, it was obvious that moneylending had brought the Jews no great fortune but only a bare livelihood, for they had not been able to build many houses of stone for themselves, or to acquire land and people as pledges. "Since the Jews, after all, are also creatures and creations of God Almighty," Josel asked the Estates to exercise "human patience and compassion" in their dealings with them and not to revoke their ancient freedoms.

Pertinent historical sources do not indicate whether he ever received a reply to this appeal.

Josel had another special mandate to fulfill at the Augsburg Diet on behalf of his brethren in the Alsace: namely, to bring about an amicable settlement of the dispute in which they had been engaged for decades with the Imperial town of Colmar.[14]

Colmar, the most important city in the Alsace after Strasbourg, had expelled its Jews in 1510. As a result the Jews, as was the custom at the time, settled in neighboring small towns and villages and continued to do business with the burghers of Colmar from their new homes. They were the most numerous visitors at weekly markets and annual fairs, and there, as the Magistrate bitterly complained to Josel, they traded in new clothes and dealt in foreign currency, by-passing the regular exchange offices.[15] Finally, at the Regensburg Diet of 1541, Charles had yielded to the importunings of the Magistrate and issued a mandate whereby admittance to the territory of the city was subject to his permission.

While this decree did not in any manner bar the Jews from entering the city, a new regulation was enacted in 1544, which strictly prohibited them from doing business with the resident burghers of Colmar.

Since Josel's efforts to effect an "amicable and peaceable" settlement met with failure, he brought the dispute of his brethren with the town of Colmar before the Emperor at Augsburg in December, 1547, claiming that the town had utterly misconstrued the Decree of 1541.

Taking up Josel's argument, the Emperor sharply reprimanded the Magistrate of Colmar for his willful distortion of the clear terms of the Edict of 1541, and for having subjected the Jews to needless oppression and residence bans "under the mask of having been given by law the freedom to do so."[16]

Josel argued[17] that since the two parties in the dispute differed with regard to the interpretation of the regulations of the Imperial decree, an end could be put to this unpleasant situation only if an unequivocal official explanation of the mandate were to be handed down. Charles thereupon had his counselors study the freedoms of the city of Colmar as well as the privileges of the Jews, and admitted that Josel's complaint was justified. On January 4, 1548, in a detailed interpretation of his earlier decree,[18] the Emperor specified that if the Jews as a body were to promise not to engage in unfair business practices, the Councillors of Colmar would have no right to forbid them access to the city.

When Josel returned to the Alsace in the summer of 1548, he requested the Magistrate of Colmar, through the intercession of the *Landvogt,* to enforce this Imperial decree to the letter.

The Councillors, however, in hopes that the Emperor would not refuse a hearing to the Catholic city which had remained loyal to him in the Schmalkaldic War, sent the Syndic Wendeling Zippern to Speyer, where Charles was staying in the late summer that year. But despite his piteous pleas that the city would be ruined if the Jews were to be permitted to attend the annual fairs, Zippern's mission met with utter failure.

In the meantime, Josel, annoyed at not having received a straightforward answer, declared to the *Landvogt*[19] that he, Josel, had to insist upon obedience to the Imperial decree. He did so neither out of spite nor with the intention of causing damage and expense to Colmar, but solely in the interest of his brethren, who had to know what their attitude toward the city should be. "For my intention is nothing but honesty and peace . . . [and] although we are not of the same faith, we are still human beings, created by Almighty God to dwell in the midst of other men on earth."

The "straightforward answer" of the Councillors of Colmar came in the person of the Town Clerk, the eloquent and clever Balthasar Hellu, whom they dispatched to Brussels in an attempt to win the support of the Imperial counselors, the Emperor's father confessor, and even that of the Chancellor for their cause.

Hellu kept a detailed diary of his journey which clearly sets forth the attitude that prevailed at the Emperor's Court with regard to the Jews at the time.[20]

In a number of audiences, the younger Granvelle, Bishop of Arras, endeavored to make it clear to the emissary from Colmar that the terms of the Privilege of 1541 did not in any manner justify a complete expulsion of the Jews from the precincts of his town and that it was the Emperor's will to keep the Mandate of 1547 in force. True, the city had the right to combat usury by Jews, but it was slander to claim that the city was being ruined by their business practices. The Jews, he pointed out, were human beings like all others and therefore were entitled to support themselves and to make a living.

With a good deal of annoyance, the Town Clerk reports

to his Magistrate an incident which he himself had witnessed. He had been invited to dinner at the home of one of the Imperial counselors. In the course of the evening, probably in connection with Hellu's mission, the Jewish problem was discussed. Among the guests was one Herr von Sickingen, a former Chancellor of the Elector Palatine. The host reminded that gentleman that in the old days, at the Court in Heidelberg, he had had little good will for the Jews. "Whether or not I was kindly disposed toward the Jews at the time or not," von Sickingen replied, "I do not know. But I beg leave to say that if I were to become involved again in some matter having to do with the Jews, I would take care not to say anything against them nowadays, because I would be sure from the start that it would be useless to do so."

While the emissary from Colmar spun the threads of his plot in Brussels, Josel, too, did not rest upon his oars. Pressed by his brethren, who reminded him of his duty as their *manhig* and of the oath he had taken, he decided to take legal steps against Colmar and to cite the city before the Imperial Supreme Court of Justice. It was with a heavy heart that he made this decision, and he did not act alone. He had the support of the most respected Jewish leaders of the Upper and the Lower Alsace: Aaron of Tuerckheim, Menlin of Wintzenheim, Gershon of Ammerschweiler, Isaac of Dangolsheim, Loeb of Surburg and Seligmann of Hagenau.

The summons, dated December 19, 1548, was sent to Colmar by the Supreme Court of Justice of Speyer at the request of these Jewish leaders.[21] It pointed out that, as subjects of the Roman Empire, the Jews had the right, based on special privileges and regulations, to dwell among the Christians and like the Christians, they, too, were entitled to protection under the law. The Magistrate of Colmar, it was charged, had heeded neither the general privileges of the Jews nor the special decrees of December, 1547, but had infringed upon these Imperial prerogatives and refused the Jews access to the city, to which they were entitled by time-honored tradition. Since the Burgomaster and Councillors of Colmar had deprived them, *civibus Romanis,* of this ancient right, they, the authorities of Colmar, were requested to appear before the Supreme Court of Justice (*Reichskammergericht*) twenty-four days after receipt of the summons to justify their action.

Nevertheless, Josel made one more attempt at an amicable settlement. He proposed to the Magistrate to have the dispute settled by a court of arbitration prior to the date set for the Supreme Court hearing. Only when the city persisted in its stand did he authorize his attorney, Moritz Breunle, who practiced before the Supreme Court, to conduct the case in his behalf. The Councillors of Colmar chose Licentiate Schwapach to represent them.

Schwapach argued that the city had been entitled by the Imperial decrees of 1510 and 1541 to follow the course it had taken. Breunle, probably on Josel's instructions, pointed out in reply that these mandates had been obtained surreptitiously, without the Jews having been given a legal hearing. Breunle also strongly contested the validity of the accusation of usury, which had a paramount place in Schwapach's charges, maintaining that by the terms of all the privileges issued by the Emperor and the Estates, the Jews had been expressly permitted to engage in moneylending. Moreover, the Commander of German Jewry had prescribed severe penalties for Jewish transgressors of the usury laws. And why, Breunle demanded caustically, should only the Jews be made to suffer for their transgressions? Why was justice not meted out also to those Christian wholesalers who bought up quantities of wine and wheat from far and wide to force up prices? Was not this monopoly even more ruinous to the poor man than the money trade of the Jews of which Colmar was constantly complaining?

Josel was obliged to make a number of journeys on horseback to Speyer in connection with this affair. However, we do not know the outcome of the case, since the records stop with the year 1551.

What seems of more historical significance than the decision of the court is the legal terminology which Josel employed at that time.

In his dispute with the Imperial town of Oberehnheim in the 1520's, he had referred to the Jews as the serfs of the Imperial Chamber. In subsequent petitions, he had described them as members or appurtenances of the *Reich* and of the Emperor; in other words, as the property of the sovereign. But in the Colmar dispute, they were defined as subjects of the *Reich, cives Romani;* they were no longer merely a *Regal* of the sovereign, with whom he could do as he pleased, but *cives Romani,* and hence citizens of the Roman Empire of the German Nation.

Does this mean that Josel drew the legal inferences from the Edict which had been enacted in Speyer in 1544? Or had the judges of the Supreme Court, who had been trained in Roman law, used these terms of their own accord in the document by which they cited the town of Colmar before the Supreme Court of Justice at Speyer?

In his opinion in favor of the books of the Jews, Reuchlin had declared that the Jews "should be protected by the Imperial Jewry Privileges as subjects of the Holy Roman Empire."[22] He had also demanded that their synagogue and possessions be secured and that no force should be used against them any more than against the Christians. For the members of "both these sects are citizens of the Holy Roman Empire and of the Imperial Realm, the Christians by their election of the Electors and the Electorates, and the Jews by their own will and their declaration that 'We have no King but the Emperor' (John 19.15)."[23]

The great jurist had recalled the Roman law which prevailed in the era of the pre-Christian emperors, when the Jews still had the full rights of Roman citizenship, albeit with several restrictions. He had demanded that the Jewry-Laws of the Middle Ages be repealed and replaced by the ancient Roman Law. This did not mean that he wanted to free the Jews from all the special laws to which they were bound and to render them equal, as a religious community, to all the other subjects of the *Reich*. But he had plainly insisted, for the sake of justice and right, that they be given equality under the law as full-fledged citizens, as *concives imperii Romani*. "Though they may be the enemies of our faith," Reuchlin wrote, "they are not our enemies; i.e., of the Roman Empire."[24]

In his memoirs and in the *Sefer Ha-Mikneh,* Josel spoke in grateful and admiring terms of Reuchlin, that "great and wise man" who had saved his people. Now that the Emperor, as Reuchlin put it, thought of himself as *universorum morum in re publica legifer et arbitrator,* as the rightful heir to the Caesars of ancient Rome, was it not only natural that Josel should recall those words which had left such a deep impression upon him? Was it not only natural that he should think the time was ripe for the demands of Reuchlin to be translated into reality? Was there not a chance now that the *servi camerae* might rise from oppression to stand proudly once again as *concives imperii Romani?*

There is hardly any doubt that the new drive of the city of Colmar and of the other cities against Jewish usury was occasioned by the activities of the Jews in the field of finance, which had been given renewed impetus and official sanction by the Edict of Speyer.

At a time when the Christians, too, were investing their

funds profitably in the banking establishments of Upper Germany, when the influx of gold and silver from the mines of Hungary, the Tyrol and the newly discovered lands across the sea gave rise to a new technique of finance and thus also of speculation, when the money markets of Antwerp, London, Augsburg, Strasbourg and Frankfort began to flourish and Imperial and Provincial laws eased the penalties for usury, it was impossible to entirely exclude from the money trade the very people who were most familiar with its laws.

The Final Decrees of the former Imperial Diets (*Reichstagsabschiede*) prior to 1548 had contained provisions strictly prohibiting Jews from charging interest. By contrast, the Final Decree of the Imperial Diet (*Reichstagsabschied*) of 1548 provided that Jews should be permitted to "charge *Wucher* [interest; lit. "usury"] at the rate of five per cent to enable them to earn their sustenance."[25] While this provision lessened the effectiveness of the Privilege issued at Speyer in 1544, which had permitted the Jews to charge higher rates of interest than the Christians, it was the first time that the right of the Jews to charge interest at all was accorded recognition in principle by an Imperial law. From that time on the use of the term *Wucher,* which until then had been applied indiscriminately to any type of interest on loans, regardless of amount, was restricted to denote rates of interest in excess of the ceiling set by the law.

These transactions did not merely involve petty loans to peasants and artisans for pledges, but larger sums of money lent to wealthy burghers, knights or communities, made mostly in the form of promissory notes, debentures, or obligations. It was at that time that the term *Aktie,* or share, was first coined.[26]

This new type of moneylending became the butt of sharp criticism from the Estates assembled at the third Imperial Diet of Augsburg which Charles had convoked for July 1550.[27]

Complaints were rife that the Jews "were issuing separate promissory notes for the loan as such and for the interest due therefrom,"[28] or selling their promissory notes to Christians, and registering bonds in the name of the Christian purchasers who then would sorely press the "poor, defrauded debtors" and frequently evict them from house and home.[29] To counteract these abuses, Paragraph 78 of the Final Decree of the Diet (*Reichstagsabschied*) enacted on February 14, 1551, forbade Jews to draw up a bond or debenture in the presence of any other witnesses save the rightful authorities of the city in which the Christian party to the transaction resided.

"Nor shall any Christian in the future purchase from a Jew a share or claim against any other Christian, nor shall any Jewish creditor cede such shares or claims to another Christian party or make contractual provisions in case of the loss of such claim."[30]

On January 23, 1551, Josel lodged a protest at Augsburg in behalf of the Jewry of the *Reich* against the provision in the *Reichstagsabschied* by which "promissory notes made out in favor of Jews should have no legal force without the full knowledge and consent of the authorities."[31] On January 31, he requested once again that the Jews should not be burdened by one more police regulation,[32] but he did not succeed in bringing about the desired change in the provisions of the *Reichstagsabschied.*

In the middle of March, 1551, Josel returned to Rosheim to settle several disputes between the *Landjudenschaft* of Lower Alsace and the Magistrate of Strasbourg. At that time he probably also discussed with the representatives of the Jewish communities the provisions of the *Reichstagsabschied* of Augsburg which had a crucial bearing on the economic situation of every Jew. For that June, Josel went back to Augsburg, where the Emperor held court all summer long, and presented Charles with two memorials: one had been composed by the "representatives of all Jewry," and the other by Josel himself.[33]

The deputies of the Jewish communities complained that the new police regulations might create the impression among the Christians that they were not obliged to pay their debts to the Jews, because the loan transactions had not been made in the presence of the legally constituted authorities. Moreover, they claimed that the provisions of the *Reichstagsabschied* constituted a great hardship and posed a real threat to their economic survival. For the provision that their loan transactions had to be legalized in the presence of the Christian authorities of the debtor's place of residence meant in many cases that the Jewish creditors had to travel such great distances and pay such high protection, customs and toll duties that they could make no profit from their moneylending. They therefore requested a modification of the police regulations to the effect that any loan agreement made between a Jew and a Christian should be considered legally binding as long as the bond had been drawn up in the presence of reputable witnesses.

Josel backed the petition of his brethren by a special letter, in which he wrote that if that provision of the *Reichstagsabschied* were really enforced, all the Jews would be compelled to leave the *Reich* "on account of starvation." In that case, not only would the Jews lose all the amnesties and freedoms which they had obtained at such great sacrifice, but the Emperor, too, would be deprived of those special privileges to which he was entitled with regard to the serfs of his Imperial Chamber.

The answer from Charles to the petition is no longer extant. There only is a brief entry in the records of the *Reichshofrat*[34] to the effect that a declaration was to be drawn up to accede to the wishes of the Jews "to be permitted to draw up their contracts in the presence of reputable witnesses." However, the provisions concerning the issuance of bonds were to be carried out in accordance with the terms of the *Reichstagsabschied.*

Josel had still another reason for returning to Augsburg in the summer of 1551. He had been concerned for some time about the situation of the Jews of Wuerttemberg. In that state, which was torn by political and religious strife, it had not been possible to enforce the privilege of 1510 by which the Ducal counselors were at liberty to revoke the residence rights of the Jews and to forbid them from engaging in business, money trading or making loans on immovables. The citizens of the Duchy could not be prevented from borrowing money from Jews in neighboring territories at high rates of interest and compound interest.

In 1550 a new ruler, young Duke Christopher, took the throne of Wuerttemberg and proposed to solve the problem by expelling all the Jews from the *Reich.* Unable to carry his point, he made plans to bar them at least from his own Duchy.

It was of vital necessity that the Jews should not lose their freedom to travel through this state. The *Hofgericht* (Manorial Court) of Rottweil,[35] to which Jews from all over the *Reich* frequently had to resort, was in Wuerttemberg. In addition, the territories of Baden, Franconia, Bavaria and the Lake Constance and Danube regions all bordering on the Duchy had good-sized Jewish settlements which would be in danger of losing contact with one another if the proposed decree were passed.

Josel himself had been refused a letter of safe-conduct from the government of Wuerttemberg in 1530. Now he had to make every effort to gain personal access to young Duke Christopher, especially since, only a short time before, two Jews travelling to the *Hofgericht* of Rottweil had been arrested by Wuerttemberg officials and released only after paying a heavy fine.[36]

Josel realized that the problem of Jewish moneylending was crucial in a country without access to the sea or maritime commerce, with a simple, uncomplicated, and practically all agrarian economy. In a conversation at Hagenau with the Chancellor of Wuerttemberg,[37] Josel had openly admitted that the peasants and the linen weavers of Wuerttemberg, who were unfamiliar with the circulation of money, were suffering considerable harm at the hands of Jewish moneylenders. He had tried to make it clear to the Chancellor that the officers of the Jewish communities had made a thorough study of these abuses at various conferences and had proclaimed a "great and mighty ban" to be placed on anyone violating the usury laws of the *Reich* in general and the Augsburg "Articles" in particular.

At the time of the Augsburg Diet, he discussed all the aspects of the problem in writing with Johann Fessler,[38] Chancellor of Wuerttemberg, and with Christopher himself.[39] He believed he had reason to assume that the Duke, who had only come to the throne a short time before, was still not familiar with the Jewry laws of the *Reich,* and therefore did not know that, by the terms of all the privileges conferred upon them, the Jews had been given express permission to use the Imperial highways. He explained to the young prince that the Edict of 1530 was not to be construed to mean that all Jews were to be forbidden to travel through the Duchy. The Emperor, too, as the "fountainhead of all justice," had intended to have the freedom conferred upon the Duchy of Wuerttemberg enforced only in the case of those who had engaged in dishonest practices, and certainly had not wanted to penalize people who had been forced in these "fast-moving, troubled times" to travel from one province to the other in order to make a living. Josel solemnly promised that in the future the subjects of Wuerttemberg would not be harassed by the orders of foreign courts and that all court cases would be conducted before judges residing in the Duchy. He expressed the hope that the Duke and his counselors would accept his proposals at a personal conference, for he, Josel, had dealt for some fifty years with Emperors, Kings, Electors and Princes as Commander of Jewry "in the fear of God and according to the dictates of decency," and had managed to settle many controversies and disputes in this manner.

No less a personage than Johann Obernburger, Secretary to the Emperor, expressed his support of Josel's petition, stating that he had found all of Josel's transactions at the Diets and at the Imperial Courts to have been "honest and sincere for a Jew" and that he kept every promise he had made in behalf of the Jews.[40] As a result, Josel was invited in August to appear in Stuttgart in person.

On August 11, after five days of negotiations, a mutually binding agreement was signed between Duke Christopher and the "Advocate and Commander Josel, a Jew from Rosheim" as the authorized representative of *Reich* Jewry "by virtue of the power vested in him."[41]

By the terms of this agreement, any legal proceedings by Jews against subjects of Wuerttemberg, either at the Imperial Supreme Court of Justice (*Reichskammergericht*) or at the *Hofgericht* at Rottweil, had to be stopped immediately. All legal action already begun was to be settled out of court by the Ducal bailiffs. Failing a satisfactory settlement, the Jewish plaintiff was to appeal his case to the Ducal court or some other court of justice in the state of Wuerttemberg.

Persons violating the terms of the agreement were not to be given safe-conduct for traveling through the state. Anyone desiring to enter the Duchy had to apply to the bailiff for a personal escort against payment of a specified fee. The use of passports was restricted to indigent Jews who had taken a pauper's oath. No Jew was to do business while traveling through the state except to buy and sell merchandise for cash if he happened to pass a free market place.

We still have an interesting letter, addressed by rabbis and *parnassim* who had met in Frankfort at the time to their "veteran leader."[42] The German translation of a Hebrew original was sent by Josel to the Duke prior to the opening of these negotiations to convince Christopher that he, Josel, intended to act "in honesty and sincerity," mindful of the responsibility which he had taken upon himself in behalf of *Reich* Jewry.

In his memoirs, Josel stressed over and over again that he carried out his missions "by order of the rabbis and scholars of the *Reich*," "with the consent of the [Jewish] communities," "with the concurrence of our sages" or "on the urging of the public."

In 1530, too, when he was working on a plan for new Jewish Ordinances, he had called the deputies of the Jewish communities throughout the *Reich* to Augsburg in order to deliberate on the new constitution, article by article.

All these remarks indicate that Josel always remembered that he was acting only as the representative and authorized agent of German Jewry, to whom he felt duty-bound to render an account of all his activities.

But this document, dated July, 1551, is our earliest source of information on the relationship which existed between the Commander and the Jewish communities, and on the political role of Jewry as a group under Josel's leadership.

The Hebrew original of this document was a detailed reply to a letter which Josel had sent from Augsburg to the representatives of the German Jewish communities. In that communication, which has been lost, he reported to them his negotiations with Duke Christopher and the Counselors of Wuerttemberg, submitting to them the basic outline of the agreement which he intended to sign with the Duke, and inviting counter-proposals from them if his plans and discussions did not meet with their approval.

In their reply, the deputies took up Josel's report point by point. They took due note of the information and wrote that they approved of the proposals which Josel had made to the Ducal Counselors. They had no objections to them and suggested that he attempt to have them carried out in the form he had outlined, except in one respect, where, they said, they would recommend more rigorous action. They felt that any Jew who dared to circumvent the resident courts and cite a Christian party before the Imperial Court to the detriment of the common welfare, should have his passport suspended until such time as he should have made restitution, at his own expense, for the damage he had caused.

We see, then, that Josel never undertook a mission which he had not been authorized to carry out by express order of the *parnassim* of the Jewish communities, and that he conscientiously reported to them on every phase of the negotiations which he conducted on their behalf. However, he reserved for himself the "power and the authority" to make agreements and to accept Final Decrees at Imperial Diets (*Reichstagsabschiede*). No one had the right to engage in political activity on behalf of the Jews as a group without his knowledge.[43] *Reich* Jewry had only advisory privileges; the responsibility for the execution and enforcement of the action rested solely with the Commander.

These scanty reports give us reason to assume that, at that time, an organic union had been formed of all the more important communities and corporate bodies of Territorial Jewry, with representatives meeting at regular intervals to discuss the problems created by political, economic, social and religious developments and to plan steps to avert threatening dangers. Josel makes mention of a number of such meetings in Worms, at which a stern ban was pronounced on all violators of the Augsburg "Articles," and the Hebrew letter of 1551 had been sent by the rabbis and *parnassim* from one such conference which was held in Frankfort.

This was the first time in the history of German Jewry that the Jews of the Reich were willing to give up their zealously guarded autonomy to submit to one powerful personality and to unite into a closer community. Josel sought to prevent the complete disintegration of the communities, which bickered with one another and were torn by dissension from within. He probably envisioned a sort of Jewish *Reichsliga,* which would imbue the Jews of the south and of the west with a new community spirit and common resolve, much as the Emperor had conceived of and attempted to weld the Estates of his Empire into a more tightly knit confederation under his leadership.

Shortly before signing the agreement with the Duke of Wuerttemberg, Josel had to affix his signature to a document which legally confirmed the expulsion of the Jews from Upper and Lower Bavaria. Information on the circumstances which led to this move is incomplete.[44] All that is definitely known is that several Jews, the brothers Isaac and Hayum of Stadtamhof near Regensburg, Abraham of Cracow (a goldsmith by trade), and one Simon Puzl from The Hague had been arrested and detained in Munich, and were threatened with investigation under torture. The nature of the charges against them was not made known. In order to save these prisoners from the rack, Josel traveled to Munich at the request of the corporate body of Jewry. There, on July 1, 1551, he signed a "most unusual reciprocal obligation" with the government of Bavaria. In return for the release of the four Jewish prisoners, he made a solemn promise that in the future no Jew would make application for the right to reside and settle in Bavaria. Jews with outstanding debts in Bavaria were to authorize Christians to collect in their behalf. Jews obliged to travel through Bavaria had to promise to acquire an escort, to spend only one night in the Duchy, and not to do any business while traveling through the country. Foreign Jews found guilty of usury or fraud were not to receive legal aid and their outstanding debts were to be forfeit to the Duke. By the terms of this agreement, all the freedoms, privileges and letters of protection previously issued to the Jews of Bavaria were declared null and void. After taking an "oath according to proper Jewish custom in keeping with the Law of the *Reich,*" Josel signed his name to the document in Hebrew. Paulus Aemilius, a convert who was a professor at the University of Ingolstadt, translated the signature as "Joseph, the son of Gershon, who is called Joselmann Roschaim."

The agreements which Josel signed in July and August of 1551 with the Dukes of Bavaria and Wuerttemberg were indicative to some extent of the fate that awaited the Jews in all the larger states in general. Basically, these reigning princes who made ready to consolidate their sovereign powers were planning to follow the lead of the Imperial towns in dealing with the Jews. Not only Protestant states such as Saxony and Wuerttemberg, but also Catholic ones such as Bavaria, endeavored to get rid of their Jews.

The motivations for the simultaneous action of the territorial sovereigns were not only religious but also political and economic in nature. In the agreement which Josel had been compelled to sign in Munich, it was expressly stated that Duke Albrecht V had decided at the insistence of the territorial Estates to expel the Jews from Bavaria. The host desecration trial which had been held in the March of Brandenburg in 1510 also had been preceded by demands from the Estates that the Jews be expelled from the March.

That era of incipient territorial sovereignty was also the period of the beginnings of the dualist form of the State. The efforts of the reigning princes toward centralization of their powers and unification of their territories were countered by a drive on the part of the Estates, representatives of the nobility, the clergy and the burghers to gain a share in the government and to effect a partition of executive authority.

Indeed, these elements had practically become the sovereign lords in several states. This was especially the case in Wuerttemberg, where, in the disastrous era following the expulsion of Duke Ulrich, the Estates had succeeded in ensuring for themselves their freedoms by written agreement, and in Bavaria, where they had offered bitter resistance to the absolutist inclinations of the powerful Chancellor Eck.

But the main exponents of resistance were the cities. Even as subject cities, they still adhered to their ancient privileges, the *Meilenrecht* (freedom of the town extending one mile around), the *Bannrecht* (feudal economic privilege), corporate monopoly, and the rights of pre-emption. They bitterly fought against the free monetary system of the great bankers and industrialists, and particularly against the role of the Jews in commerce and moneylending.

Even in countries where they sought to effect a balance between the conflicting interests of urban and rural regions, of nobility and bourgeoisie, the reigning princes found themselves compelled again and again by serious financial embarrassment to side with the moneyed cities, on whose grant of supply they depended.

We can thus understand why, in the beginning, the policy of the evolving territorial states toward the Jews did not differ from the policy of the city-state, which had brought so much disaster to Jewry.

The third Imperial Diet to be held at Augsburg was the last Diet which Josel attended and the last held under the personal chairmanship of the Emperor. At the time, neither of the two men was aware that the struggle which they had begun—each for a different cause—at the first Diet of Augsburg had come to an end, and that the outcome had not been favorable for either party.

Late in August or early in September of that year, Josel left the city where the Diet had been held, and made the return journey to the Alsace on horseback. In those early autumn days, as he observed the flight of the birds from the chill of the north to the sunny south, he was unaware that the mighty Eagle Emperor, beneath whose pinions he had sought to secure shelter for his people, would soon take flight himself, with broken wings, to the warmth of his own homeland in Spain.

CHAPTER TEN

THE END

JOSEL signed his name as "Commander" of *Reich* Jewry for the last time when he made his agreements with the Dukes of Bavaria and Wuerttemberg. He was neither the first nor the last Jew to bear that title. In the decades before him and through the centuries after him, the heads of the corporate bodies of Territorial Jewry *(Landjudenschaft)* frequently made use of this title, or were addressed as such by the non-Jewish authorities. But Josel is the only Jew to have gone down in history simply as "the Commander." It is as the sole bearer of this title that he lives on in the memory of his grateful people, an honor and distinction considered the rightful due of Josel alone.

The position of Commander had evolved for him without his having sought it. He himself grew with it, even as his life was interwoven with the office. It had become a unique and necessary institution, whose origin and evolution can be readily understood as an outgrowth of the particular political situation that prevailed in the *Reich,* the economic circumstances there, and the social conditions of the era of the Reformation. It is a little more difficult to explain why the imagination of the people of his generation should have endowed this rational administrative institution with a special aura, and ascribed to it a unique magic power to settle disputes, alleviate distress, free prisoners, and obtain reprieves for those condemned to death. The reason was not that the people of that period were more susceptible to the miraculous than others, or that they believed in magical powers which could alter the destinies of men. Certainly, they did not regard Josel as a Faustian character, as an Agrippa von Nettesheim, as it were, "who was able to change things by his command." The secret is not rooted in the supernatural or in the miraculous. The answer lies in the personality of Josel himself, whose moral strength was felt to have the same profound effect which was attributed to prayer: the "power to open and close the gates of destiny."

From the very beginning, Josel was completely identified with the office that he held. He infused it with all the love and devotion in his heart, so that it became one with the man who held it. The holder of the office came to be regarded as an ideal and a symbol, while the institution in turn came to signify an exemplary way of life, measuring itself by the standard of eternal laws; it was a way of life deserving to be followed and emulated.

Josel has not set down his own thoughts with regard to his calling. But the historical figure with whom he most closely identified was Moses, to whom God had said: "My presence shall go before thee, and I will lead thee."[1] It was Josel's firm conviction that the leader was responsible, to the point of complete self-sacrifice, for the people that was entrusted to his care with regard to both its physical and spiritual existence. At the same time he believed that the people, too, had a responsibility toward the leader of its choice, to do him credit in the eyes of both God and man by its own conduct and attitude. Josel conceived of leader and nation together as an inseparable unit, on whose mission it worked together to achieve moral perfection, so that the most perfect of nations might be equal to the most perfect of leaders, and the most perfect of leaders might match the most perfect of nations. In this way, the nation might set an example for all other nations on earth to emulate.

But precisely because he had set the highest moral standards for his own people, Josel also became their severest critic and judge. Tenderly though he helped and cared for all those in distress, he was merciless in his dealings with those who jeopardized the welfare of the community by their conduct. In his *Sefer Ha-Mikneh,* in which he impressively warned his brethren against the traitors and informers in their midst, he quoted an anathema, worded in very sharp terms, by which such offenders were permanently excluded from the Jewish community. He made frequent and angry mention of the "erring and foolish people who have no good and amicable mind,"[2] who "did not lead a life of truth and righteousness as their fathers had done before them,"[3] and who conducted themselves in an "unseemly and shameless" manner to the detriment of their community.[4]

In his correspondence with the Magistrate of Strasbourg, Josel reports on a number of occasions that he excommunicated Jews who failed to abide by Jewish law or to observe agreements, who had bought up stolen articles, appealed to non-resident courts of justice, or charged exorbitant interest rates. In one of his last letters to the Councillors of Strasbourg,[5] Josel avowed upon his Jewish conscience and in accordance with true fact that he had pronounced excommunication upon Jews who had violated the agreement he had made with the city. He could do no more than that, he declared. For the Jews, he said, had no other secular form of punishment beside such excommunication, and he who failed to observe this decree for a period of four weeks was liable to the confiscation of all his property, which would then be forfeit to the Emperor's Fiscal Agent.

However, Josel demanded that Christian judges apply that same stern impartiality in their dealings with greedy and foolish Christians who had wronged Jews, no matter what the defendant's position. "For truth and justice are virtues in every station in the eyes of Almighty God."[6]

Contrary to the assumptions of some, Josel never considered himself a commander in the military sense of the term. Although there was a soldier-like strain in his character, his was the bravery of a chivalrous nature, the impetuous ardor of a warrior inspired by a sacred mission. The loyalty with which he kept the oath of office he had taken was neither the loyalty of a general to his supreme commander, nor that of a feudal lord to his vassals. It was the loyalty which had served from generation to generation to unite the wise teachers of his people with their disciples in question and answer, the rabbis with the community of Israel in prayer and penitence, and the Hassidim with their followers in mystical communion.

Josel, who started out as one Jew among many in an Imperial town, broadened his horizons to become a Jew of the *Reich* and finally gained the stature of a European Jew in the truest meaning of the term, showing the same deep concern for the fate of the Jews of Bohemia, Moravia, Silesia, Poland and Algiers and for the destinies of the Sephardim as he did for the welfare of his German brethren. The closing years of his life were spent almost entirely in the seclusion of tiny Rosheim, where he was once again merely the leader of the Jewry of the region (*Landjudenschaft*) of Lower Alsace, even as he had been in the beginning. It is true that he must have found at last the peace and solitude for which he had yearned during the years when he tirelessly rushed through the territories, carried on his disputations, and delivered speeches at Imperial Diets, or waited in the antechambers of chancellors and ministers to present his petitions. But old age brought him tragedy, years of disappointment and despair, and the realization that the work to which he had devoted his life would not endure. He saw that the protection against enemies from without which he had attained for his brethren, and the inner security which he had helped them to develop would both be wrecked by forces which he was powerless to avert.

History was to take a course different from that which he had expected, and the future destinies of the Jews were to be determined by forces other than those to which he had sought to commit them. The collapse of the Holy Roman Empire of the German Nation was to clear the way for the dominion of the modern, secular, absolutist, nationalist totalitarian states. These states were political entities which, unlike Charles V, no longer felt duty-bound as bearers of a sacred tradition of justice and morality to protect the Jews, but exploited or abused them for their individual purposes according to the iron dictates of political expediency and the impersonal principles of economic policy.

During those years, when Josel dwelt with his family within the walls of quiet Rosheim, he never ceased to give thought and send anxious communications to the *Reich* outside, not only in order to guard his brethren from danger, but to preserve their Protector himself from catastrophe.

Prior to the opening of the Imperial Diet of Augsburg, Margrave Hans von Kuestrin, and the Dukes Albrecht of Prussia and John Albrecht of Mecklenburg, the Emperor's Protestant adversaries, had already formed a defensive alliance for the purpose of combatting the hated "Interim" and re-establishing the German *Libertät.* Early in 1551, Maurice, Elector of Saxony, the most energetic but also the most unscrupulous and inscrutable of that younger generation of reigning princes, joined this alliance even though he was still in the Emperor's service as an Imperial Commander at the time, and unflinchingly continued to assure Charles of his loyalty and devotion.

The alliance was made for the purpose of restoring the ancient elective Emperorship and the true Christian faith, of freeing Landgrave Philip, Maurice's father-in-law, from captivity, and of abolishing the "brutal, intolerable and unbearable servitude which is like that in Spain."

In that same year the rebellious princes contacted King Henry II of France, whose greatest desire was to resume the policy of his father, Francis I, against the Emperor, and, with the help of the opposition party within the German Estates, to put an end to the power of Charles forever.

In October, 1551, a secret agreement was signed between the allied princes and the emissaries from France at a hunting lodge of the Elector Maurice in Lochau Moor where, six years before, Charles had won his victory over the Schmalkaldians. By the terms of this treaty the German cities of Metz, Toul, Verdun and Cambrai, those most important bridgeheads and fortresses on the borders of the *Reich* which formed the main line of communication between the hereditary lands of Charles and the Low Countries, were ceded by the allied princes to the King of France as the future *Reichsvikar.* In return, Henry promised to aid the princes in their struggle against the common enemy with funds, weapons and troops. This treaty, an act of open treason against the Emperor and the *Reich,* was solemnly confirmed at Chambord in January 1552.

In March of that year, while the Turks once again threatened the Provinces of King Ferdinand in the East and the troops of the allied princes were massing in Franconia, the King of France invaded Lorraine. He seized the cities which had been promised to him and made a surprise attack on the mighty fortress of Metz, forcing its surrender.

The people of the Alsace were seized with real panic. Wedged in between the swiftly advancing troops of the King of France, whom Schaertlin von Burtenbach, the former commander of the Schmalkald army had joined, marching with his troops from Basel, threatened by the Spanish mercenaries massed in the Low Countries, and not quite certain about the dangerous game of Maurice of Saxony, the governments found it extremely difficult to make the right decision in this precarious situation.

While the authorities and the Estates of the Alsace held meeting after meeting in order to plan "how to save the Country" and devise measures of mutual defense, and while the city of Strasbourg, courted by both France and Charles V, was recruiting mercenaries and arming the peasants, fate, to use Josel's favorite expression, overtook the Emperor.

Charles had gone from Augsburg to Innsbruck in order to be near the Ecumenical Council of Trient, hoping to bring about a last-minute settlement of the religious dispute.

It had been a matter of general knowledge for some time that Maurice, Elector of Saxony, was working hand in glove with France, and that it was the aim of Henry II and the Protestant princes to capture the Emperor, dead or alive. But Charles was "like one rapt in sleep and dreams," as an old folk song expressed it.[7]

It was inconceivable to Charles, but lately the all-powerful lord of Europe who had laid down the law for Christianity, that the reigning princes of the *Reich* should rise in treacherous revolt against the sovereign they themselves had chosen. He refused to believe that Maurice of Saxony, on whom he himself had conferred the title of Elector and whom he had charged with the task of laying siege to Protestant Magdeburg, should have been capable of ceding German territories to the most bitter enemy of the *Reich* and of endangering the life of his own Emperor. In those days, Charles was incapable of making decisions, of making up his mind as to whether to "endure great outrage or to expose himself to great danger."[8] His gout, which at times hindered his every movement, added to his anguish. He suffered deep and frequent depressions; he felt alone, helpless and betrayed, and abandoned by all. He no longer trusted his brother Ferdinand, who had always been on good terms with the German princes and who was even then negotiating with Maurice in Linz, in an attempt to intercede between him and his brother.

The Catholic allies, too, proved cautious and pusillanimous, and did not offer to help. The Electors of Mayence, Treves and Cologne were "exceedingly weak and miserable," and feared an attack by the French on their territories. Bavaria, which was always willing and ready to harm the House of Habsburg, remained neutral, as did the Protestant Duke of Wuerttemberg, whose country Charles had just saved from the demands of Ferdinand.

Innsbruck itself was an open city. The Imperial troops were stationed far away, in Italy and in the Low Countries. The Emperor was left completely stripped of funds, since even the House of Fugger was unable to raise a loan at this critical juncture.

Maria, *Stadtholder* of the Low Countries, warned her brother of the duplicity of the Elector of Saxony, whom she considered dangerous, and pleaded with him to leave Innsbruck. Ferdinand and the Imperial counselors also attempted to persuade the Emperor to take this course, but to no avail. Charles remained stubborn, uncompromising, morose and cynical.

In May 1552, the combined enemy troops succeeded in capturing the Ehrenberg Gorge, the last remaining fortress that might have been capable of protecting Innsbruck. Only then did Charles, borne in a sedan chair and attended only by his brother Ferdinand, take flight across the Brenner Pass to Villach in Carinthia.

Josel, who himself lived amidst the chaos of the war, and who, like all the other people of the Alsace, had reason to fear that he might be plundered by the troops of either of the fighting powers or driven out of house and home with his family, followed the waning fortunes of the Emperor with profound sympathy and concern. He had felt devotion and gratitude for the great sovereign, who had always dealt kindly and justly with his brethren, and his love and compassion now went out to Charles the man, who had suffered defeat, humiliation, disillusionment and the loss of his power. At this hour, when the Emperor stood utterly alone, Josel desired to prove his loyalty to him and to bring him help and support.

It was easy for the commander of the Jews to keep informed on all that was then transpiring in the *Reich.* The Imperial commanders, including Conrad von Hanstein who was defending the city of Frankfort against the insurgents, had "set up an alert espionage service to divine the intentions of the enemy, a service primarily performed by Jews."[9] Moreover, in order to provide some relief for the Emperor, the Jews of the Rhineland had undertaken to raise a total of 20,000 florins to pay the Imperial mercenaries.

Josel, who was able to follow the advances of the French at close range and was better informed than most of his contemporaries about the attitudes of the Imperial towns of the Alsace, took more than sixty florins from his own meager savings to dispatch messenger after messenger to the Emperor and "others elsewhere," to inform Charles of the danger threatening him, to warn him against his enemies, and to plead with him not to put his life in danger needlessly at this fateful hour, but to preserve it for the sake of his people and his Empire.[10]

When rumors were rife that Charles had died, and there was reason to fear that the King of France might seize the Imperial crown, Josel spread the word everywhere that "His Imperial Majesty, thank God, was alive and well," although, as he put it, "many people did not believe me."[11]

It is not likely that Josel's warnings had any effect on the Emperor's decisions. But the loyalty of another human being who knew the meaning of insults and humiliation may have brought some measure of cheer to the sovereign, and the messages from the Alsace may have recalled to Charles the brave commander of the Jews who never shrank from any task, no matter how difficult.

Even while Josel labored to bring about a change for the better in the Emperor's fortunes, he did all he could to save his own town of Rosheim from disaster.

All reports from that year of 1552 are agreed that this war, in which the German princes fought against the head of the Holy Roman Empire, had been conducted with ruthless cruelty and savagery.

"Not even the enraged peasants," a contemporary chronicler reports, "committed such atrocities and cruel arson in 1525 or took such bestial delight in torturing and tormenting the poor people and in bloody villainy as did those in this war of 1552, to the shame of all mankind. And [worst of all] the men who dealt in this manner with members of their own nation, and have brought down so many curses upon their own heads that those who come after them will groan beneath the burden for a long time to come, were Princes of German blood."

The fiercest of all the robber knights among those princes of German blood was Albrecht, Margrave of Brandenburg-Kulmbach. A member of the Protestant alliance, he acted independently from his allies "like a mad, wild monster"[12] to spread just as much havoc in the wealthy Protestant cities as in the Catholic Episcopal sees of Franconia, on the Danube, on the Rhine and on the Main.

In the fall of 1552, he overran Treves and Luxembourg, and the rumor spread that he was approaching the Bishopric of Strasbourg and intended to set fire to all of the smaller towns.

Even as he had done in the Peasants' War, so now, too, Josel placed his political experience and diplomatic skills at the service of the town of Rosheim. He offered to the Magistrate a loan of all the gold and silver in his possession in the value of 400 florins, and advised him to call on the other citizens to follow his lead "so that if the enemy should come and demand a war contribution, we may be able to turn him away."[13]

The Alsatians were spared the fate of the Frankish and Rhenish provinces, but they were witness to the final bitter struggle that was fought out between the Emperor and the King of France.

To the surprise of all the world, Charles quickly regained his bearings after his humiliating flight across the Brenner Pass. He rallied his troops, obtained loans and thought out ways and means to separate the warring princes from Henry of France. To be sure, he was now aware of the import of this revolt of the Estates, and no longer nursed hopes that he would succeed again in defeating the oligarchy of the princes. But he had regained sufficient authority to reject the demands of the *Reich*'s Estates assembled at Passau, to defer any decision concerning a settlement of the religious problem until a general Imperial Diet could be held under his chairmanship, and to propose that, in return for the release of the Landgrave of Hesse and the abrogation of the "Interim," the insurgents should disarm and break with

Henry II. As a result of this move, France was the only remaining enemy power with which he now had to contend and against which he could prepare to strike a decisive blow.

His first objective was to storm the doughty bulwark of Metz, which the French had put in an excellent state of defense and manned with the best of their troops, so that, by occupying the city, he might be able to put an obstacle in Henry's path to the *Reich* and to keep communications open between Germany and the Low Countries.[14]

It was an ill-starred venture from the very outset. It was much too late in the season for embarking on a lengthy siege, and it was most difficult during the long autumn rains and the cold winter months to cater to the needs of the Spanish troops, who were not accustomed to the northern climate and complained about inadequate pay as well.

The French put up a heroic defense. Charles was unable to capture the fortress, and in January, 1553, he saw himself compelled to acknowledge defeat and to withdraw from the theater of war.

Wounded in his pride, his conscience deeply troubled, and even more abjectly humiliated than he had been at Innsbruck, he retreated to Brussels, depressed, subdued, and already contemplating abdication. Convinced that he would not be able to crush the schism in Germany and to suppress the opposition of the Estates, Charles left the *Reich* to his brother Ferdinand, leaving him to settle the religious controversy to the satisfaction of the opposing princes. Charles never set foot on the *Reich* again, and no longer took an interest in the fortunes of the serfs of the Imperial Chamber who were part of that *Reich*.

Shortly before Josel was born, Charles of Burgundy, the Emperor's great-grandfather, had lost the battle of Nancy and met his death there. The events at the end of the Burgundian War had provided the long-awaited excuse for the Imperial cities of the Alsace to drive out the Jews or at least to place sharp restrictions on their business activities. This lost battle had wrought a complete change in the personal fortunes of Josel's parents as well as in the social and economic situation of the Jews in the Alsace.

When Josel was nearing the end of his life, the great-grandson of Charles the Bold lost the decisive battle of Metz, again with disastrous consequences for the Jews. The defeat at Metz put an end to the Emperor's dream of reviving the universal concept of Emperorship from the Middle Ages, and of setting up a united *Imperium Romanum* within which Jewry would have received protection as a political unit in its own right. It also meant the end of the "highest honor instituted by God on earth" in which Charles, as the most faithful steward and advocate of God, had sought to include also the Jews of the *Reich*.

Even as the beginning and the end of Josel's life, bounded by the battles of Nancy and Metz, joined to close the circle, so, too, the aged commander's final struggle was the last link in a long chain of battles which he had begun as a young *parnas* and *manhig*.

Josel relates in his memoirs[15] that immediately after the death of Maximilian in 1519, the burghers of the village of Dangolsheim had expelled their Jews and incited neighboring communities to follow suit. At that time, Josel, with the help of the *Unterlandvogt,* had managed to dissuade them from their "evil plans" and the Jews were permitted to return to their homes.

Thirty-four years later, the burghers of Dangolsheim felt that they again had cause for complaint. They deplored the fact that the number of Jews in Dangolsheim engaging in lucrative pursuits had grown from four married couples to ten. All of these, the burghers asserted, were earning their livelihood by usury and moneylending, so that half of the inhabitants of the village were in debt to them and had lost almost all of their landed property.

The Imperial village of Dangolsheim was part of the *Landvogtei* of Hagenau which had reverted to the Palatine branch of the Wittelsbach dynasty in 1530. Thus it was to the Elector Frederick II, the *Oberlandvogt* of the Lower Alsace, that the Magistrate turned for help. He asked Frederick for permission to expel the Jews from Dangolsheim, declaring that he would be willing in return to pay a higher tribute to the government than the Jews had paid heretofore.

Frederick II of the Palatine, who at one time had been a brilliant courtier and a friend of the Emperor, had converted to Protestantism only a few years before. Now he was an old man, badly disillusioned with life and without a will of his own. He had dealt kindly with the Jews in his own Electorate, and would have been willing to maintain a similar policy in the Alsace. However, he was not strong enough to resist the pressure applied by the *Unterlandvogt,* who sided with the citizens of Dangolsheim and who had complained about the ruinous usury practiced by the Jews there. Moreover, this was the "time when police regulations were in flower," when rulers everywhere began to watch the business activities of the Jews more narrowly, to set standard rates of interest and to put contracts made by Jewish creditors with their Christian debtors under the control of the authorities.

Accordingly, in April, 1553, the Elector ordered the *Landvogt* of Hagenau to report to him how many Jews were living in Dangolsheim, how much tribute they were paying, and when and from whom they had obtained their letters of safe-conduct.

The following month he commanded the Jews themselves

to submit to him an itemized list of their loans, and forbade them in the future to charge interest or to sell their possessions.

In a letter addressed to the Count Palatine,[16] Josel strongly protested against this decree. The Jews, he wrote, were willing to report the amounts of principal as well as interest due them from citizens of Dangolsheim. The other provisions of the decree, however, were inconsistent with all the Imperial and Palatine privileges issued to the Jews, and their enforcement would bring disaster upon all the Jews in the Alsace.

In reply, Frederick named a commission to lower the interest rate to five per cent and to uphold the right of residence in Dangolsheim of all those Jews who had obtained letters of safe-conduct from the Emperor or his ancestors. Josel therefore traveled to Heidelberg in July 1553 in order to clear up the questions at issue by way of a personal conference.

At this meeting, the Elector assured Josel that it was his wish to have the Jews and Christians dwell together in peace and that he had no intention of infringing on the traditional rights and privileges of his Jewish subjects. Nevertheless, he felt that it was in order to have the Jews expelled from Dangolsheim, since the Provincial Governor had advised him to "relieve the unfortunate Christians from this gnawing burden."

Josel tried to persuade the Count Palatine to have the matter investigated one more time by his own Court before making a final decision. When his request was refused, he appealed to the Imperial *Kammergericht.* During his second visit to Heidelberg he explained to the Elector that he had been forced to take this step because "many poor, plain Jews, widows and orphans, have appealed to me, Josel the Jew, as their commander, begging me to take action in keeping with my duty." However, he did everything possible to avoid taking recourse to the Supreme Court of Justice, and to persuade the Palatine Councillors to give the citizens of Dangolsheim and the Jews a hearing before a court of arbitration in Heidelberg, and not to issue the edict of expulsion until that time.

This request was granted. On March 12 a meeting was held in the capital, with five representatives of the Jews in attendance. Since the discussion could not be concluded in one day, a second meeting was scheduled to be held, again at Heidelberg, on April 15.

That winter of 1553-54, as he traveled back and forth on horseback between Rosheim and Hagenau, Speyer and Heidelberg, Josel's thoughts were not centered solely on the problem of his brethren in Dangolsheim. He had reason to be concerned also about his own situation and that of the Jews in the town of Rosheim, where he had lived for four decades.

He had always lived in peace with the citizens of Rosheim. As he stated on one occasion, he had rarely gone to law with them, and could honestly say that he had helped the townsmen and advised them in times of political stress. It was at Rosheim that he would convene meetings of the Lower Alsatian *Landjudenschaft,* sit in judgment, try the guilty, mete out punishment, arbitrate disputes and comfort the downhearted. It was to Rosheim that messengers had come from all over the *Reich,* and emissaries from Bohemia, Moravia and Silesia, to call on him for help. Here he had raised his children, married off his daughters, observed the Sabbaths and the festivals, done business, studied the works of the philosophers, and written his memoirs. It was from Rosheim that he had set out countless times to travel on horseback into the wide world at all seasons, in ice and snow, in sunshine and in rain. It was to Rosheim that he would return after absences of many months, after victory or defeat, happy to see the gentle mountain slopes of home again, where the bright clouds shone over the beechwoods in the sunset sky. He would ride through the massive gates, built to last an eternity, guarding the town from enemy invaders, past the skillfully wrought well with its iron wheels attached to heavy chains which pulled the water buckets up and down, past the sprawling grey Vosges stone edifice of the Church of Saints Peter and Paul, and through the broad main street lined with the trim timber-framed homes of the Councillors and wealthy burghers, ornamented with gables and oriels, balconies and windows set in fine frames. At last he would turn into a narrow street which is known as the Judengasse even today, and alight in front of one of the three-story houses with dark, tall, pointed roofs, brown galleries and a wide gate, a house which sheltered him for a little while from the great world outside whence he had come.

But in the last several years, the good relations between the Christian and Jewish inhabitants of Rosheim had been dealt a severe blow. Rosheim was the only Imperial town in the Alsace besides Hagenau that still had not expelled its Jews. In the early 1520's, Josel had succeeded in thwarting the endeavors of the people of Rosheim, who were determined not to be outdone by Colmar and Oberehnheim. But beginning with the early 1540's, clashes between the Jews and the Christians of the town had been steadily on the increase. The Jews of the town were harassed at night, and Jewish traders from elsewhere were prevented from entering the town or molested on the free Imperial highways. Eventually, Josel succeeded in bringing about an agreement between the Magistrate of Rosheim and the Jews, mediated through the Arbitration Court of Hagenau, Schlettstadt and Oberehnheim, by which eight Jewish couples and their kin were to be permitted to live in the town and to employ three Jewish schoolmasters.

But almost simultaneously with Josel's efforts to save the town of Rosheim from being forced to make a war contribution to the treasury of the Margrave Albrecht Alcibiades, the conflict flared up again. During one of his absences from the town, the windows, shutters and doors of Josel's own home were smashed in the middle of the night, and his wife and children were taken ill from the shock. The Magistrate had the four townsmen responsible for the raid locked up in the prison tower for several days and fined them one pound of Strasbourg currency. But at the same time he ordered the schoolmasters, including Josel's son Jacob, either to leave the town or to pay a heavy fine. When the schoolmasters did not comply with his order, he had the silver goblets in Josel's house impounded. Although he was in possession of an Imperial letter of protection securing for his sons and his sons-in-law the right to reside in the town,[17] Josel attempted to settle the dispute amicably. He proposed that the two parties submit their case for arbitration either to the *Landvogt,* or to the Magistrate of Hagenau, and to accept the resulting decision.

The Magistrate's answer was to forbid one Aaron, one widower Joseph and Josel, whose son-in-law David was living in his house as his business and political representative, to shelter their offspring in their homes for more than four nights. If they failed to obey the Magistrate's order, their sons and sons-in-law would be driven from Rosheim by the town beadles.

This time again, in January 1554, the threat was made while Josel was away at the Court of Heidelberg. The mob abetted the Magistrate by hurling stones into the homes of the Jews during the night. When the victims reported the incident to the mayor the next morning, the latter's terse reply was: "We cannot sit here and guard you; if you cannot abide this, then leave our town."[18]

When Josel returned from his journey, he became involved in a heated debate with the Councillors concerning the legal interpretation of the agreement that had been made between the town and the Jews. Josel pointed out that by the terms of the agreement, only non-resident and foreign Jews were forbidden to settle in Rosheim in the place of a deceased resident Jew and that the sons and sons-in-law of resident Jews clearly had the right to do so. The Magistrate, on the other hand, insisted that no Jews at all should be permitted in the future to settle in the town, for otherwise neither the townspeople nor their children would live to see the Jews die out. The Councillors did not deny that Josel had given aid and support to their town during the Peasants' War and in the war with the French. However, they added disparagingly, Josel had done this not out of concern for the townspeople but only for his own benefit and for the benefit of the Jews. Had he and his brethren enjoyed the same rights and freedoms as the other subjects, they would have cared little for the welfare of the Christians.[19]

Once, in an outburst of anger, Josel threatened the Magistrate that he would have recourse to the Supreme Court of Justice (*Kammergericht*), even if it should cost him a thousand florins. Yet, he begged the Magistrate of Hagenau "in his great distress" to hold another court day and to give a hearing to both parties so that each one might get its due.

This petition, from Josel to the Magistrate of Hagenau, is the last surviving document from his hand, his political testament, as it were. In his usual way, he prefaces his case with a survey of the historical background of the relations between the town of Rosheim and its Jews, the mounting tensions of the past years, and finally the open outbreak of the conflict which led to a breach of the agreement that had been signed under the aegis of the city of Hagenau. In a few dramatic and emotional words, he renders an account to the Councillors, but primarily to himself, of his past life. He describes his activities at the Imperial Diets and at the Supreme Court of Justice, his discussions with Emperors, kings and local authorities, his political dealings at the time of the Peasants' War and the war with the French, his efforts to preserve the time-honored privileges of the Jews and to make peace between Christians and Jews so that the possession they both cherished in common, their human dignity, would remain inviolate.

This final document from the hand of Josel recalls in many respects his first official petition from the year 1522, in which he made a complaint in behalf of lower Alsatian Jewry against the Imperial town of Oberehnheim. However, the two petitions differ in one important respect. This last letter contains no references to the Emperor and expressions of hope that he will protect the serfs of his Imperial Chamber. Moreover, it is couched in different terms. The language is not urgent and impassioned, challenging and demanding, but bespeaks wisdom, detachment, wistfulness and resignation. Josel no longer looks forward, but only backward. He knows, too, that his life has come full circle and that the beginning and the ending are the same. He realizes that the inimical forces against which he pitted himself have risen again, and that they will recur again through all the ages to come, each time in another guise and form.

He had gone forth as a fiery young rider to wage war on death and the devil. His sole armor had been purity of mind, and he had had no weapons beyond the steadfastness of his soul and the compassion in his heart.

Now, old and tired, he still rode through the dark valley of shadows, but it was the way that "leads from strength to strength," and he was convinced that it was the road to the Sanctuary.[20]

Death overtook him as he was preparing to ride to Heidelberg to save the Jews of Dangolsheim from expulsion. On April 6, the Jews of Dangolsheim informed the Elector Frederick that they would be unable to attend the meeting which was to be held at the Palatine residence around the middle of that month, due to the fact that their leader, who had pleaded their cause at the Elector's court, "had departed this life in death."[21]

Thus, in all probability, Josel died late in March or early in April, 1554. It was the season of the most beautiful festival of the Jewish year,[22] the feast of revelation and liberation on which the Jews honor the memory of the man who "preserved his generation by his exhortations and prayed for his people that God might be gracious unto it."[23]

Several memorial books from that period describe for us in simple and sincere words the reaction of the Jews to the news of the passing of their commander.[24]

"May God remember the soul of the venerable prince, our teacher Joseph, son of Gershon, of blessed memory, who was called by the name of Joselmann, together with the souls of Abraham, Isaac and Jacob, because he spared neither his honor nor his property and ofttimes risked his life to intercede for the protection of the community and of individuals. For a period of over forty years he attended the courts of kings and princes and kept expulsion, oppression, persecution and murder far from the Israelite nation. He also obtained letters of protection at the court of the Emperor, may His Majesty be exalted. For all this he accepted neither favors nor rewards. He did it solely for the love of God and of Israel. May his portion therefore be with the other shepherds and princes in Israel and may his soul be bound up in the bond of eternal life with the other pious in Paradise."

ACKNOWLEDGMENTS

This work is based in part on studies of manuscripts, records and documents in the Bodleian Library, Oxford; in the *Archives of the City of Strasbourg* and the *Archives Départementales,* Strasbourg; the *Hauptstaatsarchiv* of Wuerttemberg, Stuttgart; the *Badische Generallandesarchiv,* Karlsruhe; the *Archives of the Germanische National-museum,* Nuremberg, and in the *Oesterreichischen Staats-archiv, Abteilung Haus-, Hof-, und Staatsarchiv,* Vienna. Most of the source materials from the Alsace, including those in the municipal archives of Colmar and Oberehn-heim, have already been exploited in the last decades of the nineteenth century by Jewish and non-Jewish historians. A number of documents have been superbly edited by I. Kracauer, H. Bresslau and L. Feilchenfeld. The *Haus-, Hof-, und Staatsarchiv* of Vienna made available to me an abundance of previously unpublished source material which was most meaningful for the proper evaluation of Josel's political activities as Commander of German Jewry. These were mostly unpublished records of the Imperial Diets, including the Reichstagsakten from the *Erzkanzlerarchiv* in Mayence, the *Judicialia Miscellanea,* and the *Protocolla Rerum Resolu-*

tarum of the Reichshofrat, and the *Reichsregister* of Ferdinand I.

My sincere thanks go to the directors and the archivists of all the above institutions, particularly of the *Oesterreich Staatsarchiv* in Vienna, for their tireless assistance in searching out and gathering the source material, for their valuable advice, written and verbal, and for their careful preparation of copies, photostats and microfilms.

Thanks are due also to the officials of repositories such as the *Archives Générales,* Brussels; the *Geheime Staatsarchiv,* Berlin-Dahlem; the *Hauptstaatsarchiv* of Bavaria, Munich; the *Landesregierungsarchiv* of Tyrol, Innsbruck; the State Archives in Marburg, Nuremberg and Wuerzburg, and the Municipal Archives in Mayence, Mergentheim, Nuremberg, Speyer, Worms and Wuerzberg where, despite diligent study, pertinent source material could not be located.

I wish to record my special indebtedness to my friends at the Hebrew Union College-Jewish Institute of Religion, Cincinnati, Ohio, without whose generous assistance Chapter Eight of this volume could not have been produced in its present form. The late Dr. I. Sonne undertook the translation into German of the most important chapters of the *Sefer Ha-Mikneh,* a manuscript whose reading presented considerable difficulty. His interpretation of numerous puns, allegories and allusions greatly contributed to my understanding of Josel's philosophical treatise. Dr. A. Guttmann, who also translated several pages of the *Sefer Ha-Mikneh,* checked the talmudic passages I have quoted; Dr. M. Tsevat made the first complete rendering of Josel's *Memoirs* into German and aided me in my study of the Neubauer Catalogue; Rabbi I. Newman translated several printed Hebrew texts, and Mrs. Dora Landsberger rendered valuable assistance in the reading and correction of the printer's proofs.

With a deep sense of gratitude, I wish to express my

heartfelt thanks to Miss Gertrude Hirschler for her meticulous and thoughtful work in translating and interpreting the difficult German text, for her ever patient cooperation and her fine understanding of the complicated historical, social, economic and religious problems of the sixteenth century.

I am also deeply indebted to Dr. Solomon Grayzel, and Mrs. Evelyn Weiman, who read and reread, revised and corrected the English manuscript methodically and carefully, and gave me their invaluable assistance and constructive counsel.

Finally, I hereby express my sincere gratitude also to the officials of the Leo Baeck Institute, particularly Dr. Max Kreutzberger, for their active interest in my work and their technical assistance throughout.

NOTES

PREFACE

1. Leo Baeck, *This People Israel: The Meaning of Jewish Existence* (The Jewish Publication Society of America, 1965), p. 292.

INTRODUCTION

1. Carl J. Burckhardt, *Gedanken ueber Karl V* (Munich, 1954).

CHAPTER ONE: THE BEGINNINGS

1. For discussions of Josel's ancestry, see the following: E. Carmoly, "Ein allgemeiner Anwalt der Juden im deutschen Reiche," in *Israelitische Annalen* (publ. by M. Jost, Frankfort, 1839), p. 94. Elie Scheid, "Joselmann de Rosheim," in *Revue des Etudes Juives,* XIII (1886), pp. 62-84, 248-259. Moritz Stern, "Joselmann von Rosheim und seine Nachkommen," in *Zeitschrift fuer die Geschichte der Juden in Deutschland,* III (1889), pp. 65 ff. David Kaufmann, *R. Ja'ir Chajjim Bacharach (1638-1702) und seine Ahnen* (Treves, 1894).
2. Ludwig Geiger, *Johann Reuchlin, Sein Leben und seine Werke* (Leipzig, 1871), p. 106; Wilhelm Maurer, "Reuchlin und das Judentum," in *Theologische Literaturzeitung,* no. 9 (1952), pp. 535 ff.
3. Karl von Amira, *Das Endinger Judenspiel* (first edition, Halle, 1883); Isidor Kracauer, "L'Affaire des Juifs d'Endingen de 1470. Prétendu meurtre de Chrétiens par les Juifs," in *REJ,* XVI (1888), pp. 236 ff.
4. I. Kracauer, "Rabbi Joselmann de Rosheim," Part I, "Journal of Joselmann," in Hebrew and with French summary, *REJ,* vol. 16 (1888), pp. 84-105.

5. From a song by Ermoldus Nigellus, eighth-century poet. Quoted in *Deutsches Elsass, Deutsches Lothringen. Ein Querschnitt aus Geschichte, Volkstum und Kultur,* published by Otto Meissner (Berlin, 1941).
6. L'Abbé J. Gyss, *Histoire de la Ville d'Obernai* (Strasbourg, 1866); Elie Scheid, *Histoire des Juifs d'Alsace* (Paris, 1887); Jacqueline Rochette, *Histoire des Juifs d'Alsace des Origines à la Révolution* (Paris, 1938).
7. "Memorbuch von Niederehnheim," in *REJ,* vol. XIII (1886), p. 63.
8. *Memoirs,* Part 2.
9. Scheid, *Alsace,* Pièces Justificatives, XXIV.
10. Scheid, "Histoire des Juifs de Hagenau sous la domination allemande," in *REJ,* vol. II (1881), pp. 73-92; vol. III (1881), pp. 58-74; vol. IV (1882), pp. 98-112; vol. VI (1883), pp. 230-249.
11. Ludwig Feilchenfeld, *Rabbi Josel von Rosheim. Ein Beitrag zur Geschichte der Juden in Deutschland im Reformationszeitalter* (Strasbourg, 1898), p. 7.
12. Kaufmann, *Bacharach,* p. 9.
13. Anton Lourié, *Die Familie Lourié (Luria)* (Vienna, 1923).
14. Moritz Stern, "Die Blutbeschuldigung zu Fulda und ihre Folgen," in *ZGJD,* vol. 2 (1888), pp. 194-199.
15. Ernst Cassirer and Paul Oscar Kristeller, *The Renaissance Philosophy of Man* (Chicago, 1948).
16. *Sefer Ha-Mikneh.*
17. *Josephi oder Josels juden trostschrift an seine brueder wider Buceri buechlin sine die et consule,* Feilchenfeld, Appendix XVI, p. 180 ff.
18. Max Freudenthal, "Die Eigenart der Wormser Gemeinde in ihrer geschichtlichen Wiederkehr," in *ZGJD,* vol. V (1933-1934), pp. 103-104.
19. A. Sulzbach, *Die Ethik des Judentums. Auszuege aus dem "Buche der Frommen" des R. Jehuda Hachassid* (Frankfort, 1923). G. Scholem, "Die 'Frommen Deutschlands': Ein Kapitel juedischer Religionsgeschichte," in *Almanach des Schocken Verlags auf das Jahr 5694,* no. 1 (Berlin, 1937-1938), pp. 53 ff. *Idem, Major Trends in Jewish Mysticism* (New York, 1946).
20. R. von Liliencron, *Die historischen Volkslieder der Deutschen vom 13. bis 16. Jahrhundert,* vol. III (Leipzig, 1867).
21. H. Pflaum, *Die religioese Disputation in der europaeischen Dichtung des Mittelalters,* first study: *Der allegorische Streit zwischen Synagoge und Kirche* (Geneva, 1935).
22. W. M. Schmid, "Zur Geschichte der Juden in Passau," in *ZGJD,* vol. I (1929-1930).

23. Leopold Donath, *Geschichte der Juden in Mecklenburg von den aeltesten Zeiten (1266) bis auf die Gegenwart (1874); auch ein Beitrag zur Kulturgeschichte Mecklenburgs* (Leipzig, 1874).

CHAPTER TWO: LEADER OF PROVINCIAL JEWRY

1. Raphael Straus, *Die Judengemeinde Regensburg im ausgehenden Mittelalter. Heidelberger Abhandlungen zur mittleren und neueren Geschichte,* vol. VI (Heidelberg, 1932).
2. Otto Stobbe, *Die Juden in Deutschland waehrend des Mittelalters in politischer, sozialer und rechtlicher Beziehung* (Brunswick, 1866), p. 16.
3. A. Bachmann, *Aus den letzen Tagen Kaiser Friedrichs III. Mitteilungen des Instituts fuer Oesterreichische Geschichtsforschung,* vol. VII (1886), quoted in Raphael Straus, *Die Judengemeinde Regensburg,* p. 15, note.
4. R. Straus, "Der Regensburger 'Ritualmordprozess,' 1476-1480," in *Menorah,* 6th year (Vienna and Frankfort, 1928).
5. Hermann Dicker, *Die Geschichte der Juden in Ulm* (Rottweil a.N., 1937).
6. Scheid, *Histoire des Juifs d'Alsace,* Pièces Justificatives, XXVI, p. 312. I. Kracauer, "Rabbi Joselmann de Rosheim," in *REJ,* XVI, p. 102. Edict of Oct. 22, 1497.
7. Dicker, *op. cit.,* p. 74.
8. He had made such loans to one Viax Bonn and his wife, both of Bertschweiler, who certified that they owed him the sum of 50 florins; also to one Martin Fell of Oberehnheim, and to a man from Boersch, whose heirs refused to remit the amount owed. Feilchenfield, *op. cit.,* p. 10.
9. *Memoirs,* Part 3.
10. *Ibid.*
11. Folk Song. See W. Grau, *Antisemitismus im späten Mittelalter* (Munich and Leipzig, 1934), p. 34.
12. From a sermon by Jakob Strauss, Swiss preacher in Eisenach. Quoted from Friedrich von Bezold, *Geschichte der deutschen Reformation. Allgemeine Geschichte in Einzeldarstellungen,* ed. by W. Oncken, 3rd section, Part 1 (Berlin, 1890), pp. 458 ff.
13. Oskar Frankl, *Der Jude in den deutschen Dichtungen des 15., 16., und 17. Jahrhunderts* (Vienna, 1905). Hermann Sinsheimer, "Shylock—die Geschichte einer Figur," in *Jahrbuch fuer juedische Geschichte und Literatur,* vol. XXXI (1938).
14. From a folk song.
15. *Memoirs,* Part 5.
16. Friedrich Holtze, *Das Strafverfahren gegen die Maerkischen Juden im Jahre 1510. Schriften des Vereins fuer die Geschichte*

der Stadt Berlin, XXI (Berlin, 1884). Werner Heise, *Die Juden in der Mark Brandenburg bis zum Jahre 1571. Historische Studien,* no. 220 (Berlin, 1932).

17. Ludwig Geiger, "Die Juden und die deutsche Literatur, IV: Die Juden und die deutsche Literatur des 16. Jahrhunderts," in *ZGJD,* II (1888), p. 313.
18. *Memoirs,* Part 5.
19. *Sefer Ha-Mikneh.* On Pfefferkorn, see Max Freudenthal, "Dokumente zur Schriftenverfolgung durch Pfefferkorn," *ZGJD,* III (1931), pp. 227 ff. Meier Spanier, "Zur Charakteristik Johannes Pfefferkorns," *ibid.,* VI (1936), p. 209 ff.
20. *Der Judenspiegel* (1507); *Die Judenbeichte* (1508); *Der Judenfeind* (1509).
21. *Sefer Ha-Mikneh.*
22. *Memoirs,* Part 5.
23. *Sefer Ha-Mikneh.*
24. *Memoirs,* Part 5.
25. *Sefer Ha-Mikneh* and *Memoirs.*
26. Yitzhak Fritz Baer, *Galut* (Buecherei des Schocken Verlags, Berlin, 1936), p. 61.
27. *Fortalitium fidei* [Fortress of Faith] *contra Judaeos, Sarcenos aliosque christianae fidei inimicos,* written by Alfonso de Spina, a Franciscan monk in Spain, and published in 1485 and again in 1495 in Nuremberg, also attracted considerable attention at that time. Baer (*Galut,* p. 48) describes it as "the earliest epitome of a Jewish history written from the anti-Semitic point of view."
28. *Opus aureum ac novum a doctis viris diu expectatum domini Victoris a Carben—in quo omnes Judaeorum errores manifestantur* (Cologne, 1509).
29. Scheid, *Alsace,* Pièces Justificatives, XXV.
30. *Ibid.,* XXVII.
31. Abbé J. Gyss, *Histoire de la Ville d'Obernai* (Strasbourg, 1886).
32. Markus Lehmann, *Rabbi Joselmann von Rosheim. Eine historische Erzaelhlung aus der Zeit der Reformation,* 2 vols., vol. I (Frankfort on the Main, 1880), pp. 159 ff.; and Feilchenfeld, *op. cit.,* p. 96.
33. *Memoirs,* Part 4.
34. *Clag gemeiner judischait wonend in der landvogti Hagenaw gegen burgermeister und rat der stadt Ehenheym,* Obernai Archives (n.d.). In Feilchenfeld, *op. cit.,* Appendix II, pp. 146 ff.
35. *Memoirs,* Part 4.
36. This is also Feilchenfeld's view. *Archives du Département Bas-Rhin,* Série C, 8, and Feilchenfeld, *op. cit.,* Supplement XXIX.

37. Fritz Baer, "Gemeinde und Landjudenschaft. Ein Beitrag zur Geschichte des juedischen Organisationswesens," in *Korrespondenzblatt des Vereins zur Gruendung und Erhaltung einer Akademie fuer die Wissenschaft des Judentums, 2nd yr.* (1921). *Idem, Das Protokollbuch der Landjudenschaft des Herzogtums Kleve* (Berlin, 1936).
38. Letter from Josel to the Magistrate of Strasbourg, June 8, 1552. *Archives de la Ville de Strasbourg,* Records of the Senate *(Rathsprotokolle),* III, 116, fasc. 38.
39. Quoted in Feilchenfeld, p. 84.
40. Document dated February 9, 1552. *Archives Départmentales—Archives du Département Bas-Rhin,* Strasbourg, Série C, 78.
41. Petition to the Magistrate of Strasbourg, dated November 15, 1553. *Archives de la Ville de Strasbourg,* Records of the Senate (*Rathsprotokolle*), III, 117, fasc. 38.
42. *Ibid.*
43. In 1536. *Archives de la Ville de Strasbourg,* G.U.P., 174, no. 22; and Feilchenfeld, *op. cit.,* p. 37.
44. *Memoirs,* Part 7.
45. *Clag gemeiner judischait . . .*
46. *Memoirs,* Part 4.
47. *Clag gemeiner judischait . . .*
48. Mandate of August 18, 1514. Issued in the town of Gmuenden. Rappoltstein Family Archives. Quoted in Lehmann, *op. cit.,* vol. I, pp. 216 ff.
49. Bulletin of Baden Historical Commission, Supplement to the *Zeitschrift fuer die Geschichte des Oberrheins,* N.F., XXIV, 31, pp. 20 ff.: "Innsbruck. In response to their complaint, the Emperor Maximilian issues to the Bishop of Strasbourg and the [Masters] of Andlau the privilege of ordering all Jews and Jewesses to leave the territory of the villages of Blienschweiler, Mittelbergheim, and Nothalten by the following Pentecost. Those who will continue to do business in these villages shall wear a yellow ring on their outer garment and shall not be permitted to stay there overnight." In *Mitteilungen des Gesamtarchivs der deutschen Juden,* vol. II, no. 2, pp. 144-145.
50. *Memoirs,* Part 7.
51. *Ibid.*
52. *Ibid.*
53. Feilchenfeld, *op. cit.,* Appendix 1. Mandate of December 4, 1516.
54. Lehmann, *op. cit.,* vol. I, p. 207.
55. H. Bresslau, "Zur Geschichte der Juden in Rothenburg . . . ," in *ZGJD,* III (1931), pp. 301 ff.

56. Guenther Franz, *Der deutsche Bauernkrieg,* vol. I (Munich and Berlin, 1933-1935), p. 132.
57. *Memoirs,* Part 8.
58. In 1520 the Jews were also expelled from Weissenburg. Cf. Moritz Stern, "Die Vertreibung der Juden aus Weissenburg," in *ZGJD,* I (1929), pp. 297-303.

CHAPTER THREE: THE "COMMANDER"

1. *Memoirs,* Part 9.
2. Max Freudenthal, "Zur Geschichte der Judenprivilegien Kaiser Maximilians II. auf dem Reichstag zu Augsburg," *ZGJD,* IV, pp. 83 ff.
3. Gyss, *op. cit.,* vol. I, pp. 387 ff.
4. On December 16th and 18th, 1520. *Die Reichsregisterbuecher Karls V.,* published by the Kaiser Wilhelm Institute for German History in cooperation with the *Haus-, Hof- und Staatsarchiv* in Vienna (Vienna and Leipzig, 1913, 1930).
5. *Ibid.*
6. *Clag gemeiner judischait . . .*
7. Gyss, *op. cit.,* vol. I, pp. 378 ff.
8. L. Geiger, *Johann Reuchlin,* p. 311.
9. *Deutsche Reichstagsakten unter Karl V.,* prepared by Ad. Wrede, vol. II, pp. 355 ff. *Der Reichstag zu Worms* (Gotha, 1896).
10. M. Wiener, *Regesten zur Geschichte der Juden in Deutschland waehrend des Mittelalters,* vol. I (Hanover, 1862). Gerson Wolf, "Zur Geschichte der Juden in Deutschland, Part One: Die Anstellung der Rabbiner," *ZGJD,* vol. III (1889), pp. 159 ff. Moritz Stern, *Koenig Ruprecht von der Pfalz in seinen Beziehungen zu den Juden* (Kiel, 1898). Idem, *Die israelitische Bevoelkerung der deutschen Staedte. Ein Beitrag zur deutschen Staedtegeschichte,* vol. VII, *Worms*; no. 1: *Die Reichsrabbiner des 15. und 16. Jahrhunderts* (Berlin, 1937). James Parkes, *The Jew in the Medieval Community. A Study of his Political and Economic Situation* (London, 1938), p. 245.
11. *Memoirs,* Part 10.
12. *Clag gemeiner judischait . . .,* n.d.
13. *REJ,* XVI (1888), pp. 103 ff. Also Gyss, *op. cit.,* vol. 1, pp. 387 ff.; and Lehmann, *op. cit.,* vol. I, pp. 268 ff.
14. Eugen Taeubler, "Urkundliche Beitraege zur Geschichte der Juden in Deutschland im Mittelalter," *Mitteilungen des Gesamtarchivs der Deutschen Juden,* IV (Leipzig, 1914), pp. 31-62; V (1915), pp. 127-148, Section II: *Zur Geschichte der Kammerknechtschaft,* 4th year, pp. 54 ff. Guido Kisch, *The Jews in*

Medieval Germany: A Study of Their Legal and Social Status (Chicago, 1949).

15. E. Taeubler, *Mitteilungen,* IV, pp. 54 ff.
16. *Ibid.*
17. Irmgard Schmidt, *Das goettliche Recht und seine Bedeutung im deutschen Bauernkrieg,* Dissertation (Jena, 1939).
18. Alfred Stern, "Die Juden im grossen Deutchen Bauernkrieg 1525," *Juedische Zeitschrift fuer Wissenschaft und Leben,* 8th year (1870), pp. 57 ff. Franz Ludwig Baumann, *Quellen zur Geschichte des Bauernkriegs in Oberschwaben* (Tuebingen, 1876). Guenther Franz, *Der deutsche Bauernkrieg,* vols. I and II (Munich and Berlin, 1933-1935).
19. Franz Ludwig Baumann, *Quellen zur Geschichte des Bauernkriegs aus Rothenburg an der Tauber. Bibliothek des Litterarischen Vereins in Stuttgart,* CXXXIX (Tuebingen, 1878).
20. *Memoirs,* Part 11.
21. Letter from Josel to the Magistrate of Hagenau, 1554. *Archives du Département Bas-Rhin.* Bas Rhin, Série C, 78.
22. *Memoirs,* Part 11.
23. Letter from Josel to the Magistrate of Hagenau, 1554. *Archives du Département Bas-Rhin.*
24. *Ibid.*
25. *Memoirs,* Part 11.
26. *Ibid.*
27. *Memoirs,* Part 12.
28. *Ibid.*
29. M. H. Friedlaender, *Zur Geschichte der Blutbeschuldigungen gegen die Juden im Mittelalter und in der Neuzeit* (1171-1883), 3rd ed. (Brno, 1883). David Kaufmann, "Die Maertyrer des Poesinger Autodafé von 1529," *Monatsschrift,* vol. 38 (1894), pp. 426 ff. Hugo Hayn, *Uebersicht der (meist in Deutschland erschienenen) Literatur ueber die angeblich von Juden veruebten Ritualmorde und Hostienfrevel* (Jena, 1906).
30. *Memoirs,* Part 13.
31. Actually, there were only 30.
32. M. Stern, *Die paepstlichen Bullen ueber die Blutbeschuldigung* (Berlin, 1893). Solomon Grayzel, *The Church and the Jews in the 13th Century. A Study of Their Relations During the Years 1198-1254, Based on the Papal Letters and the Conciliar Decrees of the Period* (Philadelphia, 1933).
33. Joshua Trachtenberg, *The Devil and the Jews. The Medieval Conception of the Jew and Its Relation to Modern Anti-Semitism* (New Haven, 1943).

34. Salo W. Baron, *The Jewish Community, Its History and Structure to the American Revolution,* vols. I-III (Philadelphia, 1942).
35. Moritz Stern "Die Versammlung der Juden zu Worms im Jahre 1510," in *ZGJD,* vol. III (1889), pp. 248 ff. Harry Bresslau, "Zur Geschichte der Juden in Rothenburg an der Tauber," *ibid.,* pp. 301 ff.
36. M. Wiener, *Regesten zur Geschichte der Juden in Deutschland waehrend des Mittelalters,* vol. I (Hanover, 1862), pp. 71 ff. Gerson Wolf, "Zur Geschichte der Juden in Deutschland," *ZGJD,* III (1889), pp. 159 ff. Moritz Stern, *Koenig Ruprecht von der Pfalz in seinen Beziehungen zu den Juden* (Kiel, 1898). James Parkes, *The Jew in the Medieval Community* (London, 1938), pp. 247 ff.
37. The best source of information on the functions of the *Reichsrabbiner* is a later document dealing with the "Appointment of Three Judges After the Death of the *Reichsrabbiner* Samuel of Worms," entitled *Der Juedischait im Heilligen Reich erlangte Bewilligung von wegen Halltung dreyer Richter, so under inen des ubl Juedischer Ordnung nach straffen,* Nuremberg, March 28, 1543, *Reichsregister Ferdinands I.,* vol. 6, folios 21 r. - 22 v. *Oesterreichisches Staatsarchiv, Abt. Haus-, Hof- und Staatsarchiv* (Vienna). Moritz Stern, "Der Wormser Reichsrabbiner Anselm," *ZGJD,* V (1935), pp. 157-168.
38. Letter from Frederick III to the Magistrate of Nuremberg, January 16, 1488. *Archives of the Germanische Nationalmuseum* (Nuremberg).
39. *Replice et conclusiones des kais.-fiscals ctra Joesel juden von Rossheim, so sich nennet regirer gemeiner judischeit im reich,* Pres. Speyer, November 4, 1536. *Archives du Département Bas-Rhin,* F. 2615, Wetzl. 454, A. Copied in Feilchenfeld, *op. cit.,* Appendix XIII, pp. 173 ff. Elie Scheid, "Joselmann von Rosheim," *REJ,* XIII (1886), Appendix, pp. 254 ff.
40. *Ibid.*
41. Reichshofrat, *Judicialia miscellanea,* J 1, fasc. 6, conv. 1, fol. 8. *Oesterreichisches Staatsarchiv, Abt. Haus-, Hof- und Staatsarchiv* (Vienna).
42. 1541. *Archives du Dép. Bas-Rhin,* Série C, 78.
43. Feilchenfeld, *op. cit.,* Appendix IV.
44. *Ibid.,* Appendix XII.
45. See Feilchenfeld, *op. cit.,* p. 20, and Moritz Stern, "Die Versammlung zu Worms," *ZGJD,* III (1889), p. 250, note.
46. The same opinion is advanced in Feilchenfeld, pp. 13 ff.
47. Feilchenfeld is in agreement.
48. Feilchenfeld, Appendix XXVII.

CHAPTER FOUR: CRITIC AND REFORMER

1. *Die Reichsregisterbuecher Kaiser Karls V.*, ed. by Kaiser-Wilhelm Institut fuer Deutsche Geschichte in cooperation with the *Haus-, Hof-, und Staatsarchiv* (Vienna and Leipzig, 1913-1930), "1530 Mai, Innsbruck: Jesal von Rossheim, und Jud."
2. *Memoirs,* Part 14.
3. For Peutinger, see *Konrad Peutingers Briefwechsel,* compiled, edited and interpreted by Dr. Erich Koenig, *Veroeffentlichungen der Kommission fuer Erforschung der Geschichte der Reformation. Humanistenbriefe,* I (Munich, 1923).
4. Bezold, *Geschichte der Deutschen Reformation,* p. 703.
5. A. E. Adcock, *Renaissance and Reformation (Judaism and Christianity),* vol. II (London, 1937), p. 7, ed. by H. Loewe. Franz Kobler, *A Treasury of Jewish Letters: Letters from the Famous and the Humble* (Philadelphia, 1953): Letter from Isaac Zarphati to his brethren in Germany.
6. *Memoirs,* Part 14.
7. *"Geleit. Judischeit im Reich und in Germanien wohnhaft; Schutz; Geleit. Generalmandat ins Reich, bes. Landvogtei i. Un. Elsass allgem. Priv. Bestaetigung fuer die Juden betr."* (Safe-Conduct for Jewry residing in the *Reich* and in Germany; Protection; Safe-Conduct; General Mandate for the *Reich,* particularly the *Landvogtei* of the Lower Alsace; general confirmation of Privilege for the Jews), *Reichsregisterbuecher.*
8. For the Imperial Diet, see: Eduard Wilhelm Mayer, "Forschungen zur Politik Karls V. waehrend des Augsburger Reichstags von 1530," *Archiv fuer Reformationsgeschichte. Texte und Untersuchungen,* 8th year (1916).
9. Josel's "Letter of Consolation to His Brethren."
10. Reinhold Lewin, *Luther's Stellung zu den Juden. Ein Beitrag zur Geschichte der Juden in Deutschland waehrend des Reformationszeitalters (Neue Studien zur Geschichte der Theologie und der Kirche)* (Berlin, 1911). Hartmann, Grisar, S. J., *Luther,* vols. 1-3 (Freiburg i. B., 1911). *D. Martin Luther's Werke,* Complete Critical Edition, *Tischreden,* vol. I (Weimar, 1912). Louis Israel Newman, *Jewish Influence on Christian Reform Movements,* Columbia University Oriental Studies, vol. XXIII (New York, 1925). Heinrich Bornkamm, *Luther und das Alte Testament* (Tuebingen, 1948). Armas K. E. Holmio, *The Lutheran Reformation and the Jews* (Hancock, Michigan, 1949). Gerhard Ritter, *Luther, Gestalt und Tat,* 5th ed. (Munich, 1949).
11. "Letter of Consolation."
12. *Mit sampt einer gruendtlichen und warhaften Anzaygunge/*

aller Satzungen/ Ceremonien/ Gebeten/ Haymliche und offentliche Gebraeuch/ deren sich dye Juden halten/ durch das gantze Jar/ mit schoenen und gegruendten Argumenten wyder jhren Glauben. Durch Anthoninum Margaritham/ Hebrayschen Leser der loeblichen Stadt Augspurg beschrieben und an tag gegeben M. D. XXX. (With a true and detailed listing of all the precepts, ceremonies, prayers, private and public rituals which the Jews observe throughout the year, with good and well-founded arguments against their creed. By Anthony Margaritha, Lecturer in Hebrew, of the celebrated city of Augsburg, Augsburg, 1530. I had access only to the 1705 edition, entitled: *Der gantze Juedische Glaube/ mit einer gruendlichen und wahrhafftigen Anzeigung aller Satzungen/ Ceremonien/ Gebeten/ heimlich—und oeffentlichen Gebraeuchen/ deren sich die Jueden das ganze Jahr ueber bedienen/ nebst schoenen und gegruendeten Argumenten wider ihren Glauben beschrieben und zusammengetragen von Antonio Margaritha, einem bekehrten Jueden/ und weiland Lectore oder Lesern der Hebraeischen Sprache bey der Hochloebl. Universitaet Leipzig/ Itzo aber allen Christlichen Liebhabern zu einem grossen Nutz und Erkaentnis der Juedischen Blindheit/ auffs neue nach den alten editionibus uebersehen/ und mit einem vollkommenen Register vermehrt/ nebst M. Christiani Reineccii S. S. theol. Baccal Vorbericht von des Antonii Margarithae Juedischen Familie/ Bekehrung/ Leben und Schriften,* Leipzig, 1705. (The Whole Jewish Faith, with a true and detailed listing of all the precepts, ceremonies, prayers, private and public rituals which the Jews observe throughout the year, with good and well-founded arguments against their creed, written and compiled by Anthony Margaritha, a converted Jew and former Lecturer in Hebrew at the Most Celebrated University of Leipzig, now re-edited after the older text, and supplemented with a complete Index, also with an introduction by M. Christiani Reinecce, Bachelor of Theology, concerning Margaritha's Jewish family background, his conversion, his life and letters, to benefit all lovers of Christianity so that they may recognize the blindness of the Jews, Leipzig, 1705. See also Josef Mieses, *Die aelteste gedruckte deutsche Uebersetzung des juedischen Gebetbuchs aus dem Jahre 1530 und ihr Autor Anthomius Margaritha* (Vienna, 1916).

13. *Sefer Ha-Mikneh.*
14. *Ibid.* and "Letter of Consolation," and letters to the Magistrate of Strasbourg of May and July 1543. Published by Harry Bresslau, "Aus Strassburger Judenakten, II: Zur Geschichte Josels von Rosheim," *ZGJD,* V (1892).

15. Tosefta Sanhedrin 13.2 and *Otijjot de Rabbi Akiba,* paragraph 7.
16. Jerus. Talmud, Shebi'it 4.2.
17. Deuteronomy 10.19.
18. Leviticus 19.34.
19. Leo Baeck, *This People Israel,* p. 47.
20. Letter from Josel to the Magistrate of Strasbourg, July, 1543. See Bresslau, "Aus Strassburger Judenakten," in *ZGJD,* V (1892), pp. 332 ff.
21. "Letter of Consolation."
22. *Sefer Ha-Mikneh.*
23. *ZGJD,* V, pp. 332 ff.
24. *Memoirs,* Part 15.
25. Badisches Generallandesarchiv, Karlsruhe, Dept. 67, *Bestand Kopialbuecher,* vol. 894, fol. 152. Issued in Augsburg on August 12, 1530. Entry in the *Reich Registerbücher* reads: "1530 *Aug. Judenschaft im R. Best. d. Priv. K. Sigismund fuer die Juden in den R. Staedten i. Elsass."* ("August 1530, Jews in the Reich . . . Privilege issued by the Emperor Sigismund for the Jews in the Imperial Cities of the Alsace.")
26. Letter from Charles to his brother Ferdinand, dated September 26, 1541: *"Car l'argent ce lieve pour moy et en puis disposer a mon plaisir."* ("Because the money is mine to do with as I see fit"). Karl Brandi, *Kaiser Karl V.,* vol. II: *Quellen und Eroerterungen* (Munich, 1941), p. 306.
27. Max Neumann, *Geschichte des Wuchers in Deutschland bis zur Begruendung der heutigen Zinsengesetze* (1654) (Halle, 1865), pp. 344 ff.
28. Bezold, *op. cit.,* p. 405.
29. The nineteen Imperial cities were Strasbourg, Regensburg, Augsburg, Ulm, Reutlingen, Noerdlingen, Schwaebisch-Hall, Gmuend, Memmingen, Biberach, Kempten, Dinkelsbuehl, Kaufbeuren, Wangen, Isny, Schwaebisch-Werd, Aalen, Bopfingen, Gingen. Ludwig Mueller, "Aus fuenf Jahrhunderten. Beitraege zur Geschichte der juedischen Gemeinden im Riess," *Zeitschrift des historischen Vereins fuer Schwaben und Neuburg* (1899-1900).
30. Final decree of Provincial Diet of Wuerttemberg (known as *"Zweite Regimentsordnung"*): The Jews were not to be allowed in the Province, and neighboring provinces were requested to do likewise. Business transactions between non-resident Jews and subjects of Wuerttemberg involving pledges, securities or bonds were declared null and void and the Jews were permitted to collect only the capital involved. Copy from the Hausarchiv of

Stuttgart, Records of the Provincial Diets of Wuerttemberg, Series 1, vol. I, no. 12, p. 50 in *Mitteilungen des Gesamtarchivs der deutschen Juden,* vol. V, p. 188.

31. *Keysers Caroli V. Privilegium vor das Hertzogthum Wuerttemberg, wegen der Juden, und dass die Herzoge zu Wuerttemberg geaechtete Personen recipiren doerfen,* issued on October 15, 1530. Library of University of Tuebingen.
32. Karl Eduard Foerstemann, *Urkundenbuch zu der Geschichte des Reichstags zu Augsburg im Jahre 1530,* vol II: *Vonn Judenn wucher* (Halle, 1833).
33. Raphael Straus, "Die Judenfrage auf dem Augsburger Reichstag von 1530," in *Bayerische Israelitische Gemeindezeitung,* 6th year (1930).
34. Feilchenfeld, *op. cit.,* Appendix IV.
35. Eliezer ben Nathan of Worms, about 1150.
36. Isaac ben Moshe Or Zarua, about 1250.
37. Guido Kisch, "The Jewish Law of Concealment," *Historia Judaica,* vol. I (1938), pp. 1-30.
38. Cf. R. Straus, *Die Judengemeinde Regensburg* . . .
39. Mishna, Baba Kamma, 10.9.
40. Mishna, Baba Kamma, 10.3.
41. Jakob Strieder, *Jacob Fugger, The Rich Merchant and Banker of Augsburg, 1495-1525* (New York, 1931).
42. *Artikel und Ordnung, so durch Josel juden von Rossheim, gemeiner juedischer regierer, aufgericht und beschlossen worden, gehalten im reichstag zu Augspurgk im jar 1530* ("Articles and Regulations drawn up and decreed by Josel, Jew of Rosheim, Governor of all Jewry, at the Imperial Diet at Augsburg in 1530"). Feilchenfeld, *op. cit.,* Appendix III. A copy of this document, without the introduction, is in the Haupstaatsarchiv of Wuerttemberg with the records of the Lands in the possession of the Teutonic Order: B 287 *Judenschaft (im Deutschordensgebiet und auswaerts),* fasc. 3/4, *Die Artikel und Ordnung, di durch Josel Juden von Rosshen, gemeyner juedischer Regierer, aufgerichtet und beschlossen worden. Gehalten im Reichstag zu Augsburg im Jahr alls man zalt 1530* ("The Articles and Regulations, which were drawn up and decreed by Josel, Jew of Rosshen, Governor of all Jewry, at the Imperial Diet at Augsburg in the year 1530"). Another copy is available in the *Archives de la Ville de Strasbourg,* Strasbourg, under G.U.P. 115 to 174, no. 19.
43. *Archives de la Ville de Strasbourg,* G.U.P. 115-174, no. 19 and Feilchenfeld, Appendix III.
44. Feilchenfeld, Appendix VI.

CHAPTER FIVE: MEDIATOR AND LIBERATOR

1. *Memoirs,* Part 16.
2. No reference to Josel was found in the *Papiers d'Etat et de l'Audience,* no. 1627/1, *Correspondance générale 1531-1536,* no. 1669/1 and 2, *Correspondance avec l'Empire, 1531-1555,* or in the *Secrétairerie d'Etat allemande,* no. 88, *Correspondance générale 1531-1549,* which are kept at the Archives Générales, Brussels.
3. Marianne Beyer-Froehlich, *Die Entwicklung der deutschen Selbstzeugnisse. Deutsche Literatur, Sammlung literarischer Kunst und Kulturdenkmaeler in Entwicklungsreihen* (Leipzig, 1930).
4. *Memoirs,* Part 16.
5. As did Feilchenfeld, who cites these passages in his work, pp. 138 ff.
6. *The Holy Path.*
7. Hugo Bergmann, *Die Heiligung des Namens. Jawne und Jerusalem.* Collected Essays (Berlin, 1919).
8. *Archives du Dép. Bas-Rhin,* F. 2615, Wetzl. 454, no. 5, and Feilchenfeld, *op. cit.,* p. 56.
9. *Memoirs,* Part 17.
10. *Copeien der juden irer privilegien, so sie itzo in der eil behanden gehabt* (Copies of privileges issued to Jews), *Archives du Dép. Bas-Rhin,* E. 1406. P. Scheffer-Boichorst has published in the *Mitteilungen des Instituts fuer Oesterreichische Geschichtsforschung,* vol. X, pp. 459 ff., a document drawn up by Frederick II on January 3, 1216, dealing with the Jews in Regensburg. This document, which is now part of a miscellany of the *Bezirksarchiv* of Strasbourg, incorporates a sizable part of a document drawn up by Frederick I, probably in 1182. This discovery is particularly significant because of the statement "*sollvetur curam gerentes omnium Judaeorum in imperio nostro degentium qui spetiali praerogativa dignitatis nostrae ad imperialem cameram noscuntur pertinere . . .*" contained in the document. In 1531 [should read 1532], Jessel, Jew, from Rotzem, made application *Judaeorum totius Germaniae nomine* (in behalf of all of German Jewry), to Cardinal Campeggio, who attended the Imperial Diet of Regensburg, for confirmation of the Charter issued by Frederick II, which request was granted. Harry Bresslau, in *ZGJD,* III (1889), p. 394.
11. E. Taeubler, *Mitteilungen des Gesamtarchivs,* IV, pp. 31 ff.
12. E. Taeubler, "Urkundliche Beitraege . . .", in *Mitteilungen,* IV, pp. 40 ff.
13. Josef Segall, *Geschichte und Strafrecht der Reichspolizeiordnun-*

gen von 1530, 1548 and 1577. Strafrechtliche Abhandlungen, no. 183 (Breslau, 1914).

14. Eduard Biberfeld, *Der Reisebericht des David Reubeni. Ein Beitrag zur Geschichte des 16. Jahrhunderts* (Berlin, 1892). A. Sulzbach, *Bilder aus der Juedischen Vergangenheit. Ein Quellenbuch fuer den Unterricht und zum Selbststudium* (Frankfort, 1914). Moses Bailey, "David the Reubenite, A Messianic Figure in Three Religions," *The Macdonald Presentation Volume* (Princeton, N. J., 1933), pp. 31 ff. A. Z. Aescoly, "David Reubeni in the Light of History," in *JQR,* N.S., XXVIII (1937-1938).
15. Julius H. Greenstone, *The Messiah Idea in Jewish History* (Philadelphia, 1906; reprinted 1943).
16. *Memoirs,* Part 17.
17. David Gans, *Chronikartige Weltgeschichte unter dem Titel; Zemach David, verfasst im Jahre 1593,* first German translation from the Hebrew original, annotated by Gutmann Klemperer. With introductory and supplementary notes, publ. by D. M. Gruenwald, no. 1 (Prague, 1890).
18. Bezold, *Geschichte der deutschen Reformation . . .,* p. 708.
19. *Copia citationis mir zu ruck ufgeschribne executio,* July 6, 1535. *Archives du Dép. Bas-Rhin,* F. 2615, Wetzl. 454, no. 1. Feilchenfeld, Appendix X, pp. 167 ff.
20. *Mandatum constitutionis Jesel juden von Rosheim,* July 7, 1535. Original is at the *Archives du Dép. Bas-Rhin,* F. 2615, Wetzl. 454, no. 2. Copied in Feilchenfeld, Appendix IX, pp. 168 ff.
21. *Libellus summarius, fiscal ca. Josel juden, der sich nennt ein regierer gemeiner judischeit* (Case of Fiscal Agent"versus Josel, the Jew, who calls himself a Regent of All Jewry"). *Ibid.* See Feilchenfeld, p. 13.
22. *Exceptiones et in eventum conclusiones Joesel juden zu Rosheim ctra. den kais. fiscal. Praes. Speir 5. Julii anno 36. Ibid.,* no. 4. Copied by Feilchenfeld, Appendix XII, pp. 169 ff.
23. *Replice et conclusiones des kais. fiscals ctra. Joesel juden von Rossheim, so sich nennet regierer gemeiner judischeit im reich. Praes. Speir, 4. novembris anno 36.* In Feilchenfeld, Appendix XIII, pp. 173 ff.
24. Bernhard Wachstein, "Wer sind die Prager Munk im 16. Jahrhundert?," *ZGJD,* I (1929), pp. 141-151.
25. *Memoirs,* Part 20.
26. Probably Sabbatai Horowitz, a son of Salman Muncka, whose grandson was Sabbatai Horowitz, physician and cabbalist writer.
27. *Memoirs,* Part 20.

28. *Memoirs,* Part 20. Louis Neustadt, *Die letzte Vertreibung der Juden in Schlesien. Beilage zum Jahres-Bericht der hebraeischen Unterrichts-Anstalt zu Breslau ueber das Jahr 1892/93* (Breslau, 1893), pp. 15 ff.
29. *Memoirs,* Part 18. Josel erroneously wrote 1533 instead of 1535.
30. Alfred Glaser, *Geschichte der Juden in Strassburg von der Zeit Karls des Grossen bis auf die Gegenwart* (Strasbourg, 1894).
31. Petition to the Magistrate of Strasbourg, dated June 1531. Copy. *Archives de la Ville de Strasbourg,* G.U.P., 174, no. 26.
32. *Archives de la Ville de Strasbourg,* G.U.P., no. 21.
33. "Jews who wish to avail themselves of the right to safe-conduct in the city shall first agree not to cite the city's burghers and small farmers in the countryside before alien, non-resident courts of justice." June 25, 1535. Original in the *Archives de la Ville de Strasbourg*, G.U.P., 174, no. 21.
34. *Archives de la Ville de Strasbourg,* G.U.P., nos. 21 and 22.

CHAPTER SIX: THE COMFORTER

1. Burkhardt, *Die Judenverfolgungen im Kurfuerstentum Sachsen von 1536 an. Theologische Studien und Kritiken,* 70th year (Gotha, 1897). Reinhold Lewin, *Luthers Stellung zu den Juden. Ein Beitrag zur Geschichte der Juden in Deutschland waehrend des Reformationszeitalters. Neue Studien zur Geschichte der Theologie und der Kirche* (Berlin, 1911). *D. Martin Luthers Werke,* complete critical edition, *Briefwechsel,* VIII, no. 3152 (Weimar, 1938). pp. 76 ff. Jacob R. Marcus, *The Jew in the Medieval World, A Source Book, 315-1791* (Cincinnati, Ohio, 1938).
2. *Memoirs,* Part 22.
3. *ZGJD,* V, 307 ff.
4. *Memoirs,* Part 22.
5. *Dr. Wolfgang Capito, der erste evangelische Prediger am Jungen St. Peter in Strassburg* (Strasbourg, 1866). Hermann Baumgarten, *Jakob Sturm* (Strasbourg, 1876).
6. Letter dated July 11, 1543. Quoted in Bresslau, *ZGJD,* V, 307 ff.
7. A Latin and a German version of this letter have survived. The Latin version is printed in full in *D. Martin Luthers Werke,* VIII, no. 3152, pp. 76 ff. The German version, which was also used by Bresslau, was sent by Josel to the Magistrate of Strasbourg together with a letter written in 1543. Bresslau presumes that Josel was not responsible for the translation of the letter, but that he had received the Latin and German versions—or the German only—from Capito.

8. *Archives de la Ville de Strasbourg,* G.U.P. 174, no. 23. Letter dated May 5, 1537. See also *ZGJD,* V, 307 ff.
9. *Literae cuiusdam Judaei* (Josel Rosheim, Joselmann; i.e., Joseph Ben Gerson Lorchans of Rosheim, Lower Alsace, also known as Joseph the Jew) *Doctori M(artino) offerabantur, quibus orabat et urgebat - sicut antea saepius scripserat ad Doctorem. D. Martin Luthers Werke, Tischreden,* III, no. 2597 (Weimar, 1912), pp. 141 ff., May 27 to June 18, 1537.
10. "Letter of Consolation."
11. *Tischreden,* I, no. 953, p. 481. First half of the 1530's.
12. Letter from Josel to the Magistrate of Strasbourg, written in May, 1543. *ZGJD,* V, pp. 307 ff.
13. *Ibid.*
14. Dated June 11, 1357. Written in Wittenberg, the Monday after St. Barnabas' Day. Printed in full in *Luthers Werke, Briefwechsel,* VIII, no. 3157, pp. 89 ff.
15. Heinrich Bornkamm, *Luther und das Alte Testament* (Tuebingen, 1948).
16. *Tischreden,* I, Fall of 1532, no. 369 (Weimar, 1912), p. 162.
17. *Ibid.,* January 1533, no. 3912, p. 77.
18. *Ibid.,* first half of the 1530's, no. 741, p. 357.
19. Lewin, *Luther's Stellung,* and Julius Koestlin, *Martin Luther. Sein Leben und seine Schriften,* vol. II (Elberfeld, 1883).
20. *Tischreden,* III, May 27 to June 18, 1537, no. 3597, pp. 141 ff.
21. Siegmund Salfeld, *Die Judenpolitik Philipps des Grossmuetigen* (Frankfort on the Main, 1904). Abraham Cohn, *Beitraege zur Geschichte der Juden in Hessen-Kassel im 17. und 18. Jahrundert.* Part I: *Staat und Umwelt in ihrem Verhaeltnis zu den Juden,* Dissertation, University of Marburg (Frankfort, 1933).
22. "Proposal for tolerating the Jews, submitted to His Serene Highness, the High Born Prince and Master Philip, Landgrave of Hesse, etc., concerning the Jews." Printed in full in *Ob Christlicher Obrigkeit gebueren muege, das sie die Juden, unter den Christen zu wonen gedulde, und wo sie zu gedulden, welcher gestalt und mass. Ein Rathschlag Bucer's und sechs hessischer Prediger* ("Whether it is proper for Christian authorities to permit the Jews to dwell among the Christians, and where, and in what manner, they should be tolerated. A counsel from Butzer and six Hessian preachers") (Erfurt, 1539).
23. *Briefwechsel Landgraf Philipps des Grossmuethigen von Hessen mit Bucer,* ed. by Max Lenz, vol. I. *Publikationen aus den K. Preussischen Staatsarchiven,* vol. V (Leipzig, 1880), pp. 56 ff. N. Paulus, "Die Judenfrage und die hessischen Prediger in der Reformationszeit," *Der Katholik,* 71st year, 3rd series, III

(1891). Hastings Eells, *Martin Butzer* (New Haven and London, 1931). Heinrich Bornkamm, *Martin Bucers Bedeutung fuer die europaeische Reformationsgeschichte, Schriften des Vereins für Reformationsgeschichte,* 58th year, vol. 2, no. 169 (Guetersloh, 1952). Wilhelm Maurer, "Martin Butzer und die Judenfrage in Hessen," *Zeitschrift des Vereins fuer hessische Geschichte und Landeskunde* (1953), vol. 64.

24. "Reply by Philipp, Landgrave of Hesse . . . to his Councillors with regard to the advice [given by them] against the Jews." *Briefwechsel Landgraf Philipps des Grossmuethigen von Hessen mit Bucer,* p. 57 ff.
25. *Memoirs,* Part 22.
26. *Kurmaerkische Staendeakten aus der Regierungszeit Kurfuerst Joachims I,* ed. by Walter Friedensburg, vol. I. *Veroeffentlichungen des Vereins fuer die Geschichte der Mark Brandenburg* (Munich and Leipzig, 1913).
27. *Memoirs,* Part 22.
28. "Letter of Consolation."
29. *Memoirs,* Part 22.
30. "Letter of Consolation."
31. *Memoirs,* Part 22.
32. *Luthers Werke, Briefwechsel,* VIII, no. 3152 (Weimar, 1938), note. The Mandate states that the Elector had been moved by the "assiduous applications, pleas and offers of Jewry" to enact the decree.
33. *Memoirs,* Part 22.
34. Werner Heise, *Die Juden in der Mark Brandenburg.*
35. Heinrich Schnee, *Die Hoffinanz und der moderne Staat. Geschichte und System der Hoffaktoren an deutschen Fuerstenhoefen im Zeitalter des Absolutismus,* 1-3 (Berlin, 1953-1955), I: *Die Institution des Hoffaktorentums in Brandenburg-Preussen.*
36. *Memoirs,* Part 22.
37. "Letter of Consolation."
38. *ZGJD,* V, 317.
39. "Letter of Consolation."
40. *Briefwechsel Philipps des Grossmuethigen mit Bucer,* and N. Paulus, *Die Judenfrage und die hessischen Prediger.*
41. Published in Strasbourg on May 10, 1539.
42. Walter Holsten, *Christentum und nichtchristliche Religion nach der Auffassung Bucers. Schriften des Vereins fuer Reformationsgeschichte,* 53rd year, *Heft* 2, no. 160 (Leipzig, 1936).
43. "Letter of Consolation."
44. *Archives de la Ville de Strasbourg.* Reprinted in Feilchenfeld, Appendix XVI. The Hebrew original is no longer extant.

45. Letter from Josel to the Magistrate of Strasbourg, dated March 9, 1541. *ZGJD,* V, 320 ff. Beginning with no. 9 and ending with no. 36. *Summarischer Extrakt aus Joesslin oder Josephi Juden zu Rossheim Trostschrift an seine Brueder wider Buceri Buechlin* (Summary of Letter of Consolation from Josel of Rosheim to his brethren against Bucer's book). *Archives de la Ville de Strasbourg,* G.U.P., 174, no. 26. Also *ZGJD,* V.
46. *Memoirs,* Part 24.
47. Johann Christoph von Aretin, *Geschichte der Juden in Bayern* (Landshut, 1803).
48. *Andreas Osianders Schrift ueber die Blutbeschuldigung,* recovered and published in reprinted edition by Moritz Stern (Kiel, 1893). Emanuel Hirsch, *Die Theologie des Andreas Osiander und ihre geschichtlichen Voraussetzungen* (Goettingen, 1919).
49. *Darin ain Christ gantzer Christenhait zu schmach will es geschehe den Juden unrecht in bezichtigung der Christen Kinder Mordt, Durch Doctor Joh. Eck zu Ingolstadt. Hierin findst auch vil histori was uebels und bueberey die Juden in allen teutschen land und anderen Kuenigreichen gestift haben. Gedruckt zu Ingolstadt, MDXXXXI* ("The story of how a Christian insulted all of Christianity, alleging that the Jews were being accused falsely of murdering Christian children. By Doctor Joh. Eck of Ingolstadt. Here thou'llt also find many historical accounts of evil and foul play which the Jews have perpetrated in all the German states and other kingdoms." Printed in Ingolstadt, 1541). See also Joh. Christoph Aretin, *Geschichte der Juden in Bayern* (Landshut, 1803). Also "L. Geiger," in *ZGJD,* II, 328 ff.
50. *Memoirs,* Part 23.
51. On the Imperial Diet of Regensburg: F. Roth, *Zur Geschichte des Reichstags zu Regensburg im Jahre 1541. Archiv fuer Reformationsgeschichte. Texte und Untersuchungen,* 3rd year, (1905-1906) pp. 18 ff.
52. *Memoirs,* Part 23, and *Reichstagsakten,* Fasc. 7, *Reichstag zu Regensburg 1541,* Conv. VII, Records of Imperial Chancery for March-August 1541, *Haus-, Hof-, Staatsarchiv,* Vienna.
53. Lehmann, vol. II, pp. 226 ff. On July 20 of that year, the Emperor ordered the Alsatian town of Landau not to carry out its plans for the expulsion of its Jews without prior approval from a court of arbitration to be constituted of the Regional Governor and members of the Magistracy of Hagenau. *Archives du Dép. Bas-Rhin,* Série C. 78, and Feilchenfeld, p. 79.
54. *Memoirs,* Part 25.
55. *Ibid.* Josel records that in 1547 he was forced once again to act

as mediator between the disputing parties in Prague. "However," he reports, "when I was in Prague on the first day of Tammuz of this year (1547), I was informed by (the Jews of Prague) both by letter and verbally, that several families had reverted (to their former ways) and had resumed the quarrel. I thereupon reprimanded them officially until they finally agreed to keep the peace."

CHAPTER SEVEN: THE APOLOGIST

1. A letter from Dr. Martin Luther against the Sabbatarians, addressed to a good friend (1538). *D. Martin Luthers Werke,* vol. 50 (Weimar, 1914).
2. This tract was composed in the fourteenth century and was prepared for publication in 1520.
3. *D. Martin Luthers Werke,* vol. 53 (Weimar, 1920), pp. 411 ff.
4. In May 1543, *Joesslin Jud zu Rossheim im Nahmen der uebrigen Juden an die Statt wegen eines buechleins so Dr. Martin Luther . . . wieder sie ausgehen lassen. De anno 1543* ("Joesslin Jew of Rosheim in the name of the other Jews to the city regarding a booklet published against them by Dr. Martin Luther. In the year 1543"). *Archives de la Ville de Strasbourg,* G.U.P., 174, no. 23. See also *ZGJD,* V, 321 ff.
5. Vol. 53 (Weimar, 1920).
6. Communication from Josel to the Magistrate of Strasbourg, dated July 11, 1543. *Archives de la Ville de Strasbourg,* G.U.P., 174, no. 23. At the Imperial Diet of Worms several Catholic deputies sharply criticized what they called "Luther's seditious writings and books." They said that his tract "against the Jews which he recently published *(Of the Shem Hamphoras)* was a hateful book, as cruel as if it had been written in blood, and it incited the mob to robbery and murder . . ." . . . "It has also been seen that the people behaved atrociously in many places in accordance with these teachings, striking at the lives of many innocent people." Janssen, *op. cit.,* vol. III (1883), p. 539.
7. Dated July 11. *ZGJD,* V, 332 ff.
8. Scheid, *op. cit.,* Pièces Justificatives, no. XXXVI.
9. *Memoirs,* Part 26.
10. *The Holy Path, Jossif Ometz,* paragraph 482. *The Holy Path* had already been written in 1531. However, as Feilchenfeld presumed, Josel inserted into this work at a later date accounts of several historical events, such as the ritual murder incident of 1544. He also added the penitential prayer of Rabbi Avigdor of Prague, which was only written in 1542, when the Jews were expelled from Prague. See also Lehmann, vol. II, pp. 252 ff.

11. *Privilegiorum Universorum, Teutoniae Nationis, Hebraeorum Confirmatio:* Gegeben in Speyer 3. Aprilis 1544. Signed by Carl Naves, Obernburger. Badisches Generallandesarchiv, Karlsruhe, Sec. 67, *Bestand Kopialbuecher,* vol. 894, fol. 171-176. This document was incorporated also in the certificate of renewal which was issued to the Jews of the *Reich* by Maximilian II on March 8, 1561, and again by Rudolf II on June 15, 1577. An entry in Reichshofrat. *Protocolla rerum resolutarum* XVII, vol. Ia, fol. 89, for May 23, states that "The requested document was issued to Josel the Jew." *Oesterreichisches Haus-, Hof-, und Staatsarchiv,* Vienna.
12. This view has been expressed by Bresslau.
13. *Memoirs,* Part 28.
14. Karl Brandi, *Berichte und Studien zur Geschichte Karls V. Nachrichten von der Gesellschaft der Wissenschaften zu Goettingen aus dem Jahre 1930, Phil. hist. Kl.,* (Berlin, 1930), pp. 250 ff.
15. The payment of the golden tribute penny was never imposed on the Jews of Frankfort. I. Kracauer, *Geschichte der Frankfurter Juden,* vol. I.
16. This should read 1544.
17. *Memoirs,* Part 27.
18. I. Kracauer, "Procès de R. Joselmann contre la ville de Colmar," in *REJ,* XIX (1889), pp. 282 ff. Basing his information on material in the *Archives du Dép. du Bas-Rhin,* Strasbourg, Kracauer gives the date as August 7. On the other hand, there is an entry in the Records of Imperial Diets, Fasc. 16, Convol. III, fol. 224, *Oesterr. Haus-, Hof-, und Staatsarchiv* as follows: *Der judischeit quittung umb die 111 mfl. reinisch, so sy zu der defensif hilff erlegt haben, mit zusag, inen ire freyheit zu confirmiern.* ("Receipt issued to Jewry for the 111 Rhenish florins which they remitted as a contribution to the defensive war, with the promise that their freedom would be reconfirmed"), under date of August 6, 1545.
19. *Memoirs,* Part 27, and letter to the Magistrate of Strasbourg, from 1546. Feilchenfeld, Appendix XXI.
20. *Memoirs,* Part 28.
21. From a letter written by Charles V to his son Philip. Bezold, *op. cit.,* p. 767.
22. At this Imperial Diet, Josel submitted to Charles a complaint that, although the Jews had an Imperial letter of safe-conduct entitling them to stay in the city during the Imperial Diet, the Magistrate of Regensburg permitted them to remain there only from eight o'clock in the morning until four o'clock in the after-

noon. He requested that they be permitted to remain from six o'clock in the morning until six o'clock in the evening, as had been the custom of old. *Records of Imperial Diets,* Fasc. 20, fol. 88-88v. - Imperial Diet of Regensburg, 1546, *Oesterreichisches Haus-, Hof-, und Staatsarchiv.* The citizens of Regensburg had already protested at the Diet of Worms against the Privilege of Speyer, which had been "issued to the Jews at their request." They asked that their agreement with the House of Austria be permitted to remain in effect; according to this agreement Jews were barred from doing business in the city. Their request was granted. *Actum Wormbis in consilio regis, 5 Aprilis 1545. Records of Imperial Diets,* Fasc. 16, Imperial Diet of Worms, 1545. Convolut. III, fol. 28.

23. From pamphlets of that period. Bezold, *op. cit.,* pp. 774-775.
25. *Memoirs,* Part 28.
26. *Supplication Joeslin juden als bevelchabers der ganzen judenschaft an m. Hn der st. Strassburg, ersucht dieselben, dass sie bei ihren bundsverwandten verfuegen wollen, dass die juden ohnbeschedigt pleiben und bei ihren freiheiten gelassen werden moegen. Muss a. 1546 geschickt worden sein, als der schmalkald. Krieg angieng.* ("Petition from Joeslin, Jew, as Commander of all Jewry, to my Lords of the City of Strasbourg, requesting that they prevail upon their allies that the Jews be allowed to remain unharmed and to retain their freedoms. This petition must have been sent in 1546, when the Schmalkaldic War broke out.") Copy. *Archives de la Ville de Strasbourg,* G.U.P., 174, no. 26.
27. Records of the Magistrate, 1546, fol. 444. *Archives de la Ville de Strasbourg.*
28. *Archives de la Ville de Strasbourg,* Records of the Magistrate, III, fol. 127; and Feilchenfeld, p. 65.
29. Records of the Magistrate, fol. 438.
30. *Supplication Joeslin juden . . .*
31. *Archives de la Ville de Strasbourg,* Records of the Magistrate, fol. 444. See Feilchenfeld, pp. 65-66.
32. *Memoirs,* Part 28.
33. *Memoirs,* Part 29.
34. *Sefer Ha-Mikneh.*
35. *Memoirs,* Part 29.
36. *Memoirs,* Part 28.

CHAPTER EIGHT: HISTORIAN, PHILOSOPHER, EDUCATOR

1. Josel comments as follows on an ancient manuscript of which he incorporated several passages into his *Sefer Ha-Mikneh*: "There

were other great and wonderful things which were recorded by earlier generations, each in the manner in which they had been handed down to him. But I did not deem these worthy of being written down. It was only in the case of true and accurate documents that I did not hesitate; I copied them to preserve them for future generations." *Sefer Ha-Mikneh.* The *Sefer Ha-Mikneh* (literally "Book of Acquisitions") is now in the Bodleian Library, Oxford (no. 2240, col. 773; Ms. Opp. 712). Adolf Neubauer gives a detailed description of the manuscript in his *Catalogue of the Hebrew Manuscripts in the Bodleian Library and in the College Libraries of Oxford* (Oxford, 1886), pp. 773-774.

2. Leo W. Schwarz, *Memoirs of My People* (Philadelphia, 1943).
3. *Sefer Ha-Mikneh.*
4. *Memoirs,* Part 2.
5. *Ibid.*
6. *Memoirs,* Part 26.
7. *REJ,* XIII (1886).
8. Benzion Netanyahu, *Don Isaac Abravanel, Statesman and Philosopher* (Philadelphia, 1953).
9. *Memoirs,* Part 2.
10. Yitzhak Fritz Baer, *Galut,* (Schocken Verlag, Berlin, 1936), p. 61.
11. *Sefer Ha-Mikneh.*
12. *Sefer Ha-Mikneh.* Tr. by I. Sonne.
13. A play on words and on the name Luther. The Hebrew for "impure," in Ashkenazi pronunciation, is *lo-toher.* Tr. by I. Sonne.
14. Bodleian Library, Oxford, no. 2240; Ms. Opp. 712.
15. P. 138. See also Feilchenfeld, pp. 140-141.
16. Adolf Neubauer, *Catalogue of Hebrew Manuscripts.*
17. These nine chapters were published in Hebrew by Adolf Neubauer in "Texte aus Joselmanns Sefer Hamikneh," in *Israelitische Letterbode,* vol. IV (Amsterdam, 1880-1881).
18. "The expulsion [of the Jews from] Ulm was caused by talebearing in which they strove to outdo one another until Satan helped them lift up their hands to bring great distress to the Gaon Rabbi Moshe Zart [perhaps Meschi]. Finally he was forced to abandon his own faith and to fall in with them [i.e., the Christians]. Then joy and jubilation swept through the camp of the informers and of his adversaries, and bitter weeping racked the ears of Israel, of the communities and of the provinces. But the Lord saw it and He knew of the distress of his soul and of the duress under which he lived. Moreover, the heart of the teacher

did not forsake him. He was helped to overcome his unbelief, and he succeeded in going to the Holy Land and in returning [to his faith] with true repentance . . . As for those informers, the evil spirit came upon them so that they ended their days in turmoil . . . and their names went down in ignominy. Their descendants met an unnatural death. The citizens of Ulm wandered on the path of their shame to which they had come because of the Gaon's return to his old faith. In their wrath they conspired with nine evil neighbors to have the Emperor Maximilian expel [the Jews] utterly and soon. It was a difficult situation." (Herman Dicker. . . .) The expulsion took place in 1599.

19. In this chapter, Josel cites several other illustrations as proof that God will wipe out the informers, whose "beginning is distress and whose end is destruction." He tells of one Samuel Enschheim (who probably came from Ensisheim in Alsace), a noted and even erudite person who turned informer and converted to Christianity at the age of seventy. Next, he recalls a well-bred but wicked man in Frankfort who also embraced Christianity and who had his child taken from his wife's custody when she refused to follow his lead. He speaks of one Gershon Heildorisch, who was the first of the informers in Worms, of Hoechlin of Posen, a Polish Jew who denounced the Jews as proselytizers, and finally of Jacob Boneida, a wealthy Jew from Posen who, when thrown into prison on charges of fraud and talebearing, promised to convert to Christianity when his father died; and he kept this promise.
20. *Wahre und einfaeltige Historia Stephani Isaaci. Allen frommen Christen und Liebhabern der warheyt zu nutz in Druck verfertigt im jar M.D. XXCVI* (A true and simple history of Stephen Isaac. Printed in the year 1586 for the benefit of all devout Christians and lovers of truth.) See Marianne Beyer-Froehlich, *Aus dem Zeitalter des Humanismus und der Reformation. Deutsche Literatur. Deutsche Selbstzeugnisse,* vol. V (Leipzig, 1931).
21. Royall Tyler, *The Emperor Charles the Fifth* (Fair Lawn, N. J., 1956), p. 94.
22. Neubauer, *Catalogue of Hebrew Manuscripts.*
23. *Sefer Ha-Mikneh,* on Job 33.13-17. Tr. by L. Sonne, who pointed out to me that Josel for the most part followed the philosophy of Gersonides here.
24. *Sefer Ha-Mikneh,* Treatise 4, pp. 110-114.
25. Exodus 33.14 as paraphrased in the *Sefer Ha-Mikneh.*
26. *Sefer Ha-Mikneh,* opening of Part 8.
27. *Ibid.,* fol. 192.

28. Franz Rosenzweig, in *Almanach des Schocken Verlags auf das Jahr 5695,* pp. 60 ff.
29. Proverbs 4.5; see Neubauer, *Catalogue of Hebrew Manuscripts.*
30. Moshe Ben Maimon, *Guide of the Perplexed,* tr. into German and annotated by Adolf Weiss, vols. I-III (Leipzig, 1923-1924).
31. Feilchenfeld, *op. cit.,* p. 140.
32. Translation by Sonne. *Sefer Ha-Mikneh,* p. 275a. Josel then proceeds to copy almost all of the final chapter of the *Moreh* (Part III, Chap. 50), pp. 275-289 of the *Sefer Ha-Mikneh.*
33. Franz Spunda, *Paracelsus. Menschen, Voelker, Zeiten. Eine Kulturgeschichte in Einzeldarstellungen,* ed. by Max Kemmerich, vol. VI (Vienna and Leipzig, 1925). Henry M. Pachter, *Paracelsus, Magic into Science* (New York, 1951).
34. *Archives de la Ville de Strasbourg,* G.U.P., 4, no. 23.
35. Josel's Commentary on Exodus 33.1-18. Tr. by Sonne.
36. Karl Joel, *Wandlungen der Weltanschauungen. Eine Philosophiegeschichte als Geschichtsphilosophie* (Tuebingen, 1918).
37. *Paracelsus,* quoted in Joel, *supra.*
38. Saying of Rabbi Moshe Leib. See Martin Buber, *Vom Geist des Judentums* (Leipzig, 1916), p. 190.

CHAPTER NINE: THE ADVOCATE OF GERMAN JEWRY

1. *Social Germany in Luther's Time. The Memoirs of Bartholomeo Sastrow,* tr. into English by Albert D. Vandam (New York, n.d.).
2. Reichshofrat, *Judicialia miscellanea* J.1, fasc. 60, fol. 51-53. *Oest. Haus-, Hof-, und Staatsarchiv.*
3. Reichshofrat, *Protocolla rerum resolutarum* XVII, vol. 2c, fol. 70v. *Judicialia miscellanea* J.1, fasc. 60, fol. 57-58 (1548): January 30, 1548, Augsburg. Draft of the Order issued by Charles V *"an statt Rossheim und flecken Turckeym pro judischait in der landvogtei Hagenau."* (To the city of Rosheim and the village of Turkheim with regard to Jewry in the bailiwick of Hagenau.) On the insistence of Josel, the Emperor commanded Konrad von Fleckenstein, *Landvogt* of Hagenau (under date of February 6, 1548) to see to it that the cities observed the Imperial mandate and that the Jews should not be insulted, terrorized, and oppressed in the future. *Judicialia miscellanea* J.1, fasc. 60, fol. 54-56 (1548): *Die judischait inn der landvogtei Hagenaw betreffendt* (Concerning Jewry in the bailiwick of Hagenau). *Oest. Haus-, Hof-, und Staatsarchiv.*
4. Printed with seal. Stuttgart State Archives, Rep. A 56, B8, no. 5.
5. Salomon Stein, "Zur Geschichte der Juden in Schweinfurt und dem Vogteidorf Gochsheim im 16. Jahrhundert," in *Jahrbuch*

der Juedischen Literarischen Gesellschaft, vol. IV (Frankfort, 1906), pp. 1 ff.

6. *Joesel jud von Rosheim von wegen der armen judischeit so noch wonen in obgedachten marckt Gochtsheim* ("Joesel, Jew, of Rosheim, with regard to the unfortunate Jews still living in this above-mentioned market town of Gochtsheim"), undated (probably middle of January). Reichshofrat, *Judicialia miscellanea,* J.1, fasc. 60, fol. 51-53.
7. *"ist bewilligt (Josels Gesuch) pro conservatione regaliarum. Caes. Mt. XVII, Januarii 1548."* ("Josel's application for the preservation of the privileges is hereby granted. Imperial Mandate XVII January 1548"). Reichshofrat, *Judicialia miscellanea* J.1, fasc. 60. fol. 51-53. *Oest. Haus-, Hof-, und Staats archiv. Ibid.: Koncept des Mandats an den Schutzherrn (Juden zu Gotschhaim pleiben lassen), dat. Augspurg den 17. tag januarii anno 48.* ("Draft of the mandate to the Protector to allow the Jews to remain in Gochsheim, given in Augsburg, January 17, 1548.")
8. Stein writes that "The original of the letter to the burgomaster of Gochsheim, with Rabbi Josel's seal (a bull with great horns—see Deut. 33.17—and the imprint of the name Joseph in Hebrew) is kept in the Archives of Wuerzburg." At the present writing the letter could no longer be located.
9. Reichshofrat, *Protocolla rerum resolutarum* XVII, vol. 2c, fol. 230v.: *Decima nona aprilis 1548. Josel jud umb duplicat seines schutzbriefs* (April 19, 1548. Josel, Jew, applies for a duplicate of his letter of protection). Moritz Stern, who recovered the original of the document in the *Germanischen Nationalmuseum* in Nuremberg and reprinted it in M. Stern, "Joselmann von Rosheim und seine Nachkommen," *ZGJD,* III (1889), 65 ff., gives the date as Augsburg, February 28, 1548. The document, which is no longer extant, is described by Stern as follows: "The document, which contains a transcript of Joselmann's letter of protection, is written on parchment, in booklet form, on seven folios, and is now in the Archives of the *Germanischen National-museum* in Nuremberg under the no. 4984. Attached to its heavy twisted white and red silken cord which holds the leaves together is the green seal, inside a wooden capsule and damaged in several places. The letter of protection for 'the Jew Josel of Rosheim and his sons and sons-in-law, together with their wives, children, servants, households and all their possessions and property,' was issued by Charles V in Augsburg on February 28, 1548." This is the date which was also given in subsequent certificates of renewal issued to Josel's descendants; e.g.,

in a document issued by Maximilian II on December 6, 1570, for Josel's sons Gershon and Moses.

10. Reichshofrat, *Protocolla rerum resolutarum* XVII, vol. 2c, fol. 217v. Entry dated April 16: *Josel jud von Rosshaim wegen gemainer Judischait umb bevelh, die ungehorsamen Juden so sich irer ordnung nit halten und auf der rabbi straf nit geben wollen, das sy nachmals inen gehorsamen. Item umb bevelh wider die, so die Auflag irer teyls zu erlegen sich waigern. Soviel den ersten puenkten belenngt, sollen sy die ordnung einpringen und so die ersehen und rechtsmaessig befunden wirde, soll inen dieselb sub poena confirmiert werden. So vil den andern puncten betrifft, sollen sy verzaichnis der auflag anzaigen.* (Josel, Jew of Rosheim, on behalf of all Jewry, asks for an order that such disobedient Jews as refuse to observe their regulations and to abide by the penalty decreed by the rabbi, shall be made to obey them in the future. Moreover, he asks for an order with regard to those Jews who refuse to pay their share of the tax. As for the first point, the Jews shall transmit a draft of the regulations; and after they have been examined and found correct, they may be confirmed. As for the second point, the Jews shall send in a list of the taxes which they have to pay.)
11. *Reich Police Regulations,* Title 20, Paragraph 1. See Stobbe, *op. cit.,* p. 26.
12. *Gemainer Judischait im Heiligen Reich Schutz, Schirm und Glaitsbreif. Augspurg, den letzten tag Aprilis, anno . . . im achtundviertzigsten.* (Letter of Protection, Patronage and Safe Conduct issued to the Jews of the Holy Empire in Augsburg on the last day of April, 1548). Reichs Register of Ferdinand I, vol. 6, folio 92v-93v. *Oesterreichisches Haus-, Hof-, und Staatsarchiv.*
13. *Supplicatio Joesel Juden. 22 junii anno 1548* (Petition of Josel, Jew, of June 22, 1548). Signed: *Joesel judt zu Rosshaym gemainer judischait anwaldt* (Josel, Jew, of Rosheim, advocate for all Jewry). Arch Chancellor's Archives of Mayence. Records of Imperial Diets, fasc. 16, fol. 563-565. *Oest. Haus-, Hof-, und Staatsarchiv.*
14. Xavier Mossmann, *Etude sur l'histoire des Juifs à Colmar* (Colmar, Paris, 1866), pp. 21 ff. I. Kracauer, "Procès de R. Joselmann contre la ville de Colmar," *REJ,* XIX (1889), 282 ff.
15. Letter of the Magistrate of Colmar to Josel, dated August 16, 1541. Copy. Reichshofrat, *Judicialia miscellanea* J.1, fasc. 60, conv. 1, fol. 48. *Oesterreichisches Haus-, Hof-, und Staatsarchiv.*
16. *Archives du Dép. Bas-Rhin,* E. 1406, pp. 133-139. Dec. 23.
17. No date. Probably early part of January, 1548. Written in his

own hand. Reichshofrat, *Judicialia miscellanea* J.1, fasc. 60, conv. 1, fol. 43-45.

18. *Ibid.*, fol. 47-49, and Reichshofrat, *Protocolla rerum resolutarum* XVII, vol. 2c, fol. 13.
19. *Supplication Joesel judens von Rosheim, von wegen sein und seiner mitverwandten, den ingang zu Colmar belangen, 48, an den Landvogt.* (Petition submitted by Josel, Jew of Rosheim, in '48, to the *Landvogt,* with regard to permission to him and his brethren to enter Colmar.) Copy. *Archives du Dép. Bas-Rhin,* Série C, 78.
20. Mossmann, *op. cit.*, pp. 31 ff.
21. *Copia citationis Josel jud zu Rossheim cum consort ca. statt Colmar* (Copy of summons in case of Josel, Jew of Rosheim . . . against the town of Colmar), December 19, 1548. *Archives du Dép. Bas-Rhin,* 863, Wetzl. 1249. In Feilchenfeld, Appendix XXV, p. 198.
22. Wilhelm Maurer, "Reuchlin und das Judentum," *Theologische Literaturzeitung,* 9 (1952), pp. 536 ff.
23. *Ibid.*
24. *Ibid.*
25. Title 19, Paragraph 6. Neumann, *Geschichte des Wuchers,* p. 541.
26. Jakob Strieder, *Studien zur Geschichte der kapitalistischen Organisationsformen,* 2nd ed. (Munich and Leipzig, 1925).
27. On the Imperial Diet of Augsburg, see *Beitraege zur Reichsgeschichte 1546-1551.* Adapted by August von Druffel. *Briefe und Akten zur Geschichte des 16. Jahrhunderts,* I-IV, vol. I (Munich, 1873-1896), pp. 448 ff., 485, 516.
28. Neumann, *op. cit.*, p. 345.
29. Strieder, *op. cit.*, pp. 112 ff.
30. *Ibid.*
31. Reichshofrat, *Protocolla rerum resolutarum* XVII, vol. 10, fol. 32. We have little information as to Josel's activities at this Imperial Diet, because his memoirs make no further references to them. According to the Records of the Reichshofrat, Josel petitioned the Emperor on August 25, 1550 to *gemaine Judischait bey iren habenden Freyhaiten gnedigst handthaben und denselben zuwider ir unverhort nichts ausgehen lassen* (graciously let all Jewry retain its present freedoms and not take action against it without a fair hearing). Reichshofrat, *Protocolla rerum resolutarum* XVII, vol. 6, fol. 203. According to an entry in the records dated September 19, 1550, Josel's petition was to be addressed to the Estates of the *Reich* (*ibid.*, vol. 8, fol. 59). Another petition from Josel to the Emperor, dated October 29,

and requesting that the Emperor allow the decision, which was handed down by the Councillors several years before to Josel as Commander of all Jewry, was turned down. (*ibid.,* XVII, vol. 7, fol. 335v.). We do not know to which petition this statement refers. However, Josel succeeded in securing permission for his two sons, Gershon and Jacob, to settle in Rosheim and Tuerkheim. (*Die 11. martii 1551.* Reichshofrat, *Protocolla rerum resolutarum* XVII, vol. 10, fol. 80.)

32. *Ibid.,* vol. 10, fol. 32.
33. Gerson Wolf published these petitions in an article entitled "Zur Geschichte der Juden in Deutschland: II, Josel von Rosheim (Loans)," in the *ZGJD,* III (1889), 168 ff., without giving information as to the date, place, or the archives in which the documents were found.
34. Reichshofrat, *Protocolla rerum resolutarum* XVII, vol. 10, fol. 156. *Oesterr. Haus-, Hof-, und Staatsarchiv.*
35. Max Speidel, *Das Hofgericht zu Rottweil. Ein Beitrag zu seiner Geschichte unter der Herrschaft der Alten Hofgerichtsordnung* (Rottweil a.N., 1914).
36. Petition of Josel to the Emperor, Lehmann, *op. cit.,* vol. II, p. 308.
37. Petition of Josel to the Duke of Wuerttemberg. No place or year given. B. 287. Jewry in the Lands of the Teutonic Order and elsewhere, fasc. 3, 10. Copy. *Württembergisches Hauptstaatsarchiv.*
38. Letter dated February 6, 1551. Feilchenfeld, Appendix XXXI, p. 200.
39. Petitions dated February 22 and June 7, 1551. Original with seal. *Württembergisches Hauptstaatsarchiv,* Stuttgart, A 56, fasc. 9.
40. Letter to Chancellor Fessler of Wuerttemberg. *Ibid.* Original with seal, A 56, fasc. 9.
41. *Vertrag gegen der judischait ufgericht, d. Stuttgarten, den 11 August* a. 1551. Parchment, with seal. *Ibid.,* A 56, fasc. 9.
42. *Abgeschrift von der hebr. sprach, so von der gmain judisch. Jesall jud. ierem bevelhhaber zukomen ist.* (Copied from the Hebrew language, written by All Jewry to Jesall, their Commander), July 14, 1551. Feilchenfeld, Appendix XXVII, pp. 202-203.
43. Feilchenfeld, p. 73.
44. Research at the *Bayrisches Hauptstaatsarchiv* in Munich on Josel's activities yielded no information. The only source for this aspect of Josel's work is Johann Christoph Freiherr von Aretin, *Geschichte der Juden in Bayern* (Landshut, 1803),

pp. 52-57, in which the agreement is published. The agreement is in the *Bayrische Hauptstaatsarchiv,* Munich, 10231 (formerly *Jews in Bavaria,* fasc. 11). A copy of the reverse was made for Aretin in 1802.

CHAPTER TEN: THE END

1. *Sefer Ha-Mikneh.*
2. Letter to the Magistrate of Oberehnheim, dated October 10, 1542. Feilchenfeld, Appendix XVIII.
3. *Memoirs,* Part 27.
4. Feilchenfeld, Appendix XVIII.
5. Under date of November 13, 1553. *Archives de la Ville de Strasbourg.* Records of the Magistrate, III, 117, fasc. 38.
6. Letter dated June 8, 1552. *Ibid.* See also letter dated March 24, 1551. *Ibid.*
7. F. von Bezold, *Geschichte der deutschen Reformation,* p. 844.
8. *Ibid.*
9. I. Kracauer, *Geschichte der Frankfurter Juden,* I, p. 303.
10. Josel to the Magistrate of Hagenau. Undated copy, probably from February, 1554. *Archives du Dép. Bas-Rhin,* Série C, 78.
11. *Ibid.*
12. According to one of the Counselors of King Ferdinand. See Bezold, p. 850.
13. Josel's letter to the Magistrate of Hagenau. Undated. *Archives du Dép. Bas-Rhin.* Série C, 78.
14. Karl Brandi, *Karl V. vor Metz. Ausgewaehlte Aufsaetze. Als Festgabe zum 70. Geburtstag am 20. Mai 1938 dargebracht von seinen Schuelern und Freunden* (Oldenburg and Berlin, 1938).
15. *Memoirs,* Part 8.
16. Dated May 21, 1553. Feilchenfeld, Appendix XXIX, pp. 204 ff.
17. *Die 11. martii 1551. Josel judens sone Gerson und Jacob umb schutz und schirmb unnd das sy mogen zu Rosshaim und Turckhaim wonen in crafft ires vatters hievor erlangten freyhait, deren copy sy einbringen. So ferr sich bey der cantzley ires vatters freyheit dermassen befindt, mag sy auf die sone ernneurt werden. Die 13. martii 1551. Josel jud. Ist bewilligt mit der enderung, wie im concept angetzaigt.* (March 11, 1551. Gerson and Jacob, sons of Josel, Jew, requesting protection and patronage and permission to reside at Rosheim and Tuerkheim, by virtue of the freedom secured by their father for this purpose, a copy of which they are herewith submitting. Since this freedom conferred on their father is filed at the Chancery, it may be renewed in favor of the sons. March 13, 1551. Josel, Jew. Granted with modification as shown in draft. Reichshofrat, *Protocolla rerum resolutarum*

XVII, vol. 10, fol. 80, and vol. 8, fol. 204v. *Oesterr. Haus-, Hof-, und Staatsarchiv,* Vienna.

18. *Archives du Dép. Bas-Rhin,* Série C, 78.
19. Petition from Josel to the Magistrate of Hagenau, undated, but certainly written some time between February 20 and 24, 1554. *Archives du Dép. Bas-Rhin,* Série C, 78, and petition from the Burgomaster and Magistrate of Rosheim to *Unterlandvogt* Heinrich von Fleckenstein, undoubtedly dating from either late February or early March. *Ibid.*
20. Psalms 84.8.
21. Feilchenfeld, p. 113.
22. According to Feilchenfeld's calculations, Passover ended on March 25 in that year.
23. Josel on Moses in *Sefer Ha-Mikneh.*
24. Memorial Books of Niederehnheim and Hagenau. See Lehmann, vol. II, p. 326.

INDEX

INDEX

INDEX